THE KEY TO EVERYTHING

The Key to Everything

*May Swenson,
A Writer's Life*

Margaret A. Brucia

Foreword by Paul Crumbley & David Hoak

PRINCETON UNIVERSITY PRESS
Princeton & Oxford

Published by Princeton University Press
41 William Street, Princeton, New Jersey 08540
99 Banbury Road, Oxford OX2 6JX

press.princeton.edu

Owing to limitations of space, all acknowledgments for permission to reprint previously published and unpublished material can be found on page 234–35.

All Rights Reserved

ISBN 9780691247236
ISBN (ebook) 9780691247229

British Library Cataloging-in-Publication Data is available

Editorial: Anne Savarese, James Collier, and Emma Wagh
Production Editorial: Theresa Liu
Text and Jacket / Cover Design: Katie Osborne
Production: Erin Suydam
Publicity: Alyssa Sanford
Copyeditor: Daniel Simon

Jacket image: *May Swenson (holding teacup)*, c. 1955. Photograph by Rollie McKenna. © The Rosalie Thorne McKenna Foundation. Courtesy of the Center for Creative Photography, University of Arizona Foundation.

This book has been composed in Miller

Printed in Canada

10 9 8 7 6 5 4 3 2 1

For Peter Amram

. . . omnibus e meis amicis
antistans mihi milibus trecentis

—CATULLUS

CONTENTS

FOREWORD

FEW WRITERS CAN HAVE WORKED HARDER or persevered longer to reach the pinnacle of their craft than May Swenson. Her life is one of the most astonishing and inspiring stories in American letters. The oldest of ten children raised by Swedish immigrant converts to the Church of Jesus Christ of Latter-day Saints, Swenson left Utah for New York City in 1936, at the age of twenty-three. She would return to Utah throughout her life and retain the affection and respect of her large, nurturing family. Honoring her parents, she would never drop her membership in the LDS church, although she once told a friend, "It's not for me—religion. It seems like a redundancy for a poet" (Knudson and Bigelow 34). Her dream was to become a New York writer, and her eyes never left that prize. She succeeded like few before her.

Writing in 1994, the eminent scholar and critic Harold Bloom called May Swenson, Elizabeth Bishop, and Marianne Moore the "best women poets of [the twentieth] century" (275). This was enormously high praise coming from one of the lions of American literary criticism, but had they been alive when Bloom hailed their achievement, his words might have landed on these accomplished women's ears, as they do on ours, with a fair measure of exasperation. Elizabeth A. Frost offers a more inclusive assessment in her 2016 contribution to *A History of Twentieth-Century American Women's Poetry*: "In a career that spanned over three decades, May Swenson addressed the tensions among romantic, aesthetic, and scientific approaches to the natural world. Sometimes likened to [the work of] E. E. Cummings in its form and to [that of] Moore in its preoccupation with science, Swenson's work is consistently visual and feminist" (346).

In welcoming *The Key to Everything*, the long-awaited biographical account of her coming of age in the world of New York poetry, we can now begin to grasp the scale of May Swenson's achievement. Thanks to Margaret Brucia's early access to Swenson's unpublished diaries, we hear her story in the poet's own words. Passages from her early years in New York offer vivid glimpses into the burgeoning, often chaotic art scene of midcentury Manhattan and the competitive world of New York poetry that Swenson chose to negotiate on her long ascent from obscurity to national prominence. Also here, in language by turns humorous and heartbreaking, Swenson details the fumbling and passion of youthful sexual forays as well as more mature relationships, with both men and women. These are told in the engaging voice of the poet, full of the questing spirit that led her to embrace the diversity of Greenwich Village and fully realize her identity as a lesbian.

Swenson's first years in the city were difficult. Strongly influenced by her nineteenth-century heroes, Emily Dickinson and Walt Whitman, she encountered a poetry scene dominated by the great modernists whose work defined the 1920s and the decades that followed. Not drawn instinctively to the densely allusive style of T. S. Eliot, Ezra Pound, and Wallace Stevens, Swenson was more immediately at home with the work of William Carlos Williams, whose accessible diction and focus on ordinary life reflected her belief that poetry can spring from the familiar features of everyday experience. She found new heroes. Marianne Moore's vivid imagery and insistence on exacting description validated Swenson's own love of accuracy and precision. Robert Frost's writing about the natural world also spoke to her, particularly in his attentiveness to rural New England, which mirrored her own grounding in the landscapes of the American West. The Harlem Renaissance, then in full swing, added to the sense of artistic exuberance she associated with Manhattan. But Swenson was not strongly drawn to any particular movement or literary figure shaping American poetry. As she makes clear in a fanciful letter she wrote to the novelist Thomas Wolfe the "night before she arrived in New York City" (Brucia 46), Swenson was attracted to the city itself. "I shall come to your city—my city," she wrote. "I am coming into the thick of it" (qtd. in Brucia 46). It was the city's artistic vibrancy and freedom that charged her, and she came to immerse herself in it. Her contribution to American poetry would be as an experimental poet whose work, in its restless fascination with form and diverse subject matter, resists easy classification.

Swenson's breakthrough in national publications began with two poems about the natural world. "Haymaking" appeared in the *Saturday Review of Literature* in 1949, followed in 1953 by "Snow by Morning" in the *New Yorker*. Over her career, Swenson would publish sixty-one poems in the *New Yorker*, more than all but a handful of other poets, and a fitting achievement for someone whose first dreams were to be a New York writer. The natural world would continue to be a major poetic focus, allying her work with that of such contemporary poets as Mary Oliver and Maxine Kumin. Her accurate and precise imagery led to comparisons with Elizabeth Bishop, with whom she would maintain a close friendship and vital correspondence for nearly thirty years. While the two poets generally admired each other's work, their letters exchange lively judgments and sharp opinions reflecting their different poetic temperaments. Swenson could turn a part of almost every day into poetry. Bishop, by contrast, could circle a poem for months or years before letting it go, and often fretted over what she perceived as low productivity compared to her peers. A Swenson poem usually reveals vivid sensory stimulation, rendered in bright and clear language. Bishop's work, also prized for its naturalness of tone, is nevertheless often brooding and contemplative, plumbing deep memory to create an air of mystery or enigma. Swenson was aware of these differences and resisted critical efforts to link her to Bishop, despite her high regard for Bishop's artistry. Her concern was with being cast as a disciple—of anyone. Conversely, she would almost certainly accept being placed in a line of development that stretches from Dickinson and Whitman through Moore and Bishop, with the understanding that any close resemblances were the result of shared attitude rather than of imitative effort.

Swenson's experiments with typography and poetic form are a distinctive feature of many of her poems that helped pave the way for innovations in how poetry appears on the printed page. Reflecting her strong early feminism, one of Swenson's most anthologized works is "Women," a poem that uses a curved shape to underline her dismay at the patriarchal depiction of women as sexual objects. The feminist focus in her writing situated her in the company of other midcentury poets, such as Sylvia Plath, Anne Sexton, and Adrienne Rich, although their work differed markedly in style. Swenson dedicated her 1970 volume, *Iconographs: Poems*, entirely to shape poems, in honor of which that volume was named one of the "Books of the Year" by the American Institute of Graphic Arts (Hammer 721).

Throughout her career, Swenson wrote many humorous poems about mundane subjects, such as a trip to the dentist ("After the Dentist") or an elderly man easing himself into a beach chair

("Dr. Henderson"), while also producing work on a broad range of subjects extending from sports to art exhibits, cats, European travel, space exploration, and religion. Her poems touching on religion and spirituality emerge out of her LDS upbringing but extend into philosophical musings about evolution and our relationship to the nonhuman universe. These include one of her most anthologized poems, "Question," as well as poems like "Earth Your Dancing Place" and "God." Always delighted by riddles and puzzles, Swenson would publish two poetry collections for young readers, *Poems to Solve* in 1966 and *More Poems to Solve* in 1971. Of the many poems that fall into this category, two that stand out are "Was Worm" and "Living Tenderly."

Swenson would also become known for her many love poems, two volumes of which were published posthumously. These works are distinguished by their warmth, passion, and playfulness. Poems like "Mornings Innocent" and "Facing" exemplify this important vein in her work. Her natural inclination to write about queer desire affiliated her with James Merrill and Rich in her own generation and would win the admiration of a later generation that would include Mark Doty, Malachi Black, and Nancy K. Pearson.

Swenson was a daily poet, a busy writer whose mind was a camera pointed at the world and its contents and creatures. Her palette was vast, and her attitude remained steadfastly upbeat. Unlike many of the confessional poets who shared her poetic moment, Swenson's encounters with doubt and existential angst were not extensive or life-changing. The books that make up her main body of work consistently communicate her wish to engage joyfully with the mysteries and magnificence of the universe. These begin with *Another Animal* (1954) and include *A Cage of Spines* (1958), *To Mix with Time* (1963), *Half Sun Half Sleep* (1967), *Iconographs* (1970), *New & Selected Things Taking Place* (1978), and *In Other Words* (1987).

A selective review of blurbs that appeared on four of Swenson's books published between 1958 and 1987 shows how highly she was regarded by her contemporaries. Wedged between praise by Richard Wilbur and Howard Moss on the cover of Swenson's second book, *A Cage of Spines*, is Robert Lowell's frequently quoted quip: "Miss Swenson's quick-eyed poems should be hung with permanent fresh paint signs." In a jacket note from her third book, *To Mix with Time*, Elizabeth Bishop also identifies Swenson's originality but focuses on her infectious delight: "A great part of one's pleasure in her work is in *her* pleasure; she has directness, affection, and a rare and reassuring ungrudgingness." On the back cover of Swenson's tenth book, *New & Selected Things Taking Place*, Howard Nemerov writes that "Maybe no one, scientist or poet, has seen things . . . so clearly as she, and surely no one has made seeing and saying so nearly one." Mary Oliver's blurb on the cover of Swenson's last book, *In Other Words*, offers fond praise: "May Swenson's loving curiosity about the world comes to shining fruition in her new book. . . . I don't know when I have been led so elegantly toward thoughtful delight." Freshness, delight, sharpness of focus, and elegance: these terms testify to Swenson's command of her craft, her embrace of her readers, and the respect of her peers.

The Key to Everything is not a critical biography. It is something altogether different: a skillfully framed series of highly personal glimpses into the poet's inner life from the age of thirteen until her death in 1989 at seventy-six. Brucia's graceful contextualization of her life begins by assembling essential family history and cultural background for the experiences Swenson would go on to detail in her earliest surviving diary entries. Moving chronologically, these first accounts illuminate Swenson's early love of literature, her friendships, first sexual experiences, and the sequence of events leading up to her arrival in New York City.

Brucia's approach reveals Swenson's enormous resilience and instinct for survival. This is clearest in diary entries describing her early years in New York, navigating the art scene, mixing work and play, and balancing professional goals with her search for love and personal connection. Over more than a decade, Swenson swings from job to job and apartment to apartment, all carefully annotated in her diaries. Her career gathers momentum in the early 1950s and then begins its ascent into the highest stratum of American poetry. It is here that Swenson begins the friendship with Elizabeth Bishop that sparks their nearly thirty-year exchange of letters, certainly one of the great correspondences in the history of poetry. Brucia judiciously interweaves passages from these letters with Swenson's diaries, illuminating the daily lives and developing literary fortunes of both women. As Swenson's reputation grows, she enjoys the recognition achieved through many publications, both in major literary journals and in books.

By the time of her death in 1989, Swenson had published eleven volumes of poetry, won numerous literary awards, including the Bollingen Prize and Guggenheim and MacArthur fellowships, and served for nine years as a chancellor of the Academy of American Poets. Measuring the value of literary success and personal fulfillment, *The Key to Everything* presents a compelling account of American self-fashioning that mimics the conventional rags-to-riches story but replaces wealth accumulation with artistic achievement.

Following Swenson's death, R. R. Knudson, her last partner and a prolific writer of young adult fiction, became Swenson's first literary executor and biographer. Her initial biographical work, *The Wonderful Pen of May Swenson* (1993), was pitched to a young adult readership. Knudson quickly followed *The Wonderful Pen* with *May Swenson: A Poet's Life in Photos* (1996), a more detailed biographical portrait that she co-wrote with Suzzanne Bigelow. Building on these early works, *The Key to Everything* now takes its place as the most intimate study of the poet's life to date.

This book complements a small number of academic works on Swenson and her writings. Gardner McFall's *May Swenson: Made with Words* (1998) was the first collection to gather important interviews, essays by Swenson, and selections from Swenson's correspondence with Elizabeth Bishop. The publication of *Body My House: The Work and Life of May Swenson* (2006), edited by Paul Crumbley and Patricia M. Gantt, marked the first collection of scholarly essays dedicated exclusively to Swenson. The Library of America publication of *May Swenson: Collected Poems* (2013), edited by Langdon Hammer, was the first volume to bring together all of Swenson's nearly 400 published poems, and more than 140 previously uncollected and posthumously published poems, plus 5 of Swenson's essays on literature.

May Swenson embraced the comprehensive view, resisting specialization. In a long midcareer essay entitled "The Poet as Antispecialist," she said of poetry: "The universe, inside and out, is properly its laboratory" (688). Her approach touched all the vast world, especially its animal inhabitants. Although sophisticated and well read, Swenson believed in looking out and away, free of the filter of excessive book learning. She made light of her education and did not think of herself as a theorist or intellectual. Rather, she believed that her lack of advanced academic training in literature and poetry played to her strengths. The poet and scholar Alicia Ostriker compared her to Walt Whitman when she wrote that Swenson "is a poet of democratic vision and vista . . . a poet who is always surprising, who is not *literary*, not *fashionable*, who belongs to no school" (40–41). In her introduction to *The Poetry and Voice of May Swenson*, the 1976 Caedmon Records recording of Swenson reading selected poems, Swenson told her audience that she regarded many of her poems as "attempts to record received knowledge" as opposed to learning achieved by mental effort.

The poet Mark Doty, affectionately calling Swenson a "sly poet," examines the myriad ways Swenson uses language to get inside what he calls the "texture of reality" (198). Swenson allows us to see through her eyes but often holds her gaze aslant, asking us to ponder a mystery, inviting us to look again at something we thought we knew well. She saw people as "human particles in a culture of living change" (Swenson, "The Poet" 688). Almost all her poetry reflects the roiling process of evolution that makes each moment a novel expression of life ceaselessly seeking new form. She challenges us to "master the Great Whirl or become victims of it" (688). We need science and technology, Swenson reminds us, but "Art . . . forms the emotional and spiritual climate of our experience. Poetry can help man stay human" (688).

The poet has waited a long time for her moment. The great promise of *The Key to Everything* is a fitting tribute not only to its author, but to her subject, the incomparable May Swenson.

Paul Crumbley
Logan, Utah

David Hoak
Palm Desert, California

Works Cited

Elizabeth Bishop, praise for May Swenson, *To Mix with Time: New and Selected Poems* (New York: Charles Scribner's Sons, 1963), back of dust jacket.

Harold Bloom, *The Western Canon: The Books and School of the Ages* (New York: Riverhead Books, 1994).

Margaret Brucia, *The Key to Everything: May Swenson, A Writer's Life* (Princeton: Princeton University Press, 2025).

Mark Doty, "'Question' and More Questions," in *Body My House: May Swenson's Work and Life*, edited by Paul Crumbley and Patricia M. Gantt (Logan: Utah State University Press, 2006), 195–204.

Elizabeth A. Frost, "Visual Poetics," in *A History of Twentieth-Century American Women's Poetry*, edited by Linda A. Kinnahan (New York: Cambridge University Press, 2016), 339–58.

Langdon Hammer, "Chronology," in *Swenson: Collected Poems*, edited by Langdon Hammer (New York: Library of America, 2013), 717–23.

R. R. Knudson, *The Wonderful Pen of May Swenson* (New York: Macmillan, 1993).

R. R. Knudson and Suzzanne Bigelow, *May Swenson: A Poet's Life in Photos* (Logan: Utah State University Press, 1996).

Robert Lowell, praise for May Swenson, *A Cage of Spines* (New York: Rinehart, 1958), back of dust jacket.

Howard Nemerov, praise for May Swenson, *New & Selected Things Taking Place* (Boston: Little, Brown, 1978), back cover.

Mary Oliver, praise for May Swenson, *In Other Words: New Poems* (New York: Alfred A. Knopf, 1987), back of dust jacket.

Alicia Ostriker, "May Swenson: Whitman's Daughter," in *Body My House: May Swenson's Work and Life*, edited by Paul Crumbley and Patricia M. Gantt (Logan: Utah State University Press, 2006), 40–54.

May Swenson, "The Poet as Antispecialist," in *May Swenson: Collected Poems*, edited by Langdon Hammer (New York: Library of America, 2013), 678–88.

———. *The Poetry and Voice of May Swenson*, LP (New York: Caedmon Records, 1976).

PREFACE

THE MODERNIST POET MAY SWENSON, who was born in 1913 and died in 1989, was a storyteller since childhood. As one of her brothers remembered, "May put into words her dreams." Encouraged by her father, she kept extensive diaries for most of her life. The principal sources for this book are those records of her experiences, supplemented by her correspondence, prose, and poetry; her father's written family history and her siblings' oral histories; and interviews with May's friends, neighbors, fellow poets, and scholars of her work.

May's father, Dan Arthur Swenson, encouraged his eldest child's introspective nature. He made twenty blank books for his adolescent daughter and urged her to record in them anything she chose. Those early notebooks do not survive, but her family's memories and May's own occasional retrospective narratives in later diaries provide first-hand glimpses of May as a child and as a young adult. May's telling of her life in real time begins with her earliest surviving diary, when at the age of twenty-two she left home in the Cache Valley of Utah to forge a career and to find love first in Depression-racked Salt Lake City and then in New York City. Her own account of this challenging period unfolds in several diaries dating from 1935 until 1959 and includes an abundance of richly detailed information about May Swenson that has not been previously known, much less published. The focus of *The Key to Everything* is May's life between the ages of twenty-two and forty-six. By 1959, May had established her reputation as a poet. Her poems were appearing frequently in respected literary journals and magazines. She had published two collections of poetry and had received a Guggenheim Foundation grant.

This book begins with May's Swedish-Mormon background and youth in Utah and concludes with her death at the age of seventy-six, but the core of the book is a chronicle of her years in New York City, on a quest to succeed as a poet and to find love. There are several lacunae in the diaries during the 1940s and late 1950s, but May's correspondence with family, friends, lovers, and professional colleagues, most notably the poet Elizabeth Bishop, fills those gaps and preserves May's authentic voice. *The Key to Everything* fulfills the wish that May expressed in a diary entry of December 1952: "I want to confirm my life in a narrative—my Lesbianism—the hereditary background of my parents, grandparents, origins in the 'old country.'"

May's earliest extant "diary" is a sheaf of ruled, loose-leaf paper measuring 6 x 9½ inches and long ago separated from its original three-ring binder. That diary begins on November 24, 1935, in Salt Lake City and ends on January 12, 1937, in New York City. May's hasty, cursive handwriting, mostly in pencil but occasionally in ink, is generally legible. Her dated entries are multipage accounts of daily activities, often interspersed with personal reflections, an occasional drawing or poem, and generously peppered with wry, mordant humor. That diary begins: "Well how soon do you think I will be dead?"

The next diary starts on January 19, 1937, and concludes on December 26, 1939. Like the first, it is written on loose-leaf paper, of two different sizes. Both diaries are part of the Swenson archive in the Department of Special Collections at Washington University in St. Louis. As of this writing, May's other diaries remain in the possession of the literary estate of May Swenson.

May was a skilled typist who held several short-term secretarial jobs during her early years in New York City, where she lived from 1936 to 1967. The inexpensive notebooks she used as diaries during this period sometimes include typed insertions on standard-size paper bearing letterheads from her various places of employment. May perfected the art of appearing engaged in business matters during the workday when in fact she was otherwise occupied. She regularly alleviated the mind-numbing boredom of her daily routine—producing letters from recordings left by her boss on a Dictaphone—by instead typing her own creative work or diary entries. In mid-October 1948, May's boss suddenly entered the room where May was "working." Preoccupied by a recent quarrel with a current lover, May had just typed: "Don't stop even for a cigarette I have to solve this problem," then quickly added, "Damn theres the boss," and yanked the page from her machine for later inclusion in her diary.

In addition to May's diaries, I have quoted liberally from two of her long, autobiographical prose pieces. The first, which she called "The Long Tunnel," dating from June 1948 to March 1949, is May's self-described "novelette," in which she plumbed her subconscious.

The second, "Now and Then," dating from January 2 to July 7, 1959, is an experiment in narrative prose, which May had hoped to publish. This is a third-person account of events in the life of "Miken," a nickname given to May by her lover at the time. I also have drawn some biographical details from a third autobiographical work, May's retrospective "The Bad Luck Diary," written in December 1985, but because it dates from a later period in her life, I do not directly quote from it.

May's attitude toward her diaries changed radically over time. Initially, the diaries were strictly personal, and May's rage was formidable and relentless if anyone breached her privacy. On January 21, 1937, May discovered that her employer, a man named Paltial Rosen, had read and removed pages from the diary she kept in her office, and she became furious. Rosen apologized and returned the missing pages, but May never trusted him again. She wrote this warning to any future intruders:

> My Diary is a record of me—that <u>no one but me</u> has the right perspective for. All others who may read it will be deceived. Warning! You are deceived. . . . [S]ometimes the most significant [things] are left invisible <u>between</u> the lines. . . . It is no autobiography—It is a spilled mind on paper. And it is chaos for anyone else to fathom. Only for me. my book.

Three years later, May permitted her lover Anca Vrbovska to read her diary, but she wrote a cautionary entry addressed to Anca:

> The fact that you read this diary does not worry me; what worries me is that you will misunderstand it. Because in it I am talking to myself and so fully intelligible only to myself. . . . The moment I should discover for certain that someone else reads it, it would cease to be a diary, and become instead a more or less self-conscious and surreptitious vehicle for making an impression and maintaining a pose.

May's attitude underwent a complete reversal during her seventeen-year relationship with Pearl Schwartz. May gave Pearl free access to her diaries and even encouraged her to insert her own thoughts.

Diaries from those years include entries written by Pearl, which were usually responses to May's own observations about their relationship. May sometimes neglected her diary. In the spring of 1950, for example, May wrote, "Pearl said last night—'Your little book is dusty—you never write in it any more—I used to get your picture of us from it.'"

The May Swenson Papers in the Department of Special Collections at Washington University in St. Louis is a treasure trove. It includes May's prodigious correspondence, including with literary critic Alfred Kreymborg and publisher James Laughlin, as well as unpublished prose pieces and, of course, the poems. In 1994, five years after May's death, Rozanne Knudson, her last partner, arranged interviews with six of May's siblings. Copies of these recordings in the St. Louis collection provide invaluable firsthand memories of May. The most helpful source of information in the absence of the diaries is the archive's extensive two-way correspondence between May and her fellow poet Elizabeth Bishop. These items, about 275 in all, span the years from 1950 until Bishop's death in 1979. Although the two women primarily discussed poetry and their artistic milieu, they also informed each other about major events in their own respective literary and personal lives.

A second important archive is the May Swenson Papers, 1932–1998, in the Merrill-Cazier Library at Utah State University in Logan. This collection contains personal and professional correspondence, audio recordings, and extensive information about Swenson family history. It also includes abundant material photocopied from the St. Louis archive and the literary estate of May Swenson, including copies of the interviews with May's siblings.

In addition to primary material, I have relied on three biographical works about May Swenson published after her death: *The Wonderful Pen of May Swenson* (1993), by R. R. Knudson; *May Swenson: A Poet's Life in Photos*, by Rozanne Knudson and Suzanne Bigelow (1996); and *Body My House: May Swenson's Work and Life*, edited by Paul Crumbley and Patricia Gantt (2006). And I would not have produced this book without an invitation to do so from Carole Berglie, executor of the literary estate of May Swenson, who granted me access to May's diaries and related papers.

May was a careless speller who sometimes did not use standard capitalization or punctuation, especially when she was writing or typing quickly. So as not to impede the flow of May's quoted words, I have made corrections in brackets only when necessary for clarity and silently regularized May's use of single versus double quotation marks. I have, however, consistently corrected May's misspellings of proper names, such as Wolf[e], Sap[p]ho, Maugh[a]m, and St[ie]glitz. May's mother, known as Margaret or Greta Hellberg Swenson, who wrote frequently to her daughter, was a native speaker of Swedish and never attended school in America. Her writing is fluid but her spelling is phonetic, and I have left her misspellings uncorrected whenever comprehensible.

Quotations from May's journals and her autobiographical prose pieces written before 1959 are woven into the text as seamlessly as possible, with dates and, in the case of autobiographical prose, titles and dates included for context. All of May's words contained within quotation marks but not numbered or noted are taken from her diaries or from her autobiographical works. Some of her poems quoted in their entirety or in part have been included to add clarity to various events and experiences in her life. However, the reader should expect neither critical nor literary analysis of May's oeuvre.

In *The Key to Everything*, May's spontaneous, authentic voice narrates the compelling story of her personal and artistic growth. This book celebrates that voice.

THE KEY TO EVERYTHING

CHAPTER 1

My Life in a Narrative

THREE DAYS BEFORE CHRISTMAS 1952, May Swenson, then thirty-nine years old, was restless and dissatisfied. She had left her Mormon family in Utah sixteen years earlier to settle in New York and to establish herself as a poet. She had published a few poems since coming east, and one had appeared in the *Saturday Review of Literature*. During sessions at Yaddo, the writers' colony in Saratoga Springs, New York, May had assembled what she considered three "books" for inclusion in a volume of collected poems, but she was unable to find a publisher. In frustration, May wrote in her diary:

> In 2 months or so I must get a job again—save money. Mean-while this plenitude of leisure, solitude—the perfect environ-ment, it would seem, for creation. I'm not yet using it anywhere near fully. . . . The 3 books—Another Animal, Thing & Image, Sky Acquainted—can I do anything with them? Are they good enough? . . . I want to do new work, the chimpanzee with four hands; the kiss; the heart; the dream-machine. I want to confirm my life in a narrative—my Lesbianism—the hereditary background of my parents, grandparents, origins in the "old country"—When my brother Roy was here 2 weeks ago we talked of our childhood—the rocking horse with no ears & a real brush tail our father made.

In her diaries, May gave voice to her deepest thoughts as well as to casual observations. She wanted to "confirm [her] life in a narrative," beginning with her Swedish forebears. But May Swenson, who became one of the most important poets of her generation, never composed a formal autobiography, though she left an abundance of raw material in diaries, letters, prose, and poetry. Others have provided accounts of May's ancestry and early years in Logan, but in 1935, the voice of twenty-two-year-old May first emerges in real time from her earliest surviving diary.

❉

May Swenson's immigrant parents raised their American child to speak in Swedish and to think like a Mormon. This particular cultural fusion percolated through two generations before reaching May. Her Swedish paternal and maternal grandparents had converted from Lutheranism to Mormonism in the late nineteenth century and endured poverty and religious persecution before sailing to the United States and traveling to Utah, to Zion, the spiritual home and promised land of the Latter-day Saints.

Swen Swenson, May's paternal grandfather, was born into a Lutheran family in Grödby, Sweden, in 1850.[1] The youngest of seven children, Swen was the only one to leave his village to attend university. Determined to be a teacher, twenty-year-old Swen enrolled in a seminary in Lund, nearly four hundred miles from home. He lodged in a boarding house, where he fell in love with Thilda Pehrson, his landlady's daughter. Thilda and Swen were married in 1873. Swen became a schoolmaster near Lund, but in 1890 he suddenly and inexplicably lost his teaching position and his comfortable home in the schoolhouse. Swen and Thilda, now the parents of eight children and plunged into poverty, rented a tiny three-room cottage owned by a Mormon widow.

The Swensons, still practicing Lutherans, were visited repeatedly by LDS missionaries sent to them by the owner of their cottage. They gradually became interested in Mormonism, attracted to the church's teachings of love, goodness, and generosity, and to the emphasis on family, both in this life and in the next. They were also drawn to the concept of Zion, a holy gathering place and refuge from persecution where believers lived righteously and studied scripture to prepare communally for the imminent second coming of Christ.

In June 1892 Mormon missionaries baptized Swen and Thilda and their four oldest children. Among them was May's father, Dan Arthur, then eleven years old. Fearing local anti-Mormon sentiment, the couple had arranged a secret, late-night baptism ceremony at a lake within a dense forest. But despite their precautions, reports of the event circulated in the village, and the Swenson family incurred "the hatred of the whole [Lutheran] community."[2]

Swen, publicly scorned and consequently unemployable as a teacher, relied on Thilda, a nimble seamstress, to provide for their family. She designed elaborate aprons and wove fabric for them on a loom made by her husband, and soon the family's weaving concern became a moderately successful business. But the ever-present threat of religious persecution made the Swensons "fear for our lives if we had to leave home to do an errand."[3] The hostility they endured became intolerable and, within a year of their conversion, Swen and Thilda alerted the missionaries of their intention to immigrate to Zion, the land in the Salt Lake Valley established in 1847 as a refuge for Mormons.

A local network of Mormon missionaries—Americans about to return to their home in Zion and some wealthy Swedish Mormons planning to immigrate there—arranged to sponsor three of the Swensons' teenage children, a son and two daughters. Lutherans in the village doubtless believed that the children were destined to become victims of the "depravity of the Mormons, their practice of polygamy, and [their enslavement of] all who they could entice to emigrate to Utah (mainly young girls . . .)."[4] In fact, LDS president Wilford Woodruff had banned the practice of polygamy two years before the Swensons converted, and, according to Dan, his siblings were treated with kindness by their sponsors, who paid expenses and accompanied them to Zion. In exchange, the children worked for their benefactors as housemaids and farmhands until they repaid their debt. Three months after the departure of the last teenage child, a local Swedish couple whom Thilda had converted to Mormonism agreed to take the Swensons' seven-year-old daughter to America "for safekeeping" and to be a playmate for their own young daughter.

Swen and Thilda were desperate to leave Sweden and to reunite as a family in Zion. They sold their books, clothes, furniture, even Thilda's few pieces of jewelry to emigrate with their four sons, but the proceeds brought only enough to purchase a full-fare ticket for Thilda and three half-fare tickets for the younger children. At first Swen and Thilda planned to leave fourteen-year-old Dan with Swen in Sweden to earn money for their tickets. But Dan looked young for his age, and his parents hoped he could slip by unchallenged on a half-fare ticket to help his mother on the journey. So Dan departed with his mother and his two baby brothers, while his younger brother stayed behind with their father. Though he felt guilty for taking his brother's place, Dan realized that "mother could never have managed alone on that journey, with two babies to care for, as well as carrying the luggage."[5]

They traveled in steerage across the North Sea to Scotland, then made a three-week transatlantic crossing from Glasgow on a steamship to New York, where they boarded a train to Salt Lake City for a trip that lasted five days. Thilda suffered from recurring migraine headaches on the journey, and Dan's help with logistics proved crucial. His two older sisters, who had repaid their sponsors for their fares and were working in Salt Lake City as housemaids, met the traveling party at the train station in early September 1894. A few days later, Dan's older brother, now a farmworker, joined the rest of the Swensons. After a brief stay together in Salt Lake City at the home of a Mormon family, Thilda, Dan, and the babies continued to Pleasant Grove, about thirty-six miles south of Salt Lake, where Thilda's Swedish friends were caring for her youngest daughter.

Thilda, now forty-six, rented a house for her family on the outskirts of Pleasant Grove. According to Dan, "It was an old adobe house next to a small canal, so it was handy to get water for the household. There were two small rooms and they were alive with bed bugs."[6] Thilda supported her family by working twelve-hour days cleaning houses, doing laundry, and sewing. Within ten weeks, she had saved and borrowed enough money for her eleven-year-old son in Sweden to purchase a ticket to America. Once he arrived, she moved the family from "The Bed Bug House," as Dan called it, to another closer to town. The new house, Dan wrote, "was just a one-room dugout, with a dirt roof that leaked in rainy weather. We called the place 'The Cellar' since that was actually what the place might have been suited for, a potato cellar."[7]

Swen left Sweden and joined his family in 1896, the year Utah became a U.S. state. Dan was by then proficient in English, but having attended school only in the winter, he had barely completed fifth grade. Within a few years, the now-intact Swenson family purchased a two-room shanty on eighty acres of dry and stony land in Manila, Utah, about two hundred miles northeast of Pleasant Grove. They improved the house, cleared the land, planted fruit trees, maintained beehives, and eked out a living by raising crops of wheat, corn, potatoes, and alfalfa. Swen and Thilda managed this profitable farm with the help of their younger children, the older ones having married and moved away. Dan, meanwhile, found employment in a gold mining camp in Mercur, fifty miles from Pleasant Grove, and boarded nearby with a married sister.

On a visit home, Dan met a young man who had attended Utah Agricultural College in Logan. According to Dan, "He told me that at the school one could obtain a good education and also learn a trade. The idea appealed to me, but how could I, an insignificant immigrant, have the nerve to attain to a college education? But the seed had been planted, and by and by it began to grow. True, my companions at work, hearing of my aspirations, laughed at me and made me the butt of their jokes, telling me that I would never be going to school."[8]

In September 1901, at the age of twenty and with only a fifth-grade education, Dan traveled to Logan, 120 miles away, to register at Utah Agricultural College, where twenty-one faculty members instructed a student body of between two hundred and three hundred students. Guided by sympathetic teachers, Dan enrolled in "sub-preparatory classes" to address the gaps in his education. He performed remarkably well in English class, and by the end of his first year he was reading Shakespeare, Milton, Walter Scott, and Washington Irving, although not without considerable effort. According to Dan, "I didn't always have room in the margin for all the definitions, because I often had to look up the definitions for the definitions."[9]

Dan also became a star in the Mechanical Arts Department, where his favorite class was woodworking. He designed and built an elaborate cellarette (a small cabinet for storing wine and other alcoholic beverages), although, as an LDS member, Dan did not consume alcohol. More than sixty years later, he wrote in his autobiography, "I am sure that my plan contemplated the most elaborate piece of carving ever attempted at the College up to that time (and for that matter, since that time, if I do say so myself)."[10] Made of "quartered oak, with carved corner pieces and an elaborately carved panel for a door," Dan's cellarette, cited as "the best specimen of wood carving," received a silver medal at the state fair in 1907.[11]

Utah Agricultural College provided Dan with a solid education and a marketable trade. Upon his graduation in 1907, six years after he began his studies, Dan was hired as a picture-frame maker in a busy framing shop in Salt Lake City. At last life held promise. At the age of twenty-seven, Dan could now save a small portion of his income and dream of finding a wife and buying a house.

Dan was a devout member of the LDS Church who attended services, sang in the choir, and taught Sunday school. Prompted by his parents, he consistently contributed a tenth of his meager earnings to the church. Dan was ordained a priest and, in anticipation of serving a mission, was elevated to the status of elder in 1908, thus enabling him to perform the sacrament of baptism.[12] The Mormon community in Sweden was growing rapidly, and in 1909 Dan was summoned to return to his native land as a missionary. He and a fellow missionary traveled through the Swedish countryside preaching, selling religious books, distributing devotional pamphlets, and baptizing converts. After a year and a half of this peripatetic life, Dan was assigned to work at the mission office in Stockholm to edit the Mormon journal *The Star*, as his father had done. For the first time, at the age of thirty, Dan had a desk job. Describing his work in his autobiography, he wrote:

> I kept plenty busy at my desk, early and late, for I had much to do. . . . In addition to getting out the "Star" on time (which involved correction of the manuscript as it was set up and returned from the printer, which was done twice before the OK to print it was given) my responsibility was to wrap and address and send out a copy to each subscriber within the mission as well as to all who lived outside of Sweden, and also to have charge of all the tracts and publications and fill the orders by mail as they came in constantly from the missionaries throughout the mission. Then of course there were the meetings and sometimes concerts in the chapel to attend and an assignment to speak in meeting once in a while.
>
> At these times there were occasions when a ray of sunshine made the world seem bright. It was when Greta Hellberg could get off from her busy duties at the Old Folks Home . . . and come to attend the meeting and I could greet her and feel her soft hand in mine and look into her smiling eyes.

> I was [also] made assistant to . . . the new choir leader. . . . He
> would often send the sopranos and altos with me to my office to
> practice their parts. . . . Greta was by far the best alto. She sang
> herself right into my heart.[13]

. Margaret ("Greta") Hellberg had been born into a large family. Gre-
ta's father died when she was seven, leaving her mother to support the
family. "In 1901," Greta recorded in her autobiography, "great things
happened to us to change our lives."[14] The Mormon missionaries found
the Hellbergs, and, when Greta was twelve, she and four other family
members converted.

Shunned by friends and relatives because of her family's Mormon
faith, Greta left home for Stockholm before she turned fifteen. She
struggled to support herself, working as a housemaid, a waitress,
and a shopgirl. Greta was in her early twenties when she met Dan in
1911. Mutual love and respect and their devotion to the Mormon faith
formed the basis of their strong and enduring relationship. Greta later
wrote, "I can truly say that we two were always sweethearts."[15]

But Stockholm's damp weather weakened Dan's pulmonary system
to the point that he was no longer able to work. Having reluctantly
left Greta, Dan returned to Utah's clear air in 1912. There, his lungs
improved and he was able to perform occasional tasks for the church.
Nevertheless, he was bereft without his "sweetheart." Greta, recounting
their separation in her autobiography, recalled, "[H]e wrote to me
every day telling me of his love so I knew that he felt we should not
wait to get married since he was already thirty-two years old."[16]

Six months after Dan left Sweden, a Mormon family in Utah spon-
sored Greta by paying for her passage to America. "[It] seemed like
an eternity," wrote Dan as he awaited her arrival, "for I loved her so
much."[17] Dan and Greta were married at Thilda and Swen's house in
Salt Lake City on August 21, 1912. They sealed themselves to each other
according to the Mormon marriage rite and vowed to remain together
not merely "till death do us part" but "for time and all eternity."

Driven by perseverance, talent, resourcefulness, and faith, May's
progenitors were the authors of their own success stories. They mea-
sured their accomplishments not in material riches but in spiritual
wealth, for they were deeply religious. They accepted and internalized

LDS doctrine, sacrificed time and money to support the church, and led their lives according to Mormon principles. The Swensons also cherished their Swedish identity, keeping the language and traditions of their native country alive within themselves. These were May's ancestors, and their influence on her was profound.

Dan had maintained his friendship with his Agricultural College woodworking teacher, Professor A. J. Hansen. Upon learning that Dan had married and was back in Salt Lake City, Hansen arranged a teaching position for his prize student in the Mechanical Arts Department at the college. On a cold January day in 1913, Dan and Greta set out for Logan, eager to begin a new phase of their life together. Greta was five months pregnant.

CHAPTER 2

An Innocent Era

"OUR FIRST BABY, ANNA THILDA MAY, was born at 2:30 a.m. on Wednesday, May 28, 1913. . . . May came into the world safe and sound, and what a 'bonny lass' she proved to be, and how proud we were of our beautiful child," wrote Dan in his autobiography.[1] May was chubby, fair, and blue-eyed, with pin-straight blond hair. Officially the namesake of both her maternal and her paternal grandmothers, to her parents May was simply May. "I am born in May, and I am named May and my birthday is in May," she proclaimed as a two-year-old, and her proud father recorded his daughter's astute observation.[2]

May did not have much time to savor the exclusive attention of her doting parents. Anticipating a large family, Dan and Margaret soon moved from their tiny rental to a four-room house nearby, at 495 N 6th Street E, where more space was the move's only improvement. The Swensons' second rental house had no central heating. During the winter, Dan and Margaret lit a fire in the stove in each room at bedtime, but by morning the rooms were cold. Nor was there any internal plumbing. Water came from a hydrant outside, and a path over a bridge to a nearby canal led to the outhouse. In winter, the water often froze, and snowdrifts covered the route to the privy.[3] May's brothers were born in this house: Roy in 1915, Dan in 1916, and George in 1917.[4]

While May's parents struggled to provide for their four young children, the Great War was raging in Europe. George, their third son, was born less than five months after America entered the war. The Mormons of Utah were eager to prove their loyalty to the United States after their long battle for statehood, and many men enlisted in the 145th Field Artillery Regiment, which was sent to France but did not see action before Armistice Day. Dan, as sole support for his wife and young children, did not serve.

During May's early childhood years, her parents spoke only Swedish at home. When May entered Webster Elementary School, she could neither speak nor understand English, but she was presciently

FIGURE 1. May Swenson with her father, Dan Arthur Swenson. *Literary Estate of May Swenson.*

undaunted. Her youngest sister, Margaret, recalled her parents telling the story of May's return home after her first day at school. "Oh, it was wonderful," May reported. "They had a fountain with lemonade, and after playtime we had pink ice cream with chocolate cake."[5] Margaret said this was typical of May, who loved to give her fertile imagination free rein. May learned English quickly and did well in school, earning praise from her teachers. Gradually, English supplanted Swedish in the Swenson household, and May no longer had to juggle both languages. When her parents commended her for her early success in school, May blithely explained, according to her sister Ruth, that she appeared to be smart only because "the other kids were so dumb."[6]

The Swenson family moved again in 1921 or 1922, after Dan purchased a larger lot at 669 E 5th Street N, a hundred yards from the campus of the Agricultural College, where her father taught "mechanical engineering," which May glibly dismissed as a fancy term for "woodworking."[7] Dan, following plans and instructions in a house-building kit, constructed a six-room bungalow equipped with hot and cold running water, a bathroom, and a full basement.[8] He made most of the

FIGURE 2. Young May stands on a chair made by her father.
Literary Estate of May Swenson.

furniture himself and installed a customized kitchen sink and counter,
lower than normal and just the right height for May to help with the
dishes. Dan would ultimately expand the bungalow to a sixteen- or
seventeen-room house to accommodate his growing family.

By the time May was ten, she had three sisters: Grace, born in 1921;
Ruth, born in 1922; and Beth, born in 1923. This trio expanded to a
quartet after the birth of Margaret in 1928. A fourth brother, Lloyd,
was born in 1931 but died in infancy. Paul, born in 1935, when May
was twenty-two, was the tenth and last child.

Margaret depended on her oldest daughter for household chores
and care of the children. As May's brother George later explained,

"May was Mother's helper. I can't remember her being in any way rebellious."[9] Besides washing the dishes, May scrubbed the floors, ironed shirts, put up and stored fruits and vegetables for the winter from the Swensons' extensive garden and orchard, gave her sisters their "Dutch cut" haircuts, invented games for all the children, and, best of all, amused her siblings with imaginative stories.[10]

Ruth recalled, "I would sit on a high stool and watch her iron. She made up stories." Ruth's favorite was a story May told while she was scrubbing the kitchen floor. Their father had taken his three younger daughters to town that morning to buy shoes, an expense he could barely afford. As seven-year-old Ruth sat in the doorway admiring her new shoes, May narrated a tale about a centipede who had ten children, all of whom needed shoes. The story, besides a subtle commentary on the sacrifices parents make for their children, was a disguised math lesson. Ruth explained that May "helped me figure out the logistics—ten children, each with one hundred feet, equals one thousand feet or five hundred pairs of shoes!"[11] Her brothers were also the happy beneficiaries of May's imagination. "I remember her telling us stories . . . when I was five, six, seven, eight—something like that," said George, adding: "She was a pretty ideal older sister, in my recollection." Looking back on those years, George realized that May's storytelling was more than an attempt to amuse her siblings: "[May] put into words her dreams. And she was able to do that in talking to us—about life."[12]

May's siblings understood that being the oldest child in a large family had benefits as well as drawbacks. May's sister Margaret explained that "more was expected of May," and that helping her mother as much as she did throughout her childhood had consequences later. "May had to do a lot of housework and she hated it for the rest of her life," Margaret observed.[13] On the other hand, however, Beth, George, and Paul agreed that being the oldest gave May an edge in their parents' affection.[14] Beth said, "She being the first, I am sure she got an overabundance of love." George, perhaps a little wistfully, described his father's relationship with May: "He especially loved May because she was the first one. She got the lion's share of love to begin with." And Paul said, "She was the apple of both of my parents' eyes. She was given more free rein than the others because she was the oldest."

FIGURE 3. May and one of her brothers sit on the hood of the family's 1914 Studebaker, with siblings and friends on the running board, while May's mother stands nearby, 1925. *Literary Estate of May Swenson.*

As the family grew, the children divided themselves into groups by age. May and her three brothers (Roy, Dan, and George) formed an inseparable foursome of playmates, with May as their ringleader. One of their favorite indoor pastimes was a game they invented called "Lion," which May commemorated in an early poem (1949) of the same name:

> and I remember how I played lion with my brothers
> under the round yellow-grained table
> the shadow our cave in the lamplight

Besides building a dining room table that became their lion's lair, her father also made toys for his children.[15] George remembered, "Dad gave us older kids stick horses different from any other child's in Logan because Dad made them with a wheel on the bottom and handles on the side of the head, and he hand-drew the eyes and mouth. It was a real elegant stick horse—and that was the beginning of May's loving horses. She *loved* horses. I remember the four of us riding around and I felt

FIGURE 4. Dan and Margaret Swenson and their first seven children. Back row (*left to right*): Dan A., Roy, May, Dan H., Margaret. Front row: Beth, Grace, George, Ruth. *Courtesy Lisa Turetsky.*

really privileged—and a little smug—because no one in the neighborhood had anything like that. And yet we were just above being poor. To have that much advantage over my friends made me feel kinda good."[16]

May's frequently anthologized poem "The Centaur" is ostensibly about riding a stick horse as a child but is actually about her need to be herself. In it she is neither with her band of brothers nor showing off on her fancy horse. Rather, ten-year-old May is alone as she gallops along on Rob Roy, a stick horse she fashioned herself with a pocketknife from a growing and pliant willow branch. She melds with her horse as she gallops, and the horse gradually becomes part of her. The fusion of horse and child just happened, unanticipated, the way, as she would say later, her poems just happened.

In an interview conducted in 1977, May said:

"The Centaur," you know, is a childhood memory. The girl in this poem (who is myself) feels herself to be the horse. . . . When I was ten and I was riding this switch that I cut from a willow tree, it was really true that I felt I was riding a horse, to the extent that I became this, that I was experiencing it so vividly that it was as though I became it.[17]

At some point in her youth, May came to believe that she, like the mythical centaur, was truly a hybrid creature, that she really was "part animal," and that "running wild" was the natural thing for her to do, despite her mother's disapproval.[18] And the woods and fields around her home offered plenty of open space for this pursuit.

Logan, Utah, is situated in a ruggedly beautiful western landscape. For an imaginative child like May, the natural setting evoked a pioneer past when Shoshone, fur traders, and trappers roamed the wilderness in the Cache Valley at the foot of the Bear River Mountains. From her adolescence May sought solitude in nature whenever she could steal away from her responsibilities. She frequently escaped to the garden or to the orchard or to a stand of willow trees near the house. In a nearby field, she hollowed out a haystack to create a secret cave or climbed into the treehouse her father had made. Ensconced in these various hideaways, May read, thought, and wrote.[19] She had begun writing, she later explained, at the age of thirteen: "I didn't know that I was writing poems. But when I'd type them out their arrangement was instinctive, and I'd say to myself: 'This must be a poem. It doesn't look like a story.'"[20]

May lived on the edge of the campus of the Agricultural College, first in a rented house and then, when she was eight or nine, in the house her father built. Houses in this rural small town were close enough to permit easy contact with neighbors, most of whom were not Swedish. Helen Richards, LaNorma Jensen, and Muriel Morris were her constant companions. In summertime the girls played jacks, jumped rope, and read. Helen Richards, according to Muriel's later recollections, was "a strong, spiritual person," active in the church and steeped in Mormon doctrine. May, Helen, and Muriel were such devoted friends that they referred to themselves as "The Three Musketeers."[21]

An avid consumer of literature from her earliest years, May often returned home from the nearby Logan Library laden with children's classics like L. Frank Baum's *Oz* series and Lewis Carroll's *Alice*

FIGURE 5. May's childhood home in Logan, Utah, decorated with Christmas lights, 1936. *Literary Estate of May Swenson.*

in Wonderland as well as a wide variety of nonfiction.[22] Her friend LaNorma remembered being impressed with May's choice of books, describing them as "profound books, books of inspiration and learning."[23] And like Louisa May Alcott's Jo and Laurie in *Little Women,* May and Muriel set up a secret mailbox—a cigar box perched in an apple tree between their yards—and left messages for each other when they were children. May preserved a cherished, undated note from Muriel.

> Dear MS—Francis and I we will call for you at 3:30 by the gat an go to her hous to mak her brother let us rid the Bike. Anser emediately. Your best Friend.
>
> M.M.[24]

The Logan Library's inventory record reveals that the library added *Little Women* to its collection in 1919, when May was six.[25] What a role model and soulmate May must have discovered in Jo March: creative, free-spirited, reluctant to accept traditional norms of femininity and determined to prove her worth, against the odds, as a published author.

Dan and Margaret worked together in close partnership to keep their household running smoothly. May paid tribute to her kind and loving parents, but especially to her nurturing father, in her poem "October," written in 1975, when she was sixty-two.

> Dad would pare the fruit from our
> orchard in the fall, while Mother
> boiled the jars, prepared for
> "putting up." Dad used to darn
> our socks when we were small,
> and cut our hair and toenails.
> Sunday mornings, in pajamas, we'd
> take turns in his lap. He'd help
> bathe us sometimes. Dad could do
> anything.

May and her family lived in a bubble of Mormonism. May's sister Margaret, recalling her childhood, described a typical week in the Swenson house.[26] Her mother and father arose at 6:00 a.m. and knelt at their bedside to pray. At 7:30, the entire family gathered for a family blessing of food and breakfast. During weekdays in the academic year, the children walked to school after breakfast and Dan walked the short distance up the hill to his teaching job. May's mother read scripture until 10:00, then attended a meeting of the Relief Society (a philanthropic and educational Mormon women's organization), or visited the sick, or gathered with other women to "share spiritual messages." Returning home, Margaret did housework and prepared dinner. The children either came directly home from school or attended "Primary," "Mutual" (Mutual Improvement Association), or "Seminary," which were age-appropriate religious instruction classes. The family reconvened at 6:00 p.m. for a blessing and dinner, usually of Swedish fare. Afterward, May washed the dishes while the younger children did homework and her parents read. At 10:00 the family knelt together in bedtime prayer. On nonschool days, the schedule was the same, except that all the children performed household chores, worked with their father in the garden, or were free to play. Bath time was once a week, on Saturday evening.

Each member of the family voluntarily skipped two meals each month. Dan and Margaret calculated the cost of their food and donated that sum to the poor in their ward (the LDS term for a congregation). Also, all the Swensons contributed a tenth of their earnings to the church.

"Family night" began after dinner on Sunday with communal prayer and song, then everyone took turns reading from the Book of Mormon or the Doctrine and Covenants, after which the family knelt in prayer together. Family games and refreshments brought the evening to a close. About once each month, May's sister Margaret explained, the normal pattern varied when families in the local congregation, or ward, gathered, usually at the Swensons' house. A speaker gave a "fireside"—a talk—followed by prayers, hymns, and refreshments.

Margaret was proud of the way her parents had raised her and her siblings:

> The Church's teachings did permeate our lives when we were young. The songs, the prayers, the teachings of love and goodness and concern for others were an integral part of our growing years and helped make us what we are.

Margaret also explained that her parents encouraged their children to seek a blessing from the patriarch, an LDS official. Each personalized blessing addressed the "life pattern" the patriarch envisioned for a child. Margaret's siblings would return to the precepts of their blessing for guidance throughout their lives. May's patriarchal blessing, given to her when she was twelve, survives. The private and individual nature of patriarchal blessings, which are generally not shared with others, makes it difficult to determine how typical May's was in comparison to the blessings received by other Mormon girls at the time. But this precocious and independent little girl, the hybrid child who had galloped on her stick horse barely two years before, must have found some of her blessing difficult to accept:

> As you advance in years you will continue your labors in the midst of the daughters of Zion. . . . In due season you shall have a companion in life that will be a man of God, one upon whom you

can lean for support and for aid in the work you are called to per-
form. You will become a mother in Israel, the true spirit of moth-
er-hood will descend upon you and the gift of control will be
given unto thee, which will enable you to control yourself, your
feelings, your appetite, and subdue every passion that stands in
the way of your great progress.[27]

During her childhood and early teens, May embraced Mormonism,
at least outwardly. Her sister Beth, younger by ten years, was too young
for a specific memory of that period, but she suspected that May began
drifting from the fold in her midteens.[28] Her brother Dan, only three
years younger than May, believed she had begun questioning her faith
before high school, but he had no recollection of religious friction in
the home.[29] The next younger brother, George, felt that their mother
especially would have been sensitive to apostasy: "Though Mother
did not have a lot of formal education, she had an understanding of
things that was really unusual. She was able to see into things quite
deeply."[30] In any case, in those years May remained, as she would
through her life, profoundly influenced by Mormonism's emphasis on
the importance of family.

In an undated letter to May, written probably in the 1940s, after
both May and her younger sister Grace were no longer practicing Mor-
mons, May's mother reviewed her own conversion and professed her
faith. She also reminded her daughters of the consequences of their
departure from the church:

I thank the Lord every day that my Darling Mother listened to
the Elders way back in 1891 when they brought this glad word
to us, in our home in old Skandinavia and I too could listen and
believe. I was only 12 years old then, but I could feel and know it
was the gospel truth, and just think what it meant to us, because
of it I met your Dad who was a great missionary and a special
servant of the Lord, to bring the gospel to so many souls and,
Oh May, it was heavenly the day we could go together into the
house of the Lord, and be married for time and all eternity which
gives us also the assured blessing of being sealed as a Family
for all eternities if we only live rightious to the end. Thats what

I am striving for and praying for every day that the Lord may
bless you and Grace to understand and realize that you two must
so change your lifes, to be worthy also to come with us into the
Lords holy Temple, so that our Family Circel can be compleat.[31]

Margaret feared that May's and Grace's rejection of Mormonism
would prevent them from joining the rest of the Swenson family in
the afterlife. The future baptized children of a sealed couple, accord-
ing to Mormon doctrine, were automatically sealed to their parents
and would remain with them in the afterlife, providing their children
were faithful members of the church at the time of their own deaths.
Margaret found her daughters' lack of faith difficult to reconcile and
painful to accept. May worried about causing her parents anxiety. Her
sister Ruth observed, "May just loved our parents so much. She never
wanted to hurt them and felt bad if she did. She knew they felt bad
that she wasn't in the Church."[32]

According to Mormon doctrine, to join her parents and siblings in
the afterlife May needed to be more than "pure and righteous": she
also had to be married. If she did not marry in her lifetime, she could
become posthumously sealed to a man by proxy—surely an unsettling
thought for a person of her independence.

May had firsthand experience with posthumous sealing; her own
father had sealed himself to a second wife in 1922, when May was
nine. Dan had met a young woman, Hilja Pahjonen, in Stockholm in
1910. Hilja was attracted to him, but Dan was too in love with Mar-
garet to notice. Hilja died the following year, making it known before
her death that she would like to be sealed in the afterlife to Dan by
proxy, and Dan complied. Eleven years after her death, Hilja and Dan
were posthumously sealed in a celestial marriage rite in the temple in
Logan, with Margaret serving as Hilja's proxy.

Perhaps Dan was the first person to notice his adolescent daughter's
questioning of her faith. He surely recognized her tendency toward
introspection and acknowledged it by presenting May with twenty
small blank books that he had made. He encouraged her to use them
to record her thoughts. May later said that she used these as diaries
to discuss with herself what was happening inside her.[33] Her father's
gift inspired May to become a lifelong diarist.

May, a saver from her youth, sequestered these journals, her earliest writing, and personal letters in the cherrywood desk her father had made for her and in the cedar chest in her bedroom. No diaries and only scant ephemera from May's childhood survive. In 1968, however, Muriel Morris, May's closest childhood friend, renewed contact with May after several decades. Her letter prompted a warm reply from May in which she confirmed the wonder of their shared childhood and congratulated her friend for leading a satisfying life.

Dear Muriel: Those were innocent times—I mean our child-hood—and it was an innocent era, the first quarter of this cen-tury. And we were in an innocent place in society—the church out there in Utah. . . . You are still who you were except that your life has been added upon, having had, as you say, perhaps a very ordinary life as wife, mother and grandmother, and what a triumph to be able to write "but it has been very satisfying to me." That's it, that's all—that's the definition of success and hap-piness—that's the total, no one can get more, and a few in all the mass of mankind past and present, I suspect, obtain it.[34]

CHAPTER 3

Creature Both Male and Female

MAY ATTENDED LOGAN HIGH SCHOOL from 1926 to 1930. Although May's older siblings offered little information about her years there, Ruth recalled that May participated in LDS-sponsored programs, including "lots of outdoor nature activities before she started college." Hiking and camping were preferred pursuits, and George remembered that his sister "was very active physically." Her brother Dan, when asked about May's social life, "[couldn't] remember any time boys came to the house to take May out," and George recalled that his sister had only female friends. At home, May's responsibilities included housecleaning, but, reported Beth, "May wasn't one to do a lot of cooking." Like her sisters, May was required by her parents to take dancing lessons from their cousin Edna Swenson, known as Sunny.

May and her best friend, Muriel Morris, entered Logan High School together as freshmen in the fall of 1926. The following year, Helen Richards, the third member of their triumvirate, joined them. The 1931 edition of Logan High's yearbook, *The Amphion*, shows Helen as an attractive young woman with a dimpled chin and fashionably marcelled hair.

May's sister Margaret, who had read May's earliest and no longer extant diaries, believed that Helen Richards was May's first love.[1] The bittersweet memory of those repressed erotic yearnings persisted long into May's adulthood. Writing in her diary on October 13, 1937, she recalled her intense desire for Helen while pitying her own current suitor to whose entreaties she could not respond: "I remember my own similar devastating passion and all its nuances so exquisitely nourished and kept moist and raw like new wounds. Helen I mean mostly, when I was about 13, 14, 15."

Under May's senior portrait in her yearbook, only one achievement is noted: May won the prestigious Vernon Short Story Medal during her junior year.[2] "Christmas Day," May's prizewinning story and her first published work, appeared in the Logan High School newspa-

per, *The Grizzly*, in December
1928.[3] A hefty monetary award
of $25 (worth approximately
$425 in today's dollars) accom-
panied the honor. "Christmas
Day" is compelling, lush, lyrical,
maudlin, and creepy. A young boy
named Waldo awakens at dawn
on Christmas from a terrifying
dream about his parents. As he
sneaks downstairs to see Santa's
bounty, Waldo stumbles, making
a loud noise, and at the sight of
his gifts, he yelps with joy. But the
house remains ominously silent,
and Waldo's concern about wak-
ing up his parents turns to fear.
Returning upstairs, he discovers
his mother and father dead in
their bed. His mother's face ap-
pears "white as marble except for

FIGURE 6. May as high school student in
the backyard of her Logan home. *Literary
Estate of May Swenson.*

a faint bluish tint on the eyelids and tinging the lips," and his father's
looks "angry and yet as if in pain." The story flashes forward thirty-five
years to another Christmas. Waldo, prematurely aged, sits in a cabin
contemplating that life-changing morning when he was a ten-year-old
boy. In May's enigmatic conclusion, as the "old young man" reflects on
the tragedy, his eyes "dance with merriment one moment and dilate
with pain the next."

May's description of Waldo's dead parents was perhaps based on
her own still vivid memory of her paternal grandparents, Swen and
Thilda, laid out for burial. Swen had died when May was twelve and
Thilda when she was fourteen, the year before she wrote "Christmas
Day." These first experiences with death awakened in May a curiosity
about the subject that remained with her and surfaced frequently in
her poems.[4]

The Vernon Short Story Medal was a harbinger of May's future
recognition as a writer. In college she would strengthen her literary

FIGURE 7. Helen Richards, May's childhood friend. *Literary Estate of May Swenson.*

skills and become a vibrant and respected member of an elite circle of writers and artists.

The Morrill Land-Grant Act of 1862 established colleges on federal land to provide agricultural and technical education, especially in rural areas. Utah Agricultural College (UAC) was founded in 1888; in 1928 its name was changed to Utah State Agricultural College (USAC); and in 1957 it became Utah State University (USU). May's father taught in the Mechanical Arts Department of USAC, which was only a short walk up College Hill from the Swenson residence. Despite the land-grant college emphasis on practical skills, UAC also offered a curriculum in the liberal arts, toward which May naturally gravitated when in 1930 she joined a freshman class of 518 students—332 men and 186 women—at USAC. By the time May graduated in 1934 with a BS in English and a minor in art, the college's enrollment had nearly doubled.

As an officer of Delta Phi Epsilon, an organization that fostered the creative arts on campus and in the community, May and her fellow students arranged art exhibitions and social events to promote the work of local artists.[5] She joined the staff of *Student Life*, USAC's weekly campus newspaper, and was also a member of the Scribbler's Club, known for its left-leaning literary quarterly, *Scribble*, whose mission was "to encourage and advance the art of writing and provide means of expression for literary talent."[6] The Scribbler's Club was May's entrée into the society of dynamic student writers.

May's college years coincided with a period of campus unrest and activism. The stock market crash in 1929 struck Utah disproportionally hard. By 1933, according to an article in *Utah History Encyclopedia*, "Utah's unemployment rate was 35.8 percent, the fourth highest in the nation," and "32 of Utah's 105 banks had failed."[7] Added to financial insecurity was statewide political upheaval. Utah's Mormon-backed Republican Party, in power since statehood, gave way to the more liberal Democratic Party as Utah joined the landslide election of Franklin D. Roosevelt in 1932.

In assessing the effect of the economic "slump" on American campus life, the *New York Times* reported that the typical student in 1932 "has sold the flashy roadster and is buying second-hand books, and more than ever before he is asking for scholarship aid, low-priced dormitory rooms, and a chance to work his way."[8] The same article noted "a trend away from technical education toward cultural subjects." At USAC there sprouted "Trailertown," a ramshackle collection of trailers inhabited by students unable to afford university housing. Yet a dedicated faculty that endured pay cuts and an increased course load lifted the college to new heights of academic achievement.[9] And the steadily increasing size of the student body made for a more diverse community.

As Utah State University archivist Robert Parson observed,

Nationally, as well as locally, the 1930s produced a social climate that encouraged diversity, and challenged the more traditional culture of previous decades. Many students became critical of

American institutions during the 1930s. Some [like May and her friends] embraced the new political ideas that emerged from FDR's New Deal policies; others resisted the prevailing shift towards Roosevelt and the Democrats in 1932.[10]

May's siblings traced her falling away from the church, her smoking, her use of profanity, and the embrace of her lesbian identity directly to this period of her life, and they attributed May's altered behavior to the influence of her college acquaintances. "Her friends were not Church-approved types—they were smokers, for example," her brother Dan said, adding that he was surprised and shocked by May's "profane vocabulary."[11] A yearbook inscription from May to a fellow member of the Scribbler's Club in 1933 supports Dan's suspicion about the source of May's colorful language. "I learned my first juicy swear words at your kind knee," she wrote.[12] But surely she had rebelled, at least privately, against Mormon cultural norms long before she entered college. Her sister Margaret observed, "She struggled with the effect [of her changing attitudes toward Mormonism] on our parents. She didn't want to hurt them. She was not secretive; she just never brought it up."[13]

Regarding May's sexuality, her sister Ruth said, "Some of my brothers and sisters thought she had friends in college—in the drama department, the art department or writers—who may have gone in that direction."[14] But May reveals in her diaries an earlier attraction to females—by the time she was thirteen.

Despite their tendency to disapprove of May's USAC friends, her siblings knew little about them—except for Edith Welch, one of May's closest friends. Edith, who lived in Mendon, a town about eight miles from Logan, met May during the summer of 1930, after they had graduated from different high schools and before they entered USAC. May convinced her parents to permit Edith to live at the Swensons' house—and to share her bedroom—while Edith, who took her meals with a family across the street, attended college. This arrangement continued until Edith graduated in 1935, a year after May. In an interview years later, Edith recalled:

I paid May's father $3.00 a month for the privilege and boarded across the street for another $20.00 a month. May's family was good to me. Her mother seemed to me even then to be hard put to know how to treat her intelligent, imaginative daughter. She wanted all five of her girls to lead normal lives in the Mormon church, and May didn't seem to be fitting into the pattern. Her friends at the college were the "wrong crowd"—slightly "pink" and critical of the Mormon faith.[15]

In 1985, remembering her feelings for Edith, May wrote about riding her brother's bicycle the eight miles from her house to Edith's, and the pleasure she took in their picnics and hikes together. She also fondly recalled sharing a bed with Edith when she lived in the Swensons' house. When questioned about their sister's friendship with Edith, none of her siblings except Margaret suspected that May and Edith were lovers. But Margaret, who had read May's earliest diaries and papers and knew that "first there was Helen Richards, then Edith," was not sure "how explicit" either of those relationships had been. She recalled that May and Edith "spent a lot of time climbing mountains— out in nature. They both liked it."[16] George described May and Edith as simply "buddies" who were "on the same wavelength."[17]

In 1932 May published a love poem entitled "Fruits" in the *Scribble*. It begins, "Your love . . . / I will savor it upon my tongue all day! / like a wild tropic fruit."[18] Edith was likely May's inspiration.

Another of May's friends at USAC was Gladys Hobbs, to whom she was also physically attracted. Gladys, a fellow graduate of Logan High School who was three years older than May, had written for *The Grizzly*, and after her graduation from USAC in 1931 she became a journalist. Like Edith, Gladys wrote for Logan's *Herald Journal*, but in the spring of 1936 she relocated to Salt Lake City to work, first for the *Tribune*, and then for the *Deseret News*. In 1940 Gladys Hobbs and Donald Goodall were married in the Unitarian Church in Salt Lake City. Glad's wedding announcement in the *Tribune* described her as a "popular bride [who] is well known in social and newspaper circles."[19] May's reaction to this event is unknown, but years later, after a three-day visit with Gladys and Don in Toledo, Ohio, May commented in a letter that she "became rather bored with their company" and criticized Gladys and Don for "slipping into the bourgeois rut."[20]

FIGURE 8. May Swenson (*left*) and Edith Welch, on the Utah
State Agricultural College campus, prepare for a camping trip
at Logan Canyon. *Literary Estate of May Swenson.*

Two of May's most accomplished literary friends in college were
Grant H. Redford and Ray B. West Jr. Also graduates of Logan High,
both became USAC campus leaders who participated actively in the
Scribbler's Club and served on the staff of the school newspaper, *Stu-
dent Life*. A friend of May's noted that Grant was "romantically hand-
some, magnetic of temperament, and seemed a drama all by himself."[21]
Grant's senior picture in *The Amphion* highlights his chiseled features
and dark, curly hair; the tilt of his head and brooding expression set
him apart from his smiling classmates. Grant frequently alienated
himself from more traditional professors and peers, and, as Robert

Parson observes in his article "'Leftward March,'" he "delighted in challenging the sacred cows of the day."[22] Grant questioned LDS authority, championed free and open discussions of human sexuality, and was a steadfast critic of American militarism and warfare. May's brother Dan speculated that May had been romantically "interested in him."[23] Grant and May maintained a warm, if sporadic, correspondence throughout their lives, and Grant reliably expressed pleasure in May's major literary achievements.

In 1937 Grant accepted a teaching position at Branch Agricultural College in Cedar City, Utah. That same year, his friend Ray West joined him on the faculty, and together they launched the literary journal *Intermountain Review* (later known as *Rocky Mountain Reader*, *Rocky Mountain Review*, and finally *Western Review*). The journal was an outlet for emerging authors in the relatively new genre of western American literature.[24] In the late 1940s Grant returned to his native Seattle and taught at the University of Washington until his death, by suicide, in 1965.

Ray West graduated from USAC a year before May and attended graduate school at the University of Utah in Salt Lake City while May was living there.[25] May remained in contact with Ray and published an early poem, "Music Maker," in his literary journal in 1937 as well as several poems, including "The Centaur," during the 1950s.

When May graduated in June 1934, Edith was still living at the Swensons' house, finishing her degree; Gladys was working full-time in Logan as a reporter for the *Herald Journal;* Grant was still enrolled at USAC and a formidable presence on campus; and Ray was pursuing his master's degree in Salt Lake City. May continued to live at home and worked as a part-time reporter for the *Herald Journal*, hoping to be offered a full-time position.[26]

May's first surviving diary begins in Salt Lake City on November 24, 1935, more than a year after her graduation. A full fifty years later, however, in "The Bad Luck Diary," May revisited the weeks in Logan and the youthful heartbreak that preceded her departure for Salt Lake City, recording that in the early fall of 1935 Edith had surprised May by marrying a fellow student at USAC. Edith's new husband, and in effect May's successful rival, was Floyd Morgan, whom May knew as an accomplished playwright and a director of Shakespeare's comedies. May was devastated and found it difficult to wish the new-lyweds well. Only May's sister Margaret understood May's pain. Years later, she posited that Edith's marriage was the reason that May left Logan.[27] Edith and her husband remained in Logan for the rest of their lives. Floyd taught at USAC and Edith became an editor of the *Herald Journal.*

A few weeks after Edith's wedding, May joined her cousin Sunny in Salt Lake City. Sunny was an accomplished pianist and dancer who, during the early 1930s, had lived in the Swensons' basement apartment while she studied dance nearby. By all accounts, Sunny was lively, self-confident, and fun-loving. May's mother greatly admired her niece and "wanted May to be more like the popular, outgoing Sunny."[28] According to Swenson family lore, Sunny was the first to recognize her young cousin as a poet. When May showed her a page of an early diary, Sunny "noticed that the sentences scanned, and remarked that May was writing poetry."[29]

The first entry in May's earliest extant diary is an account of the few preceding days. May had found a job selling ads, mostly by telephone, for a magazine called *Utah.* She reported to a small group of men, her "bosses." Her "beat" included Ogden, forty miles north of Salt Lake, where, when the job required, she stayed in a hotel for several days at a time. On November 24 she had just returned to Salt Lake City from Ogden. No doubt still unsettled by Edith's marriage and uncertain about her own future, May began:

> Well, how soon do you think I will be dead? Many people have died at the age of 22 and for no reason beyond the excellent reasons Fate has. I have a feeling tho that I shall see an old age for a long stretch barren of adventure like a desert without wind and every mile like the next and level and sandy.

She mentioned that she had completed a poem, "In Jupiter Street," when she was "kicking my miserable self around Ogden." She had taken time from work to go to the Carnegie Library to compose the poem "on the stuffy scarred table" before returning to her hotel room to call prospective clients and to smoke little cigars. In her poem (published in 1952 as "Jupiter Street"), May imagined living in outer space, "eight years out from Sundown / on a dancing star." Her home was "swathed by winds," in sharp contrast to "the desert without wind" she believed was her true destiny.

May also wrote that her *Scribble* friend Gladys had come from Logan for an overnight visit. Glad and May attended a concert of the Russian Cathedral Choir at Kingsbury Hall, the vast performing arts center on the campus of the University of Utah. "They sang like Godlings. We the 5,000 gasped and beat our palms to burning," May reported.

After the concert and before returning to May's apartment, May and Glad stopped at "a little roadhouse," where May, wearing one of Sunny's "swank" hats, drank grapefruit juice and whistled Gershwin tunes ("not at the same time, of course"). In preparation for Glad's overnight stay, May noted that she had ironed a pair of wooly pajamas for her friend, for whom she felt "a prepared affection." But, to May's disappointment, there was no romantic interlude, and Glad returned home early the next morning. May was frustrated and "in the tearing hair mood—and like a dog whining inside his teeth." Toward the end of this lengthy first entry, May admitted to cheating her bosses by lying about the number of ads she had sold.

By December, May's life had fallen into a pattern of selling ads, socializing, attending concerts, going to the movies, reading Thomas Wolfe, lamenting the state of her life, drinking heavily, and flirting with men. On December 5, for example, she wrote: "I have been reeling in suckers for the 'Utah'—I'm getting quite cold blooded about it—Made about $5 in Ogden yesterday. Every word I say in my spiel is an elaborate lie. I only worked about 1 hr & a half—and less than that today—What th' hell. That's me you see." In the same entry, she mentioned that Ray West had offered to find her a date and that she had attended a Tchaikovsky concert performed by the Seattle Symphony Orchestra. She concluded by musing, "I must begin my life. Begin to die. . . . I have yet to find my love."

On December 8 she wrote, "I am reading Of Time and the River by Wolfe," and on December 11 she boasted that she was "getting to be a better liar—alias good salesman—every day." She also philosophized about drinking: "Toddys are to be sipped—whiskey gulped. A jigger or two makes some things more hazy and other things more clear."

On December 15 she recounted the events of a "business" meeting (really a social gathering) with her bosses, at which one of them, Earl Borg, took her outside and tried to kiss her. May wrote, "We skipped up and down the street to get me sober." Then she and Borg got in his car and went "to get some Spanish Fly and cigarettes to smoke" before returning to the party and drinking heavily. May explained that "Borg" was married with two children and "doesn't love his wife but is very kind to her . . . & means to make the best of it." When Borg continued to flirt with May, she was amused. "Really he was funny," May wrote, "thinking me a little inexperienced girl from the country."

Four days later, on December 19, May recorded an encounter with a fellow ad salesman, Lincoln Thompson, an accomplished pianist and composer.

> But today, Lincoln Thompson played for me. I met him on [the] street said "Hi"—and he has a tight looking face & tight mouth and tightly curled hair and his suit looks like he gets sick-drunk in it frequently. . . . He writes mediocre poetry, composes very good music.

May went to Lincoln's "swank rooms at the Newhouse" and, after hearing him play, she "gave him [her poem] Calm Weather to compose." Although May made no further mention of Lincoln ever following through with her request, she was obviously interested in having her poetry set to music.[30]

By December the seed of moving permanently to New York was already germinating in May's mind. She discussed her plans with Lincoln: "I told him all my children were going to be born in New York." But Lincoln, taking her literally, asked facetiously whether she planned to start having children "immediately upon arrival." May was, of course, speaking metaphorically; her future poems were her as-yet-unborn children. In 1953, when May's family was assembling a book about Swenson family history, May received a form to fill out, as Rozanne Knudson reports in *The Wonderful Pen of May Swenson*:

"[I]n a space on the page to list children, if any, May wrote the names of the thirty-nine poems she'd published since leaving Utah."[31]

Shortly after writing in her diary on December 19, May left Salt Lake City with Sunny to spend the Christmas holidays in Logan. She did not write again until January 1, 1936, a few days before her return. In that lengthy New Year's Day entry, May recounted the high points of her stay in Logan.

One of May's first visits was to the home of Edith Welch Morgan. "Edith," she wrote, "seems to me big and rather unfeminine, and where is the old elusive, unexplainable charm?—something in the eyes, in the mouth, and the set of the smile." Edith and Floyd talked about their honeymoon and showed May their pictures.

The Swenson family's traditional Christmas Eve dinner by candlelight, predictably, was a "delightful" family event. May brought presents for her brothers and sisters and was thrilled with Glad's gift to her of a copy of *Roget's Thesaurus*. Grant Redford telephoned May on Christmas Eve.

The following Sunday, December 29, May went downtown to the *Herald Journal* office to work on a piece she was submitting to the Logan paper. In 1931 two local newspapers, the *Journal* and the *Herald*, had merged. The offices and the production plant of the new *Herald Journal* had moved into a large building that also housed Logan's premier hotel: the Palace Hotel.[32]

> I was writing "cock-eyed world"—down at [the] Herald. It was Sunday night. Peck came in [and] we began talking [and] he told me about contraceptive that is only sure thing—the talk was strange—was glad to be informed. Said would get one for me. But costs $2.

Nothing more is known about May's piece "Cock-eyed World." Bramwell Peck was the name of the man who stopped to talk to May while she was working. Peck had been a history teacher and the debate coach at Logan High School, and May had likely been his student. A faculty picture of Peck, wearing dark-tinted glasses, appears in the 1930 edition of *The Amphion*. He was totally blind, having lost his eyesight when he was a teenager. Forty-year-old Bramwell Peck was now working full-time as a reporter for the *Herald Journal*. His successful career as a blind reporter made him something of a local celebrity. Featured in a newspaper article in 1928, his interviewer explained Peck's remarkable modus operandi:

> Peck walks all around town, guiding his steps by ear. He knows most people by their walk. He can tell by a person's step who the person is. He remembers a voice after being once introduced, and can remember names, addresses and statistics picked up on his rounds, and then typewrite them on his return to his office.[33]

And Peck himself explained to his interviewer that he used psychology to get what he wanted from people. "If you want a man to tell you something you must get him in a good mood, make him laugh and he will talk. It is my opinion that I have an advantage: I can ask questions without appearing ridiculous, since I do not see and people are always ready to explain even the most minute detail."

May matter-of-factly recounted her unplanned sexual encounter with Peck and left no doubt about who used psychology on whom on the night of December 29:

> Well later he said would I like him to give me a sexual experience. But before then we went down the basement stairs and he felt me to see what size of rubber ring [I needed]—I wasn't scared. I went immediately when he said "Come here."

Peck told May to meet him at the registration desk of the nearby Palace Hotel. As she waited for him, she felt "exhilarated and aroused" at the thought of "sneaking away to fuck with a blind man." When they learned that a room would cost a dollar (about twenty dollars today), they went to the Chamber of Commerce instead. The office was closed and the lights were off, but the janitor, who was in another part of the building, had left the door unlocked. May continued:

> He didn't care about the dark because he is blind—but I insisted on finding the light switch. I wanted to see what went in. Well—

all the rings hurt—when I lay down on the table on his coat and
he fitted them. So he said "Come here"—and he sat down and I
was to let him stick it up in me once to make me expand—and it
took a lot of persuading—but he said I won't let any spermatozoa
come. I can feel it coming. So finally I let him—and he unbut-
toned. First I just stood and stared—it was such an astonishingly
shaped thing—fat and slit and so [illegible] hair in a bush at the
base. But he tried and tried but couldn't get it in me—got it in
the wrong place—did not seem to have any erection. Well then
we hunted around for [a] couch and went in the other room. I
kicked my pants behind a chair. Well it was no use. Sweat stood
out on his brow poor man. The janitor came clumping up the
stairs. "Act like we are talking about a rehearsal"—So we did—me
rather lamely.

By the time the janitor had left, May had changed her mind, but Peck
convinced her to try again.

So I lay down on the floor. But it was no good. Couldn't get
that huge fat thing in me. He said I was terribly tight. I joked
about that. By this time I was feeling quite chummy & noncha-
lant. But I was mad because it was wasting so much time and
I ought to get back to my typewriter. We finally gave it up. I
could see that Peck felt ruefull. He said [he] had helped a lot
of girls out—getting them orientated and finding an out for
some that had got caught—not with his. I put my pants in my
coat pocket and we left. The rehearsal we agreed laughing was
a flop.

Remarkably emotionally detached while recording the details of her
uncomfortable and awkward rendezvous, May abruptly transitioned
from her experience with Peck to the subsequent success of her news-
paper submission.

I made $10 on the cock-eyed world. The next day Peck came in
and stopping at my desk said "Hello." I said "Hello" sounding a
little peeved but I really wasn't.

If Peck thought he was taking advantage of May, he was wrong; if anything, he was satisfying her curiosity. "May was interested in life's processes," her youngest sibling, Paul, observed—birth, death, and both the male and female sexual acts.[34] Just four months before her sexual encounter with Bramwell Peck, May had requested and received permission from her mother to witness the birth of her brother Paul. And, on December 5, just a few weeks before the incident with Peck, with "life's processes" on her mind, May wrote in her diary, "Sex—is secondary—creature someone both he and she or neither. I feel I am either or both. I am creature."

May's entry for January 1 continued for another two pages, turning to literary topics and her friends. She wrote about a visit with Grant to the house of a friend, Veneta Nielsen, whose poetry she admired, and about the new novels that Grant and Ray had written: "I am reading [Grant's] novel—revised. In places it is true. It is often confused & beside the point. Ray has written a novel. Grant should be a school teacher."

May next mentioned that she had finished reading *Of Time and the River*, by Thomas Wolfe, and that she thought his ending was ineffective. She concluded by looking forward to her return with Sunny to Salt Lake City. On January 5, four days later and still in Logan, May visited Gladys Hobbs and her current boyfriend, who had just returned from a trip to New York. Talking excitedly, they shared their adventures with May, further stoking her desire to travel east.

On January 10, having returned to Salt Lake City, May proclaimed in her diary, "I quit the 'Utah.'" She had applied for a job in the classified department of the *Tribune*. One week later, after an unsuccessful interview, May expressed with renewed vigor her determination to succeed.

> I've gotta find out how to be poised—always at trigger point and beautiful—for the two are synonymous—ballance and beauty. Thinking I will start now. Thinking I will conquor—Thinking glory—glory—glory—I demand it.

May's invocation of glory, here and elsewhere in her diary, is a direct echo of Thomas Wolfe. In *Look Homeward, Angel* and *Of Time and the*

River, Wolfe's alter ego, Eugene Gant, breaks away from his family in pursuit of glory as a writer, and May consciously followed his lead.[35] Believing that poetry would be the source of her glory, she wrote and revised poems feverishly. A performance of the Ballets Russes in January likely prompted her poem "At the Ballet," and Ted Shawn's all-male dance troupe, whose performance she attended with Sunny in February, directly inspired another poem: "[A]fter seeing those dancers and only half-realizing them—I could finally write this poem 'The Dancer' which is really finished." Sunny had studied under the acclaimed and innovative choreographer Ted Shawn, and her enthusiasm for dance intensified May's already considerable interest. May concluded that diary entry with her now repetitive refrain, "Restless some of these days—time passes. I want glory."

A little more than a week later, on February 11, May wrote, "no job in sight and broke and smoking sigs & reading 'Sap[p]ho' and 'Magnon [Manon] Lescaut.'" Here is May's earliest recorded reference to the poetry of Sappho, a poet she remained fond of for the rest of her life. In her later years, according to May's friend Sallie Reynolds, May could quote fragments of Sappho from memory. Also on May's reading list was Thomas Wolfe's recently published *The Story of a Novel*, his memoir about his relationship with his editor, Maxwell Perkins.

Giving vent to her frustration about job prospects, she confessed, "I wish I were a young man." On a more optimistic note, she reported that her former boss, Borg, "is actually going to town with his advertising plan—and me with him—cause aren't I just that kind of tenacious go-getter, and aren't I an idea person—? Sure!"

Earl Borg, the married man who flirted with May, was both ambitious and in step with the times. Having overseen the advertising department of the magazine *Utah* when May was on staff, Borg now saw potential in creating his own advertising agency. Radio was the new advertising medium, and he planned to air ads on the Salt Lake City radio station KSL. Earl Borg was on the cutting edge of something big, and May knew it.

Five days later, on February 16, May declared, "Earl J. Borg Ad Agency born today—yeah I come in . . . I gotta come through." Determined to succeed in her new venture, May gave herself a pep talk in her diary: "Let me learn how to be eloquent—Let me be sophisticated,

serene and smart as a whip—I want all those things. . . . If I must be
a woman let me make use of it—let me learn how to use it—I want
to get along—I want glory. . . . Hey—look at me—here I am—god or
somebody—or anybody—me—me—I want glory. Glory, every kind."
But on March 1, she wrestled with self-doubt. "In the young sun of an
afternoon working up in the avenues I sat on the coping of a church
and smoked a cigarette and felt lousy as hell cause my job's too tough
for me." But she reminded herself that Glad, who had accepted a new
job in Salt Lake City as a reporter for the *Tribune,* would arrive to start
work in just a few days. Thinking of Glad caused her to muse, "What
do you think? Shall I ever love <u>anyone</u>—"

Glad stayed at the Newhouse Hotel for a few days until she found an
apartment, and May joined her there. On March 5 and 6 she wrote, "I
slept with Glad. . . . It was too hot for a night gown. . . . Glad is pretty.
I was looking at me naked the other day—I thot [thought] 'girl, where
is thy lover?'" May and Glad slept in the same bed, but they were "not
intimate"—and Glad soon found a new boyfriend. Undaunted, May
continued to pursue Glad.

In mid-March, after a half-day of work, May had dinner, read po-
etry, and listened to popular music with friends at Glad's apartment.
"Played 'Let yourself go,' 'I'm putting all my eggs,' 'It's been so-o-o-o
long,'" May noted. The first two songs, written by Irving Berlin and
sung by Fred Astaire, were from the newly released film *Follow the
Fleet,* and the third, in his signature swing style, was Louis Prima's
latest recording. May, tipsy on "highballs," wrote, "I got feeling hid-
eous—dizzy—sick. I put my head out the window into the glittering
sleet blowing past—in the wet black shining night—I felt better and
had some black coffee—and got in bed. . . . I felt so tender looking
at Glad—and her clean childish rosy face from her bath—and in the
dressing nook—I said 'Gad, Glad, I think you're swell'—and I do."

"I'm getting so good it scares me. I've got almost $50.00 coming," she
bragged, and on March 18 she described her commute to Springville, a
town fifty miles south of Salt Lake City, and the opportunity it afforded
her to covertly observe people, a lifelong practice.

I couldn't find the alarm clock—it ringing like mad under the
bed among the shoes—but in between—Springville—I had to

fight tooth and nail—took $32.50—pissed behind a bush behind
the library and got on the 9:22 and came home. . . . I stare at
all the people. People standing in the car zones waiting—I love
to gobble them with my eyes—the inexhaustible fascination of
people, people, people—all so alike—a few so unalike—all the
people! Incredible.

Though May's work was a success, her love life was not, but not for
lack of trying. She met Grant Redford for coffee at a drugstore and
revealed cryptically that she felt nothing but a vague sense of "un-
comfortableness" upon seeing him. Perhaps they had had a romantic
interlude. May also mentioned that she was casually dating Frank, a
man she had met in town and with whom she went barhopping. On
April 5 May recounted her disastrous last date with Frank and titled
that segment of her entry "No delecasy."

[Frank] has no delecasy—that is equal to the crime of stupidity. . . .
[W]hen he would have persuaded me with a thumb in the crease
of my loin and his mouth forcing mine apart—I said enough—I
said "I'll hate you." . . . I have yet to find my love. This is important.
Death perhaps will be my only lover? Lover?

Just before Easter, May heard a concert by the renowned Austrian
pianist Artur Schnabel, who had recently completed the first ever re-
cording of all thirty-two Beethoven piano sonatas.

[W]hat is there to compare to this kind of joy? The great hall
seen from a box on the right—the hushed house, seated people
listening—turned to the square of light in which is the man and
his instrument. The spotlight falling on his white hair. He sat,
he gazed within, he let his hands come to the keys at last—so ex-
plored our souls and gave us his—thru the fingertips—trickling.

On Easter Sunday, April 12, 1936, May and Glad attended high
mass at the Cathedral of the Madeleine in Salt Lake City, "half in awe
and half in mirth." The cathedral, completed in 1909, was the seat of
the Catholic Diocese of Salt Lake City.

[W]e sat in a pew behind a flock of nuns—mumbling over their beads, their very clean and homely faces bent over their clean, limp almost nailless fingers. Like so many penguins in black and white and shapeless were they. The pageant—painted windows— the rich colored walls, Christ, naked on a cross, the mouth a half moon of agoney, the drowned eyes—this for loosing the jets of emotion, this for swelling the currents of delicious pity—. I can understand it—how millions of people <u>worship</u> this thing. The choir—this is an authentic beauty—music is truth when radiance is in the voices and trumpets and the organ—and the procession of priests & choir boys—magnificently costumed marching in the aisles. Then the hocus pocus—the insane burlesque of tradition & symbolism, on the stage the Priest's tall dunce cap, the pacing of everything, the peaked hands not suggesting prayers so much as lunicy—The bells & chants & clapping of hands—idiotic—The faultless blue sky, and the summer world in the sunshine when we came forth—was Cathedral enough for me. Oh—but the sun was warm—juicy—a juicy sun in the streets—spilling down the pavements.

May had dressed appropriately for the occasion, donning "a new flow-ered dress with a pink bow—and a new white straw hat—dainty— wearing rouge even being the sweet young thing." But though she looked the part of a devout parishioner in her Easter finery, she con-fessed the truth in her diary:

I swiped the dress—which was $12.50, wearing it out of the store under my other dress—I was afraid it would hang down & show around the bottom. I had a splitting headache which seemed [a] token of guilt. I'm glad I stole it, tho. $12.50 to my <u>good</u>.

May continued selling ads for Borg and took on another job at the *Tribune*. Though it rankled her that she did not have so prestigious a position as Glad at the newspaper, she welcomed the added income. Her goal was to save enough money to travel to New York with Sunny at the end of June.

Sunny's father had purchased a new car for his daughter, and May planned to accompany her cousin on a bus trip from Salt Lake City to Pontiac, Michigan, where, fresh off the assembly line, her car awaited her. From there, she and Sunny would drive together to Lee, Massachusetts, to attend summer dance performances choreographed by Ted Shawn at his retreat in the Berkshire Mountains. Then they planned to travel south for a few days of fun and excitement in New York City before returning to Utah.

May never told Sunny that she had no intention of returning to Utah. On May 6, however, short of funds and plagued with doubts, May wrote in her diary:

Like I said to Glad . . . "Even if I can barely get enough to get there—I'm gonna go East with Sun—I'm sick of it here—and it would at least make a better story to starve in New York than in Salt Lake City." But of course that was melodramatic—I haven't got the guts to really put myself where I might starve, But I am sick of it . . . I'm becoming jealous of Glad too—her swaggering out with a photographer, Paul, & other lackies in her train—or on assignment—and going on drinking & dancing parties with . . . the musicians of the Phila symphony.

May was aware of the devastating effect that her permanent departure would have on her unsuspecting family and particularly her mother. On May 26, two days before her twenty-third birthday, she confided in her diary: "I keep thinking of my little brother—growing up—me not there. . . . I wrote a poem 'As the Falcon.'" Published in 1938 as "Like Thee, Falcon," May's poem addresses her internal conflict: her need to soar and the importance of grounding. "I would reel in air, / infinity my marge / . . . as the falcon, return would I too / from the mist."

For the next three weeks, with her departure at the end of June looming, May's social life became frenetic. She dated a policeman named Andy and enjoyed expounding her "communistic leanings" to him. She spent a "lovely" evening consuming "sandwiches and soda pop" before a night of dancing with Clay. She went to a party to find that Glad's boyfriend, the photographer Paul, was there, but Glad was not. When Paul made advances to her, May acquiesced: "He kissed me because he wanted to kiss Glad so he kissed me see? Yes perfectly clear but why should I consent to be the goat? Unexpected side to me I guess—I understand you, Paul. It was a crazy party."

She smoked a lot, read William Saroyan's "The Snake," invoked Walt Whitman, reworked some poems, brooded over her lack of a satisfying love relationship ("And I have yet to find my love") and second-guessed her decision to go to New York ("Have been debating over and over weather to risk this no-account carcass in N.Y.—no money—no pull—nothing to grab in deep water. Seems fool-hardy in a way—again I am bogged down here").

On June 20 May hitchhiked to Logan "to see Dad about going East," never mentioning that she was setting out on a one-way trip. The familiar smell of her childhood home greeted her at the front door. She read her old diaries, which she found "boring I'm sad to say." Then, "with a mixture of eloquence and earnestness," she persuaded her father to cosign a promissory note acknowledging his loan to her of $200 and her pledge to repay him. She hitched back to Salt Lake City with $200 in traveler's checks safely in her pocket.

A few days before her departure, May celebrated with Glad, Glad's boyfriend Paul, and some of May's older friends in the advertising business, about whose behavior she sententiously observed, "Middle-aged people should never get drunk, mental note." She spent the night with Glad for the last time.

> We left the empty cups—we went home. I slept with Glad. . . .
> Glad said:—"You were cute tonight, May—so cute and bright-
> eyed. You said clever things."—how soft & downy to sleep on! . . .
> Glad and I now that we are about to part—feel melancholy and
> warm friends together. . . . And that same night we went bare-
> foot—and Glad in her pjs—up on the capitol lawn on a shadowed
> slope—and lay looking at the stars letting the wind lap our bod-
> ies—seeing nothing but the high vaulted sky and the remote glit-
> ter of the stars.

On June 27, the night before her departure, May wrote:

> new roads—a new city—life, life you are there, ferociously await-
> ing me—far—in another city. . . . I am writing in this book for the
> last time in this life before going away on a bus . . . New York is
> to be my hometown . . . New York—my city—Walt Whitman's
> and mine. You Walt Whitman & Thomas Wolfe—soon Alfred
> St[ie]glitz—soon to be in that City—

May and Sunny left for Pontiac, Michigan, early the next morning.
"1500 miles—by day and night on the bus." After passing through Wy-
oming, Nebraska, and Iowa, they arrived in Chicago on July 3, where
they spent three nights at the YWCA. They took a boat ride on Lake
Michigan, "walked the Loop," ate hamburgers at Wimpy's, and went
"slumming in China Town" with several young men. On July 6 they
rode the bus all day and night to Pontiac, where Sunny happily took
possession of her beautiful blue coupe.

Now free to travel at their own pace and on their own route, May
and Sunny drove through Canada. Fascinated by the hayfields they
whizzed past, May began "working on a poem about hayricks," which
she would publish as "Haymaking," first in Ray West's *Rocky Mountain
Review* in 1938, then in the *Saturday Review of Literature* in 1949.
May's poem is a paean to the "lean-hipped men in aisles of stubble,"
who gather "the yellow stuff of summer" into the barns so that, when
winter comes, the cows can "munch on summer." "Haymaking" cap-
tures May's lifelong fascination with nature, animals, and her own
childhood, when she hollowed out caves for herself in haystacks.

They stopped to see Niagara Falls and spent the night of July 10
in Rochester, New York. "It's hot," May wrote. May's complaint about
the heat was not idle. July 1936 marked the culmination of one of the
most severe heat waves ever recorded in U.S. weather history, causing
the death of more than five thousand people. Searing heat blanketed
the East Coast from Virginia to New York.[36] On July 9 the temperature
in Central Park reached 106 degrees, the highest temperature ever
recorded.

Sunny and May detoured near Rochester to spend a day in the woods around Palmyra, where Joseph Smith, founder of the LDS Church, had lived as a child and where, in 1820, the fourteen-year-old boy had a vision of God the Father and Jesus Christ. "We sat in the dry chestnut leaves in the 'Sacred Grove,'" May wrote. On July 13 they spent the night on Blue Mountain in the Adirondacks and then drove south, arriving at Jacob's Pillow, near Lee, Massachusetts, on July 16.

Jacob's Pillow, a name derived from the zigzag ascent (a reference to the biblical Jacob's ladder) and the pillow-shaped rock at the summit, was the Berkshire Mountain retreat and training school for Ted Shawn and His Men Dancers. Shawn had purchased the property in 1931, and he and his troupe built structures on the campus and farmed the land for food. To raise money and to promote their work, the dancers gave popular on-site tea lecture demonstrations.[37] Barton Mumaw, the company's principal dancer, was also Shawn's chauffeur, valet, and lover, but the men concealed the nature of their relationship to avoid censure.[38] May was transfixed by twenty-three-year-old Mumaw: "Mumaw—Barton Mumaw—he smiled cordial and sweet his hair swirls in the back—oh he has a fawn's ears—he has the look in his eye—obsessive dancer."

After leaving Jacob's Pillow, Sunny and May, pressing on toward New York City, spent a night near West Point, where they went "to a hop" at the Military Academy with some cadets who, according to May, "kept their guts sucked up." The next evening, Sunday, July 19, May complained in her diary, "I just about got raped on Flirtation Walk." She did not mention how she had met Bill Atwell, "from Boston and Bah Hawbah," who accompanied her on the secluded and rocky trail reserved for cadets and their escorts, nor did she mention where Sunny was at the time:

> He took me at Kissing Rock and after in a crevice & I said I was
> not mad at him after. . . . He looked outraged and his suit was
> mussed—spick & span Cadet Bill Atwell—and his short crop
> was ruffled—frustrated Bill Atwell because I wouldn't let him put
> his hand under my dress. he was panting and hot. . . . I wanted
> only truth to myself and insisted "no"—so we were mad and
> parted with chilly and over-cordial handshakes. . . . I hated him

gratefully. I was glad to hate him. . . . I had a mood—terrible with
tears and inward writhings—and I wrote to Thomas Wolf[e] a
letter. Then I went down and had a hot then an ice cold bath.

May's "letter" to her literary idol Thomas Wolfe, written in her
diary on July 19, 1936, the night before she arrived in New York City,
is almost a prayer, or perhaps a promise, from a young woman who
knew she was on the brink of becoming someone new.

Dear Thomas Wolf[e]:

Here we are—Roget and I again. He is the only lover I can
tolerate—Like you and the penny you remember—the one you
rubbed

Have you ever looked long at your hands Thomas Wolf[e]—or
your ankles so tenderly shaped and your feet on the rug when
you have undressed them when you are undressing to go to bed?
Thomas Wolf[e] have you ever said—oh incomparable I oh lover
& beloved oh creature I creature both male & female—oh lovely
one

Ashes—frail color of dust and smoke web thin as a thred rising
between my thumb and index finger and the pages of a book
strewn with words words cryptic black lines on the
white page—only these to feed on to contest my ravenousness—
Thomas Wolf[e]—

Oh I have the gaze ferocious & suave of the plush bellied panther
leaning on the bars of his cage

Oh Thomas Wolf[e]—I crouch like a panther and a snarl
meaning sweetness and rage rises in my gaze—the sweet taste
of frustration & rage is on my palate—and I lie here—splendid
and forlorn these bars on my body printed there by the shadows
of captivity

God is a word that comes up to my lips I spit it forth

    God? God! God.

Thomas Wolf[e]—this evening is the one before the day I shall
come to your city—my city I am coming into the thick of it
I come to you and the millions they the people why do I weep? I
weep

Tomorrow I enter there by the Hudson sullenly flowing

    I shall die in Brooklyn Thomas Wolf[e]

I come here to be born
    and to die

There is a boy Thomas Wolf[e]—with the stare of the obsessed
with beauty and dark hair in a swirl at the nape of his head and
standing up so quietly—his eyes so quietly gazing—his name is
Barton Mumaw and he is a dancer

I stood beside him & I was a continent away—oh sad & lovely
heart I too I too but I cannot reach over to you
    never shall I touch you
never shall the star in the south of Heaven the star stares with
lovely gaze—ever fall and clasp with that other star
riveted in the North weeping tears like golden beads the
weeping star—

The world would be better without mirrors—

On July 24 May wrote a brief note in her diary, staking a birthright
claim to her new home: "arrived N.Y. City Monday July 20–1936. Here
am I in the city of my birth—you may look for me now in these streets
and hereafter. M.S."

CHAPTER 4

The Taste of Love

A FEW WEEKS AFTER ARRIVING IN NEW YORK, May asked herself, "Am I homesick?" Her answer was, "Only when I am asleep. I have so many dreams of our place—the smell of pears in sunny autumn and lying on the shop roof above Morris's orchard and the tall disheveled grass." When she was awake, the allure of New York, her new "home town," left May little time to think about Utah and her family in Logan—or about Sunny.

May did not record at what point she revealed to her cousin that she planned to remain in New York. Nor did she mention how long Sunny stayed in the city before returning home. By July 29, 1936, the date of her next diary entry and nine days after her arrival, May had settled into an apartment on the Upper West Side with two roommates: Mary Berg, a fellow alumna of USAC, and a young woman whose first name was Louise. May had scribbled Mary's name and address and the name of a contact at the New York LDS "Mission Headquarters" on a page of her diary. There is no indication that May and Mary had been friends at school. Perhaps before leaving home May had asked Mission Headquarters in Salt Lake City or the alumni office at USAC to connect her with other Mormon women in New York with whom she could share expenses.

May's bedroom walls bore all the hallmarks of a college student's dorm room: her drawing of a monkey, unframed reproductions of favorite works of art, and a souvenir pennant.

> He is on the wall by my bed here—my monkey—and also there
> is Picasso with his naked boy leading a horse—and a cool and
> beautiful jumble by Matisse—then a banner saying Adirondack
> Mts—likewise the cigarette saucer of brown painted clay with a
> chip out—and primarily my little brother in the dented washtub
> stuck in the mirror frame—I hear him laugh each time I comb
> my hair. And this is my room—the view from the window is a

patch of brick wall. I like it here. This is New York the city of Walt Whitman, Thomas Wolfe and Alfred Stieglitz. I have $69 left.

May rented a typewriter: "It is simple & quick—no capitals—no gadgets." On Friday, August 7 she vowed, "Tomorrow I'm going to get up early. I set my mind for 7." May and her new roommates had planned to catch a train to Boston to visit a former USAC professor nicknamed "Fussy." Frank ("Fussy") Arnold, a native New Englander and legendary teacher of Latin, German, French, and English during his thirty-six-year tenure at USAC, was known for "smoothing rough edges off rural youth."[1]

Two Mormon elders, Brother Phelps and Brother Gardener (who, May noted, pronounced her home state "Utahr"), met the young women in Boston and drove them to Braintree, Massachusetts, where the professor lived with his two unmarried sisters. After the older women had plied them with cucumber sandwiches and ginger ale floats, Fussy entertained May and her friends on the porch.

> He prodded us each in turn with disconcerting questions and gave us each a token of his keen contemptible wit. Mary made a great hit with him. Louise too he liked for her femininess. And Me—he said "Have you found yourself at last?" And I replied "yes"—but this only partly true. He said "I wondered if you would turn out to be a genius or just ordinary." So do I.

May had clearly left an impression on a revered professor who recognized her intellectual potential.

May, Mary, and Louise spent Saturday night at Fussy's house and saw the sights of Boston on Sunday. Impressed by the city's illustrious and historical past, May took everything in through the lens of the hard times brought on by the Depression. "Here Oliver Wendell Holmes walked with his patriarchal beard—Now the tramps stumble up from their newspapers in the damp grass—rubbing their eyes in the gray dawn—some of them still huddled like snails on the grass in the morning."

By mid-August 1936 May had acclimated to New York. She went to the Lewisohn Stadium, a huge amphitheater seating eight thousand

and stretching from 136th to 138th Street. There she attended the Philadelphia Ballet's performance of Maurice Ravel's *Daphnis and Chloe* and *Bolero*, after which she ran thirty blocks back home to her apartment. She visited the Museum of French Art on Fifth Avenue, between 48th and 49th Streets, to which she enthusiastically vowed to return "again and again." And she sometimes spent quiet evenings with her roommates.

> One night we sat in Riverside park on the grass slope amongst all the neckers and watched the lights of Jersey across the Hudson, and the steamers sailing North on the dark Hudson. And talked nonsense and laughed a lot and it was a dusky warm night. Some tramps had their ragged fires on the shore—Louise, Mary and I— our faces were pale in the half-light—our eyes deep and bright.

May often went to the movies. On one occasion, she walked from 109th Street, down Broadway, to 45th Street, "negligently, like a Lord—for do I not own this? Are these not my streets?" She saw *The Thin Man*, starring William Powell and Myrna Loy ("squandering my money, you see!! I have $40—my rent due"). May would have paid a quarter, the equivalent of about $5.50 today, to see a movie.

As May's savings dwindled, she needed to seek employment and to break her self-indulgent pattern of going out at night and sleeping later and later each following morning. "I wish I had to get up early to a job—any job almost," she wrote on August 15. "I have been getting entirely too much sleep." The next day, she pasted into her diary the classified ad she had posted in the *New York Times*.

> WRITER, college degree, trained arts, literature, keen, healthy, physical, mental poise, age 23, do anything progressive and legitimate that nets living.

May received four responses. The first was from a woman in her late sixties, Regina Jais, who was a noted author of travel books, "sort of an Isadora [Duncan]" type.[2] Wearing slacks and a bandana, Jais received May at her home on West 11th Street. A butler served refreshments in the rooftop garden, and Jais offered May twenty dollars a week to type a manuscript.[3] May gave Jais's proposal serious consideration but pursued interviews with the other respondents.

The three men who replied to May's ad likely interpreted her offer to "do anything progressive" as an invitation for romance. Forty-eight-year-old Charles Zig Shye, who happened to be in legal difficulties related to petit larceny, arranged to meet May at his home on West 74th Street.[4] He presented himself as a "theatrical man" with an interest in drama who was looking for help with his writing. May quickly saw this unsavory character for what he was: a "sham" with a "clammy hand" who "killed my blithe mood, god damn him."

Then came Mr. Leigh, a business executive seeking a secretary. After "cross-examining" her after hours in his private office, Mr. Leigh lured May (wearing "a flowered dress" and "stolen perfume") to his leather divan, where they engaged in "all the known varieties of osculation, some savage and civilized—and other things." But May "had him guessing to the bitter end about the question of her virginity," and finally "the virgin—er—'writer'" fled from "the very common ordinary and now almost vulgar Mr. Leigh."

The last man, a Mr. Rosen, arrived at May's apartment on August 19. He explained that he wanted help writing a story called "Paltial's Dream," an autobiographical account of a mystical vision he had had at a time in his life when he almost went blind. May described him and their meeting in her diary. "Mr. Rosen came in, sat in my room, talked louder, <u>louder</u>, LOUDER. . . . [He] kept lighting his cigars a thousand times—goink, & comink." Though they reached no agreement that day, May sensed possibilities. "Mr. Rosen and maybe the impoverished 'writer' have a job!" she wrote.

Three days later, Mr. Rosen took May out for dinner. Amused and intrigued by this quirky man and his pronounced Russian accent, May titled the description of their dinner date "Darlink."

> The Saturday night of many lights and many nights and scintillating incandescent minds—hearts, too, afire. Italian dinner & dry wine—red it was. . . . Vistas opening out to me—me May Swenson. Can I fulfill his expectation, can I? . . . Anything can happen. The even hairs lying along his wrists beneath his

cuff—he kissed me. Many times. He too places such a <u>premium</u> on am I a virgin. Three men—Well—anything can happen.

May, who had a penchant for creating nicknames, referred to Paltial Rosen in her diary as "Plat." Perhaps May preferred the softer sound of "Plat" to the harsher "Palt." Similarly, she would shift the "l" when she renamed Sylvia, a later lover, "Sliver." Two days later, during another evening with Plat, something did happen.

Wine and jewels. Amber this night. . . . Today the pact was made—May and Paltial . . . Plat is my boss and collaborator—and lover, to be sure. Why not? Just like a French novel you know— and in Central Park—a dream come true—and in a little green canvas topped roadster. . . . I wonder—Plat says he wants a child by me.

May was aware of how Plat appealed to her curiosity and emotions. A few days later she wrote:

This unusual "man"—Half the time I ridicule him in thot [thought] whispers—sometimes he stirs something in me—he is quite cute about his lovemaking, and at least I am "safe" with him—standing behind the barriers of his professed self-esteem, tolerance, kindness, etc. The man is crazy about me. While presenting certain difficulties, the sensation is not baseness of in-terest. I drive him mad. I am wild for him! Whoopee! Well, May, who would have thought that you would come to such a pass. His wife—well presumably that's her problem. Still—

May agreed to collaborate with Plat for $20 a week and was to have her own private office.

Abraham Paltial Rosen, a fifty-three-year-old Russian immigrant (only a year younger than May's father, as it happened), was married for the second time and the father of three children. As May would learn, he had "worked up from a milk route on the lower east side in Brooklyn and then a newsstand" to become a successful real estate mogul. He had a spacious apartment in New York, a suburban home in Hackettstown, New Jersey, where his wife and family spent most of their time, and a showy mansion in Miami Beach.

What appealed to May about Plat, besides his kindness, was that he displayed "not the faintest sense of the elite." May could not tolerate phonies. She was, however, aware of other shortcomings in Plat. "In conversation which is his admitted personal stronghold—he is awkward, exasperating, wholly unsubtle and unaware of any of these faults. He is relentlessly arrogant, and so tactless that he steps on the toes of pride at every turn." But, though he was "often naïve—often uncouth—often foolish," she believed he was a "gentleman to the core." And May was charmed by Plat's appearance. He had "blue-shaven cheeks containing each a long dimple—very well-tailored body— bald—except for the back of his neat bulgeless head—and eyes brown delicious slits with black luxurious poignant lashes leaning over—and a pair of rimless eyeglasses." Regarding his intellect, she was not sure whether he was a "genius"—or just plain "crazy."

As May and Plat saw more of each other, the line between employer and employee blurred. On September 3, 1936, May wrote, "Plat spun a rose colored dream of Work and Play, of Duty and Love, of Joy and blessings of tragedy—'We are goink to do it!' We had each a Manhattan and gazed into each other's eyes—the clear eye of friendship—of transparent understanding."

By September 15 Plat had acquired an office for May in the Chanin Building at 122 East 42nd Street, near Grand Central Terminal. This stunning art deco skyscraper, completed in 1929, was exuberantly embellished with decorative features in terracotta, Belgian marble, bronze, and colored glass. Surely May felt a surge of pride as she turned the key in the lock of her office door, 427-B. "I have no idea where this topsy turvy whirlwind of insane adventure will lead me. . . . Meanwhile here I am, am I not? In my Home Town."

Perhaps May, an avid consumer of Hollywood fare, had seen too many romantic films set in New York. Though Plat was assuredly no matinee idol, May gave free rein to her imagination and played the part of a glamorous and sophisticated starlet. Enhancing her appearance became so important to her that she was even willing to compromise her limited savings to achieve the desired result. On a Friday in September she wrote:

He [Plat] drives home to Hackettstown [for the weekend].
Tomorrow I am to be made over at the hairdressers, at the
manicurists—and shopping—to make me a beautiful girl—My
prayer—remember? I wish I were a beautiful girl and had a mil-
lion dollars! Love makes one beautiful. I looked beautiful in the
mirror when I came in tonight. Oh life! Such honey you hold—
brimming your palm, life, and all for me.

Yet May knew she had been playacting all along. In October she
confessed the truth to her diary: "But you see I know what love is—I
know what it tastes like. So I know I do not love—yet. I have yet to
find my love." She longed to experience again the emotional attraction
she had once felt for Helen Richards, but instead the situation was re-
versed. The intensity of Plat's passion for her, though flattering, served
only as a reminder of her own unrequited love for Helen.

He is quite pitiably in love with me. I am sorry I cannot taste it a
little. I hardly feel it even indirectly, even when I think of it. And
this surprises me—for I remember my own similar devastating
passion and all its nuances. . . . Helen I mean mostly, when I was
about 13, 14, 15. Edith was never that much of a whetted knife
in the heart. And the other minor ones . . . never reached much
above middle "C" in the pitch of consciousness. The thing that
makes me visit these cobweb corners of my mind is letters of
D. H. Lawrence which I have been reading.

May feared that by continuing her relationship with Plat she was
being true neither to her quest to find real love, nor to her desire to de-
velop her poetic talent. She was only twenty-three, but she compared
her accomplishments unfavorably to those of another literary idol, the
young Lawrence. "And it is true we are alike artists, I mean inside—but
he executes," she wrote. Lawrence, by the age of twenty-seven, "had
poems and stories printed and [was] on his third novel [*Sons and
Lovers* (1913)]." And in her diary she confronted Lawrence himself,
who had died six years earlier. "You are you and I am I and we are
both the same, only I feel that I have sold myself—yea even before I
had even really found myself, been born. For it was to be born that

I came here—to New York, my hometown. But now I am on a wild goose chase again."

May consumed the works of Lawrence and read "his wife's story of him," which was Frieda Lawrence's *Not I, But the Wind*, published in 1934. On November 21 May noted that she "wrote a poem to D. H. Lawrence, dead." In "To D. H. Lawrence," first published in 2006, May imagined herself as more than the bearer of Lawrence's torch, the keeper of his flame.[5] She invited his spirit to enter her body: "Come dear, I give you dwelling, / your shade is not astray, / alert and compelling / climb up in me and sway."

During the fall, May worked diligently on Plat's project and on her own poetry. On Thanksgiving day, over lunch at the Russian Tea Room on West 57th Street, she and Plat decided that "Paltial's Dream" would take the form of a play, and together they "hatched the plot." The play would open with a prologue, a dispute between God and Satan in dialogue form. "He lays it out. I write it. I write it. Our play. We are writing a play," she recorded triumphantly. "I put in 9 hours writing yesterday." But either the subject matter did not inspire her or she was distracted by her own work. "Can't get it—the salient beginning [of the play]," she lamented. She was having better success, however, with her poetry. "Wrote 'The Prophet'—[the] other day—by-product of that other that would not emerge," and "I wrote a poem 'He Who Makes Music.'" Plat's play dragged on. For his part, Plat increasingly seemed more interested in relieving May of her virginity than in the progress of their work. May kept his hope alive.

Ever since her fiasco with Bramwell Peck, May wanted to be deflowered, and she now decided that Plat was the perfect candidate. This time there would be no fumbled attempt at copulation in a deserted office. May wanted it done adeptly and on a grand scale, with pomp and ceremony, and Plat had the physical and financial resources to make both happen. Plat eagerly planned their assignation but sought to temper May's expectations.

We straightened out the irksome little matter of my "fanaticism"—namely wanting to be made in the midst of soulful roses and ecstatic spiritual champaign (Jesus what a phrase). And I admitted my silliness. I said "What are you doing tomorrow

night? I would have time to get my hair curled by then." Plat says
we are going to have a few days in the country together before
the cold sets in.

Then she added a coy couplet in her diary, "In Indian summer—and
rustic shade—there to be for the first time made."

But the "event," according to an undated account on hotel statio-
nery inserted into May's diary, took place not in an idyllic setting but
in Newark, New Jersey, at the luxurious Hotel Riviera, where May and
Plat registered as Mr. and Mrs. Rose.

We had a whole flask of brandy. I beguiled him and we got glori-
ously—or was it snuggily—drunk. . . . And after many heavings—
and the corner of the room spinning further & further away, and
our disheveled selves flung naked in the bed together for half a
night—muttering & laughing & getting up to heave again—Then
in the beginning of dawn & soberness—it was a pointed rigid
wedge ploughing a soft groove—and very delectable I say—for
I was still drunk. Then dawn came. . . . Half day of lolling—and
cakes in bed & kisses. And then "breakfast" at 4 pm. . . . And the
train [Plat drove May to the train station in the pouring rain]
tripped on across the rails into the tunnel and I came home. This
was the honeymoon of Mr. & Mrs. P. Rose at the Riviera.

Toward the end of November 1936, May, Louise, and Mary moved
a little farther uptown to 546 West 114th Street. Their "nice modern
apartment" had "a fireplace where Santa Claus can come—and twin
beds and a bell system for visitors and . . . a black toilet top."

On December 10 May attended a much-anticipated performance
of *Hamlet*, with the acclaimed Leslie Howard in the title role. May
raved about Howard.

Today—Hamlet, The Prince of Denmark—Leslie Howard. . . .
But not a mad Hamlet. Far from it. The beauty—how he did
make it live— . . . the arched back—and the arms flung out—such
abandonment of his slim body to his passion— . . . They say
Gi[e]lgud does a better Hamlet. I should like to see him.

Louise bought tickets to see *Hamlet* with John Gielgud as the lead on December 22, a Christmas "treat" for the three of them. May wrote simply that the thirty-two-year-old Gielgud "was magnificent."

Plat was not pleased with the little that May had produced in the three months that she was in his employ. On December 5 May wrote, "What is this I have put my foot into? For it is such a huge hodgepodge of—the unbelievable stuff of which a big hash of a dream is made." Five days later the situation had not improved, and May voiced second thoughts about Plat and her ability to complete his project.

> Here I am building a thing—Paltial's Dream . . . but now Plat says [I] must eliminate [the] first page! It will be like this and worse—must be patient. . . . How will it end—sordidly? . . . I am having doubts . . . just where am I? . . . I should be well into the play by now. Is something organically wrong with me? How can I manage to admit this?

Concerned that her roommates were beginning to suspect that she and Plat were romantically involved ("Mary is wising up to me & Plat"), May concealed her behavior from them and longed for the simple comfort and unconditional love of her family. "I wish I were going to be home for Christmas to see my little brother Paul—and my mother—with the soft lines in her neck and my father—whom I love. Love is this—home—I see now the magic of the word."

Instead, May spent a quiet Christmas with her roommates, and they later hosted a New Year's Eve party at their apartment for "the kids from the ward." These were young LDS men with whom Mary and Louise had been socializing throughout the fall and who resided permanently in New York or were temporarily in the city serving missions.

On January 19, 1937, May began a new diary. Fiercely secretive, she kept her diaries in a locked cabinet in her office in the Chanin Building. On the morning of January 21, 1937, May was furious. When she arrived at her office and unlocked the cabinet, she discovered that Plat, who must have had a key, had removed some pages. "I was consumed with rage—and in a murderous mood":

We had a terrible quarrel . . . oh it was ugly—and finally he gave
me the excerpts back—I was afraid he had destroyed them—he
was awfully wrought up—and no wonder—when I re-read
some of the things I wrote. He intimated that I was perverted. . . .
Of <u>course</u> he would read it that way. Anyone would.

I am not bad. I am good. I am not perfect, but I am good. . . .
And I must erase. Tear out those pages. Write on a new page. . . .
We parted with a handshake. . . . But you didn't understand.
You saw only the lurid parts of my soul. Maybe my soul is largely
that. Maybe my honesty reveals me—reveals me as bad. Stupid
anyway.

After this outburst, May wrote a warning, in red ink, for all future
readers of her diary.

My Diary is a record of me—that <u>no one but me</u> has the right
perspective for. All others who may read it will be deceived.
Warning! You are deceived. Some things that seem to stand
out—shouldn't according to the compass of my soul—and oth-
ers, sometimes the most significant are left invisible <u>between</u> the
lines. Only I read them when I read. The juxtaposition of events
and impressions are all wrong. . . . It is no autobiography—It is a
spilled mind on paper. And it is chaos for anyone else to fathom.
Only for me. my book.

Her notice made clear that any potential, uninvited, nosy body was
at best an intruder, at worst a voyeur. And yet May preserved her
diaries even after she agreed, toward the end of her life, to establish
an archive, knowing they would become part of her collected papers.

May never regained her respect for Plat. She mocked him merci-
lessly in her diary ("He is practically illiterate—can scarcely write &
hardly read English . . . didn't even read the <u>Book of Mormon</u> I lent
him. I am disgusted with him"). Plat apologized profusely. "Why did I
act like that, so beneath my dignity," she quoted him as saying to her.

She now questioned the wisdom of engaging in close relationships
with any man. "I want always to have a woman. Don't want to get over
women," she wrote four days later. And discomfort stoked her home-
sickness. "Next summer can I go home for a while do you think? . . . My

mother has raised 10 children. My dad is a smart and careful man. I love my parents—they are finer than I will ever be." And on February 3, still fixating on the meaning of love and the importance of family, she wrote in her diary:

> See that you remember the taste
>   of love
> and the warm tear dripping upon the heart.
> See that you do not forget these:
>   tears and love.
>   greeness and home.

But comfort in thoughts of her family was tenuous. On February 13 she reacted to a letter from home: "My mother makes me feel like such a heel when she writes—she believes me to be so honorable and so smart & so industrious and all! And I am none of these things. At the end she says—I admire and respect you! This is too much. I want to weep for shame."

Through this difficult period, May neglected "Paltial's Dream" and shifted her attention to writing and revising poems and submitting them for publication. May's college friend Ray West had earlier accepted "Music Maker" for *Rocky Mountain Review*, and now she hoped for another success.[6] "I think I shall send him 'Bough in Spring' for April," she recorded.

In "Music Maker," May compares one "who makes music" to a weaver, a carver, and a weeper. The music maker/weaver leaks "a long unravelling skein of music" from his fingertips, "threading the breast with rapture"; the music maker/carver "flays the strings with his bow"; and the music maker/weeper turns "tear drops newly spilled" into jewels that dissolve into "a second weeping."

West returned "Bough in Spring." He told May that "it was cutting daisies with a two-edged ax," and he suggested that she write prose instead. May licked her wounds and defended her poem in her diary on March 3: "I thot [thought] 'Bough' was quite good—sensitive—the cadence is fine." On March 14 she completed another poem, "Sunday Exhibition—Still Life," which she described as "almost another version of 'The Short Word.'"

Before Plat left New York in early April 1937 to spend a month at his home in Miami, he exacted from May the promise that in his absence she would complete their play and write accompanying promotional material. On April 8 May eased her mounting anxiety by composing "a rabid poem about Pan stomping in the hyacinths."

Despite Plat's regular salary checks from Florida, May remained so short of funds that she resorted to her familiar modus operandi of casually shoplifting clothing that she could not afford, or chose simply not to pay for. "I swiped a dress—it's blue, white & red—wearing it out under my other. I bought some shoes, three ashtrays, cards, perfume phials, toothpaste," she wrote on April 13. Always observant of New York City vignettes, she added a lovely description of the scene from the store window where she made her small purchases. "Out of the 5 & 10 on 5th ave you can look down on the flowing bodies of the library lions & pigeons blowing like gray leaves about them & the people walking forever past & buses."

With Plat not expected back for several more weeks, May began to socialize casually with a young man named Dan, one of her room-mates' LDS friends. She thought him pleasant but intellectually infe-rior. After showing Dan her poem "Music Maker," May observed that "he pretended to be impressed but I doubt he understood it." And when Dan asked her about her relationships with the opposite sex, May dismissively told him that "there was no opposite sex."

During this time, May read books that affected her deeply, most notably Djuna Barnes's novel *Nightwood*, published in the United States in 1937. Barnes, a journalist, artist, novelist, playwright, and poet, had moved in 1915 to Greenwich Village, where she immediately immersed herself in the thriving bohemian community. Barnes's out-put was prodigious, and she created a special stir in modern literary circles with the publication of *Nightwood*, a groundbreaking work of modernist literature and a cornerstone of lesbian fiction. The Amer-ican edition featured an introduction by Barnes's editor, T. S. Eliot. "This is the stuff of which my mind is made too—like the cat's eyes it fascinates me," wrote May on April 8. *Nightwood* made her "tremble," and she even "read some of it aloud [to Dan]."

Influenced by Barnes, May began to explore the Greenwich Village art scene. On April 14 she wrote, "I went to An American Place and there was William Einstein." She wondered, "Was it Alfred Stieglitz who told me not to lean against the wall?"

It is not surprising that May encountered both the artist William Einstein and the photographer Alfred Stieglitz at An American Place, the art gallery on the seventeenth floor of the skyscraper at 509 Madison Avenue. Stieglitz had established the gallery in 1929 to promote the work of modernist artists and photographers. He had featured the paintings and drawings of Einstein and the photographs of Ansel Adams in a joint show at the gallery in late November 1936, and now, in the spring of 1937, he displayed new oils and watercolors by Arthur Dove.[7]

May raved about the current exhibit. Two days after seeing it, she wrote, "I cannot forget the railway engine by Dove—profile—he made almost an animal out of it—will I know Einstein some other day?" She recalled the hours of her youth that she had spent "[o]n the shop roof out West at home with the sun thru apple leaves warming the pages of Sti[e]glitz," where she dreamed about "An American Place, 291, Georgia O'Keef[f]e . . . [John] Marin, Marsden Hartley."

May had left Utah to experience the creative energy of New York's literary and art scene, and now had actually met both Stieglitz and Einstein, whom she called "Bill" and to whom she promised to give one of her poems. On May 2 May wrote in her diary:

> There was that day at An American Place when Einstein came in—he had read Barnes's book—and I talked with Stieglitz . . . — tufts of hair bristling from his ears. I promised E. I would bring a poem. I was sick at heart for a whole day afterward—it was so devastating—I made so many faux pas—I hated me—they were so nice to me and E. again showed me Marin's Horse and some photos by Stieglitz—one of his darkroom I loved. Another watercolor by Marin of a ship on waves & sky—all fluid and limpid with grays and blue-grays—nascent. Hartley's things were up. There was a starfish picture in a corner. And one of his ships with a 3-cornered cloud. . . .
>
> I keep thinking of Stieglitz and him [Einstein]—and me and my poem. Where am I going? What is this? Where am I? I'm not

very nice I'm afraid. I want to be beautiful. I want beauty. I want that precious thing they have there at The Place. I shall go there again, yes?

May's interest in Stieglitz and his photography no doubt motivated her to see the recently released Mexican film *The Wave*, at the Filmarte Theatre on West 58th Street. A paean to Mexico's left-wing government, the film is about poor fishermen who withhold their catch until they are paid a decent wage. The reviewer in the *New York Times* was not impressed, although he praised the score and the cinematography of photographer Paul Strand, Stieglitz's student and protégé.[8] May herself was transfixed. In her diary she wrote a lengthy and poetic description of the sea, the sunlight and clouds, the struggle of the fishermen, concluding, "I sat stone still—I was inert with my feelings—engulfed in emotion. I had it in my temples pressing—and holding my heart as if in a fist. The Wave—Bill Einstein ought to see it."

While joyfully embracing her literary, artistic, and social interests, May remained mindful of her obligations to Plat. By the time he returned from Miami on May 2, she had finished their play and written seventy-five pages of promotional material. But she rued the impending loss of freedom and was determined not to yield to Plat's sexual advances: "Plat is back. At first I thot [thought] I couldn't bear it. . . . P. wanted me to go to the country with him. I deftly wriggled out of it." Only final revisions of the play remained. Plat was pleased that their project was nearly complete but was also aware of May's changed attitude toward him. He informed her that on June 1 he intended to vacate her rented office. At the same time May learned that one roommate, Mary, was leaving New York on May 15 to return home to the West, and her other roommate, Louise, decided to move in with friends. Suddenly, everything was in flux for May. "Shifting times, these—wonder where I'll be going," she mused.

A week later, on May 10, 1937, May wrote:

I got "the sack." How childish my writing is. Plat says I will remember him in days to come. . . . There are so many overtones—

impossible to record them. I didn't cry—that was important too. I'm not going back. I'm going on—I'm going on—past the farthest ropes—no matter I'm going <u>on</u>.

Eleven days later, she pasted into her diary the new classified ad she had posted in the *Times*:

> YOUNG WRITER, keen for work, university degree, experienced author's assistant, typing, proofread, research; magazine and newspaper reporter; willing, do anything legitimate that nets living.

A week and a half later, on June 1, 1937, May began a diary entry with the words:

> Did I forget to say I had a job? Been working just about a week for Howard Ketcham, inc.—35th flr. Rockefeller Plaza (John D. died the other day). Apartment hunting after work today—Jesus it's been hot! Saw one penthouse room—little like a cell—room for a cot & washstand—but the whole roof and Manhattan in all its lovely squalor below—$20 a month. But I prefer to have the River at my door. It's my own river and I love it. . . . Must move by Saturday.

In the end, May put down a five dollar deposit on a room at 606 W 116th Street, in the Broadview Apartments, and with a woman named Lu, a friend of Mary and Louise, she moved in on June 6. "I can't see the river from here—11th floor—facing—but I know it is there—its breeze reaches me. I can hear the moo of the river boats at night. . . . I can hear the trill of birds—but can only see roofs & black girders—and a sulky piece of sky," she wrote.

May displayed determination and pluck while she repeatedly searched for apartments and employment. The new ad brought work as executive secretary, copyeditor, and receptionist for Howard Ketcham at the sleek new Rockefeller Plaza, which had opened only four years earlier. "I am <u>working hard</u>," she wrote. "Sweet acrid taste of fatigue in the brain, and tiredness—sleep is a balm. Work at 8 tomorrow. 'Howard Ketcham, Inc?'—me on phone."

Ketcham, a thirty-four-year-old business tycoon, had established a color-design agency that advised large companies on effective color choice for their branding. May was delighted with her salary and impressed with her surroundings, but she soon found her coworkers' obsession with color tiresome, even ridiculous. One day, she noted in disbelief, a colleague remarked over lunch on "the value of the mustard on the chroma of the cheese!" She was regarded, in turn, as an unsophisticated westerner.

By early July, May's hope of a lighthearted environment at work evaporated into the reality of a stressful one. "Today at the office was chaos—too much to do—& no casualness about the atmosphere—too trigger-like—and I'm no model steno. . . . I ain't got no efficiency. The boners I pull are frightful—makes me hot under the collar to remember them. The erased check episode—and the sound of his voice when the boss reprimanded me—in a low voice in a thrillingly controlled voice—not a harsh voice—but Oh my ears burned," May wrote on July 8. And the situation continued to deteriorate. On July 26 she could see the future, and it upset her. "I felt depressed. I wrote a poem about Narcissism. I think I am going to be fired soon. I am a flop—a n'er-do-well—a failure—a good for nought—lazy—incompetent, inefficient—wishy washy—unbalanced."

On August 11 May was indeed fired. She titled her diary entry: "Portrait of a girl who has just been canned."

Ketcham called me in & with very little ceremony—but a judicious sprinkling of regrets, apologies & fake reassurances—told me to go take a walk. I made a noble exit, leaving him a red-penciled article to read—about what kind of a boss not to be—then I gathered up my smock—went down on the concourse & . . . went to the automat (past the strike picket lines) and began the tale whose title lurks above—writing it on the paper which HK had penciled a job prospect on—when I ran out of paper I hopped a bus . . . & then I got the subway. At first it was pretty frightening this getting canned business . . . made my eyes smart—remembering that "Miss Swenson is no longer with us."

I haven't told anyone about it. . . . I have \$39—and owe \$5 on rent.

May had mentioned in June, when she first started working for Ketcham, that she intended to write a prose piece about her experience. "I made an outline for a story about a working girl—maybe send it to <u>Story</u>—and <u>when</u> they chuck it back, scrap it with Ray." "Story" is a reference to *Story Magazine*, a journal that emerged in 1931 from the depths of the Depression. "Devoted to the cause of the quality short story, and dedicated to the young, unpublished writer struggling for recognition," *Story* would have been the perfect venue for May.[9] Indeed, the first short stories of the young Carson McCullers, Tennessee Williams, Truman Capote, William Safire, and Ludwig Bemelmans had appeared in *Story*. But May's piece, if she ever wrote or submitted it, was not published.

May was foundering, desperate, and distressed.

AUGUST 15:
I don't know whether it is the 14 or 15. I have let myself get disordered and lost. I have begun that degeneration that is the accompaniment of idleness. . . . I saw several shows & ate a lot of chocolate candy. I am vulgar to the nth degree someways. . . . Sat on the library steps—the haughty sinewy stone lions crouching on either side—beleaguered by pigeons perched in their manes. . . . I started a letter to home—but tore it up—too sentimental. I'm going to Sunday school in the morning[.]

AUGUST 20:
Gladys wrote to me—this is the main thing. She thinks my poems are good—"Fool" I exclaimed—but it warmed my soul—that has been cold so long. . . . Glad thought my "Manhattan Moon" was marvelous. . . . I wrote to Glad . . . I said that I love her. She is the only one who believes in me. . . . Tomorrow I will write. . . . I will write about the girl who was creature & both man & woman.

On August 22 May clipped her new classified ad from the *Times* and pasted it into her diary.

YOUNG WRITER, keen for work, experi-
enced author's assistant, typist, research,
magazine and newspaper reporter, ghost
writer; university degree and references.

The ad generated an immediate response. "I rode the subway down
to the Village—Morton St.—to see a dame Anzia Yezierska—who has
a MS wants typed."

Anzia Yezierska, born in Poland, was a Jewish-American novel-
ist raised on New York's Lower East Side. Relying on her immigrant
experience, she became a prolific writer of short stories and novels
treating the theme of acculturation, especially as it pertained to Jewish
immigrant women. In 1917, divorced from her second husband and the
mother of a three-year-old daughter, Anzia had attended a seminar at
Columbia University on social and political thought. The instructor
was John Dewey, the renowned philosopher and advocate of social and
educational reform. Despite the thirty-year difference in their ages,
she and Dewey engaged in a brief but intense love affair that ended
just as Anzia's literary reputation, with Dewey's help, began to soar.[10]

Anzia's story "The Fat of the Land" had been included in Edward
J. O'Brien's *The Best Short Stories of 1919*, and the following year she
published *Hungry Heart*, a volume of collected stories, which was
released as a Hollywood film in 1922. Three years later she published
Bread Givers, her most successful novel. A few years after that, how-
ever, Anzia sank into a state of financial and emotional decline that
resulted in a mental breakdown. She was hospitalized briefly in a san-
atorium in Massachusetts and returned to New York in 1932, during
the early years of the Depression.

Anzia was now in her fifties, and her future seemed bleak. To sur-
vive financially, she joined the Federal Writers' Project, a subdivision of
the Works Progress Administration (WPA), created in 1935 as part of
President Roosevelt's response to the Depression. The FWP's function
was to provide employment for struggling writers by redirecting their
talents to works of social utility.

Initially the administrators of the FWP had difficulty determining
who qualified for employment: "Rather than try to solve the riddle
of who is a writer, the planners decided that any kind of a writer on

FIGURE 9. Anzia Yezierska, May's employer, in an undated photograph.

relief would be eligible to work in the Writers' Project—fiction writers, copywriters, poets, newspapermen, publicity writers, technical writers, and so on."[11] Eventually the ranks of the FWP swelled to include "'near writers,' 'occasional writers,' and even 'would-be writers,' whether they were educated or not, so long as they could produce anything in English."[12] Soon almost anyone who could hold a pen might qualify for a job with the FWP. But, while liberal in its definition of writers, the FWP required its employees to come from relief rolls in order to authenticate financial need. This stipulation would later become a significant impediment for May.

Upon securing employment, Anzia found herself assigned the tedious task of cataloging trees in Central Park for a New York City guidebook. By August 1937 she had left the agency and, hoping to reinvigorate her literary career, was writing a scathing denunciation of the WPA in general and the FWP in particular.

Four days after May began to type and edit that manuscript, Anzia unexpectedly arranged for May to meet her nephew.

Damn her matchmaking anyway! Anzia—had to trot out her nephew—scotch & soda-drinking guy with unblinking brown eyes—and the air of a newspaper reporter—insolent but charming—well yes—charming. So me: ankle sox & my oldest dress & carrying my hat—we go to the Brevoort on 5th Ave. & 8th & proceed to empty our hearts to each other over a dry martini & his scotch.

Despite her initial resistance, May enjoyed the company of thirty-eight-year old Arnold Kates, an executive in the advertising business. "I like him—I really like him . . . his flat is all the way to the top with a little veranda & petunias—on West 11th—the best corner of the Village," she wrote a week after meeting Arnold. By then he had taken her out to dinner several times. They attended an outdoor carnival in Washington Square and had had several, by now customary, scotch and sodas at the Brevoort Hotel bar, a popular watering hole for both the social elite and Village bohemians. May was clearly interested in furthering her relationship with Arnold. "I shall buy a blue dress with the $30 dad sent me—& a hat—and knock his eye out. . . . He quoted Browning & Milton—surprising in an advertising man—He has nice wrists too. I wish I could have an affair with him." Barely two weeks later, her wish came true.

We were at Jack Dempsey's bar and drinking our scotch & sodas—I had had two. . . . I leaned to him and said what's the chance of sleeping with you tonight? There were no buts, ifs, nor maybies he said—we were a little drunk. . . . We had a friendly time of it—he has a red toothbrush for day & a blue one for night and a black one in a box for guests. That's me.

The following morning, May lingered in Arnold's apartment after he left for work.

When he had gone—looking spruce—to the office—I sat in his rough linen lounging coat & sandals on the terrace & read thru my tumbling hair "Portrait of the Artist as a Young Man"—and after danced to the music on the radio—then I went away leaving

the key in the Laundry on the corner. I took his Joyce & Autobi-
ography of Freud with me. I had breakfast then began wandering
the village looking for an apartment. . . . The landlady has given
me notice a week—I must find a place . . . what will happen to
me? I make so little money—I shall have to live in a hole—$3 a
week will be the limit for me.

May maintained an active correspondence with Gladys Hobbs. In
a typed, five-page letter, written on September 8, 1937, May told Glad
about Anzia and Arnold.[13] This letter offers an opportunity to com-
pare May's unfiltered assessment of people and events recorded in the
privacy of her diary with her outward presentation of them in a letter
to a friend. The two accounts harmonize, but May's letter to Glad,
girlfriend to girlfriend, is far more animated and detailed.

Dearest Glad:

. . . Expected to get a wire from you saying you were skipping out
to N.Y. and for me to hunt up a flat for two. Got my last letter,
didn't you?

Oh Glad, my diary is picking up on wordage these days: I'm an
honest-to-God author's assistant now and commute to the village
every morn. Anzia Yezierska . . . is perfectly marvelous. . . . She
is writing a novel based on the WPA Writers' Project—from first
hand experience. . . . Thing is pungent as hell— . . . in the nature
of an exposee—for Christ's sake don't mention this to anyone. . . .
I said I wouldn't repeat anything to a soul. You have no soul, so
I'm sure it's alright. Anyway talking to you is like talking to my-
self—wait, I mean it!

I have gone and went and fallen in love. Met him through
Anzia, . . . an executive in the advertising department of a ship-
ping concern. . . . I wanted to meet artists, writers, not advertising
men. Arnold Kates arrived at 7, just as we were finishing work. . . .
I pounced on him viciously—asked him how he justified himself

being in the advertising business—followed by a long and impas-
sioned tirade on the stupidity, vulgarity and bunkum of advertis-
ing in particular, and all business in general, climaxed by what I
felt was a brilliant statement about the noxiousness of the whole
capitalistic system. Well, he slammed right back. . . . He took me
to dinner—to the Brevoort on Fifth Avenue and 8th—and me in
a plaid dress and ankle sox!

The next night . . . we had a drink, and then sauntered to Wash-
ington Square where we sat on the empty fountain edge. . . .
We told each other all the smutty jokes we knew—a total of six
in all—and he had some lulus in spite of the small repertoire.
And the next night . . . Arnold said we had been invited to a
Park Ave. penthouse for cocktails with a friend of his—and
first I thought I could take it, but walking up the avenue, I got
to thinking about my oxfords, and the kitcheony looking red
dress I had on under my coat—and I felt I had to make some
drastic gesture of protest. . . . So I . . . said: Let's don't go to the
penthouse. And we didn't, but went to The Russian Tea Room
instead and had Vodka . . .

Arnold asked me to spend the night. . . . I said no, because I
had to call Anzia at nine Sunday—but the real reason was that I
didn't have my kidcurlers and I knew my hair would be straight
in the morning. Jesus what a bitch.

Now all there is left is the night I had a new dress, that had been
saving up in the shop till I could get enough together to pay the
balance of the deposit. . . . We ate, and walked in the square, and
put pennies in the organ-grinder's hat, and walked aimlessly
through some streets, and stopped before a gate, and lo it was his
gate. So we went in. I didn't have my kidcurlers but I didn't care,
and in the morning I know I looked frowsy as hell and said, "I'm
sorry, but this is May Swenson in the morning," and he started to
say he liked May Swenson in the morning, but didn't finish. Our
minds had been friends for a long time; this night our bodies be-
came friends. He kept saying: I'm kissing your poetry. And I said

I didn't know whether or not I liked that. I'll bet this sounds very funny to you. But, please, don't you dare laugh. I had brought a batch of poetry with me—and he read it all—some of it outloud. And he understood—he saw what I meant! . . . But it's not just that; hungar for the body of man, which is probably pretty urgent in me from being lonely so long—it's him. Him. He is so special. He knows and feels what I feel. And he is such an excellent friend. And there is no restraint between us. . . . And he is so kind, I want to cry. . . .

If there were nothing more than this that has been. If this were the very end of it, I would be satisfied. It would be sufficient. I would not ask God to ever let me see him again. It is enough. I have looked on the face of joy.

But I am going to see him tomorrow night at 7!

Glad dearest, write me a long impersonal letter as if you had never read this.

I'm worried about you. Are you O.K.?

> I love you
> May

With Arnold's help, May found an apartment in the Village at 73 Washington Place—just west of Washington Square—a one-room, top-floor, garretlike space with a single window and a staircase in the center leading to a "hatchway" in the ceiling giving access to the roof. The tiny apartment was furnished with a table and chair, a small bed, a dresser with a mirror, and a bookcase. May loved it, especially the access to the roof, where she could read, think, write, or just look out over the city. May worked best in secluded places. As a child in Utah she gravitated to hideaways like the roof of her father's workshop, the treehouse, or her favorite apple tree. The rooftop at Washington Place satisfied this need.

FIGURE 10. May pasted this photo of Arnold Kates into
her diary entry for September 16, 1937. *Literary Estate of
May Swenson.*

May had "scads of work to do" for Anzia. While she was typing a
manuscript titled "More than Bread" (never published), which was an
apparent sequel to *Bread Givers*, Anzia worked on her exposé, "WPA:
We Poor Americans" (also never published). The more May learned
about Anzia, the more she was impressed with Anzia's acquaintances,
including the writer and journalist Martha Gellhorn, who would be-
come the third wife of Ernest Hemingway, and Djuna Barnes, whom
May called "Queen of the Lesbians." (Anzia was no fan of Barnes,
whose *Nightwood*, she told May, made her "sick.")

Although May had given Anzia some of her poems to read, she
had little confidence that Anzia would give them her full attention ("I
bet she doesn't look at them"). When May finally pressed Anzia about
her reaction to the poems, Anzia demurred, claiming that she did not
know poetry. Her confidence shaken and convinced that her poems

were "febrile" and "trivial," May complained in her diary, "I should have said aloud: 'If there was anything here—you would know it.'"

Arnold became a major presence in May's life. On weekends they rode horses in Central Park, hiked in the Palisades, and drove to Long Island for picnics and swimming. During the week, they dined out, frequented art exhibits, and socialized with a host of painters who showed their work at the newly opened Artists' Gallery.

The Artists' Gallery was a nonprofit cooperative venture subsidized by donors. Established in a Greenwich Village loft in 1936 by Hugh Stix and managed by Friederike Beer-Monti, it promoted the work of promising but struggling artists without gallery representation. Stix charged nothing to mount his shows and took no commissions from sales. A painter and sculptor himself, Stix launched the careers of many young artists, including James Lechay, Josef Albers, Willem de Kooning, and Louise Nevelson.[14]

Any previous connection between Arnold Kates and Hugh Stix is unclear, but in October, Arnold showed Stix one of May's poems, "Transition."[15] A few days later, May and Arnold attended John Opper's exhibit at the Artists' Gallery. Opper was a young Midwesterner who would later embrace abstract art but at the time was painting in a more traditional and realistic style.[16] Soon afterward, on October 17, May and Arnold spent a social evening in the Village with Stix, Beer-Monti, and two other artists, Ralph Rosenborg and Jimmy Sterling. May wrote a vivid account of the event in her diary.

> We went up to the Artist's Gallery on 8th & saw Opper's showing—met Hugh Stix to whom A[rnold] had lent my Transition. And that led to last night—the night of the Big Bender at George's—with Jimmy Sterling, Hugh [Stix], A[rnold] and I and Miss Beer from Vienna—and George himself of course . . . . The combination of corn whiskey and Black Velvet made me the life of the party. . . . Hell is when you still have to puke after there's nothing left to puke. I tried to get across to Red [Ralph Rosenborg]—he is the painter who will show after the dame from Utahr [Frances Ferry]. I don't know who stood the drinks—they appeared out of the air—and those hot pork sandwiches . . . and as they raised their glasses in a toast, I raised my hand, covering

my mouth. . . . Arnold appeared a little "stodgy" [along]side of incorrigible Hugh, his long dimples, his big loose mouth, rippling forehead—black curly hair like froth—and Red to whom I seemed to want to preach the Artist = Man + Woman theory. . . . Everybody got plastered. . . . George's is a speak[easy]—on account his license has been revoked. They said I had a surrealist mind. A[rnold] and I staggered home in the clean, clean, cold, empty air of five o'clock. . . . I had to be at Anzia's at 8–30.

Red was Ralph Rosenborg, his nickname suggested by his surname. A native New Yorker, Rosenborg was a WPA artist and a pioneer in abstract art.[17] May and Rosenborg were the same age—twenty-four. The "dame from Utahr" (May's ear for idiosyncratic speech is evident in her diaries) was Frances Ferry, a young modernist painter from Salt Lake City. Ferry had studied art in Paris and lived in New York for three years during the 1930s.[18] After seeing Ferry's work at the Artists' Gallery, May praised her "suave atmospheric canvases," calling them "beauty."

Jimmy Sterling soon became one of May's close friends. She mentioned visiting his studio and seeing his "litter of drawings," his "stacked canvasses."[19] And Sterling went to May's apartment to read and discuss her poetry. "I thrilled[,] I reveled as Sterling read my 'Dancer'—I can still remember his voice—the vibrancy of it," May recalled. Another evening, after Arnold left a party early, Sterling and May, both inebriated, returned to May's apartment, where Sterling climbed into bed with her. "It was a goofy night. I think he is impotent," May commented succinctly.

"George" was apparently the owner of the establishment where the party took place. May referred to it as a "speak" (short for speakeasy) because George, having lost his license, was selling liquor illegally.

May's diaries are peppered with accounts, such as this, of raucous evenings spent studio hopping and drinking with young artists connected to Stix's gallery. But May and her artist friends also enjoyed quieter, more reflective moments together, discussing the latest trends in art, literature, and poetry. Sometimes May sat for them as a model.

Arnold's interest in socializing with May's new friends began to wane, and he accompanied her less frequently to parties. "I was a bit peeved at Arnold for not drinking. He didn't dance and didn't ask me to dance. He looked sort of left out," May complained. But Arnold remained a reliable companion and a satisfying and exciting sexual partner. Sometimes May thought she loved him. At other times she was ambivalent.

On one occasion, after a night of heavy drinking and studio hopping with the same cast of characters, but without Arnold, May returned home late at night. In the morning, the landlady announced that she would have to vacate her room because the fire inspector had informed her that "the hatchway to the roof and fire escape must be kept clear." She gave May a month's notice. Devastated, May turned not to her gallery friends but to Arnold for sympathy and support. Anzia, however, saw May's displacement as an opportunity. After several unsuccessful attempts to find a new apartment, May wrote in her diary, "Anzia said why don't you and Arnold get hitched right away—then you wouldn't have to worry about a place to live. . . . She thinks I should try and nab him. Thank god I am free—thank god I do not owe him. . . . Anzia said he said to her that he loved me."

May did finally find a new place to live, and on December 1, 1937, she moved, with Arnold's help, to "11 Bank St. 2nd floor front." She continued to divide her free time between Arnold and her expanding circle of artist friends. Jennings Tofel, Hans Böhler, and James Lechay became frequent companions, and she developed a closer relationship with gallery manager Friederike Beer-Monti, whom she now called "Fritzie."

The expressionist painter Jennings Tofel, born Yehudah Toflevitch, had immigrated to America from Poland in 1905, when he was fourteen. A poet who wrote blank verse in English, he was also fluent in German and Yiddish.[20] May particularly liked Tofel's work. On November 23 she wrote in her diary, "I bought the Tofel drawing! He let me have it for $10. Said he wanted me to have it. I told him why I wanted it: If such a thing—so deep, so diffuse, so submerged—can be expressed as you have done here—it will mean that I too can do it. This will be proof to me—a sort of fetish. It will help me to have faith? Styx [Stix] is framing it for me."

Fifty-three-year-old Hans Böhler was an Austrian expressionist painter and a childhood friend and former lover of gallery manager

Beer-Monti. May modeled regularly for Böhler and sometimes for Sterling. In January 1938 she sat simultaneously for Böhler and Sterling—but first they "plied me with Irish Whiskeys."

> They both began to draw me—Hans left profile—& Jim facing.
> I leaned my head against the wall where I sat on the couch &
> closed my eyes—the whiskey made me sleepy. Both the sketches
> turned out badly—Hans's second one had its points.

Böhler asked May to return in a few days for another sitting. "I hope it will materialize into something definite—and perhaps lucrative," May wrote. Two months later, May was still sitting for Böhler but mentioned nothing about payment.

At another "wild" party on January 30, 1938, besides the usual crowd of revelers, such as Tofel, Stix, and Beer-Monti ("in a blue dress"), an artist new to the group—James Lechay—made an appearance. May, who attended this gathering with Arnold, was immediately attracted to Lechay.

> James LaShay [Lechay], the tall loose-limbed fellow who
> slouches a little—coarse very black straight hair and such level
> dark eyes—Arabian—a little glittering . . . lives somewhere here
> on Bank St. 43 I believe. [He] is exhibiting at the gallery be-
> ginning Tuesday. I wish I could know him. His name shouldn't
> be Jimmy. I have his Lincoln Friends medal—against Fascism
> in Spain. These are all ardent communists. . . . There was good
> music. . . . I got quite gay & had a good time. Arnold didn't. I saw
> him now & then sitting stilted a little—looking a little old. . . .
> Tuesday maybe I will see Jim LaShay [Lechay] when he opens at
> the gallery.

Five days later, on February 4, May was disappointed to learn that Lechay, who did, in fact, live at 43 Bank Street, was "married & has a kid." Further dashing May's hopes, he did not attend his own opening at the gallery. But May was enthusiastic about his pictures (especially "the farmhouse interior . . . and the one of the lilies against weather beaten boards") and was eager to learn more about him. "Fritzie said

FIGURE 11. Portrait of May Swenson by the artist Hans Böhler, 1938.

he was 32—had been a professor of psychology at Columbia—very emotional—that shock of black hair—restless fellow."

Beer-Monti was partly correct. James Lechay, born in the Bronx of Russian-Jewish immigrant parents, had graduated from the University of Illinois with a degree in psychology. He dropped out of graduate school in 1929 and returned to New York, not to teach, but to paint. Lechay's work in the early 1930s was often political in theme and in the style of social realism. Later he shifted toward abstraction. An activist for social justice, Lechay was, like so many of his left-leaning fellow artists, employed by the WPA. He was a supporter of the communist-backed Abraham Lincoln Brigade, composed of Americans fighting against Franco during the Spanish Civil War. May mentioned that he had given her his "Lincoln Friends medal," which may have unsettled Arnold, who felt "injured" by Lechay's attention to her.

After viewing Lechay's opening, May "went home and wrote a poem—'this Spring is cursed,'" about unrequited love. Posthumously published in 1991 as "Wild Water," this short poem protests the "insidious cruelty" the heart suffers when it recognizes its "thirst" for "wild water," a metaphor for passion. In the poem a cup of water is offered but suddenly withdrawn, banishing the heart to "arid land," where its thirst remains unquenched.

Although poetry readings were advertised less frequently than gallery shows, in November 1937 May went to the New School to hear Robert Frost read from his Pulitzer Prize–winning book, *A Further Range*. Of particular interest to May was his poem "Two Tramps in Mud Time." Internalizing Frost's message, May wrote in her diary. "I have to remember only one thing—'<u>Get your love and your need together</u>,'" a paraphrase from Frost's final stanza:

> Only where love and need are one,
> And the work is play for mortal stakes,
> Is the deed ever really done
> For Heaven and the future's sakes.[21]

May was surrounded by artists pursuing the parallel course of making their living by creating art. She yearned to be a professional poet and to earn her livelihood by doing what she loved. Frost's poem validated May's struggles to establish herself in New York and to become a part of its creative environment. Twenty years later, May would meet Frost under vastly different circumstances. In 1957 poet and critic John Ciardi named May the Robert Frost Fellow at the Bread Loaf Writers' Conference in Vermont. May and Robert Frost conversed that summer, poet to poet.

May was not entirely free of Plat, who stopped by every now and then to see her.

> Plat came one day—smelling of sensen and expensive cigars. . . .
> No news about the play—he said something about Max Rhine-
> hart seeing it—but I think that was made up. He went away, then
> came shambling back. Offered me money, which I refused; I said
> I was well-off—no worries (I had 18 cents in my purse to last me

2 days) then he began kissing me. It was like those awful nights in the Chanin office. . . . I have not seen him since. When he was necking me he said "I still love you May. I can't help it." . . . Why oh why do I have this tiresome fascination for old men? . . . Why do old men fall for me?

When Anzia met Plat on one of his visits, she thought him "a frightful bore." Nevertheless, May went out with Plat for an occasional dinner and sometimes to Radio City Music Hall. After repeated pleas on his part, she "agreed to work for him 2 nights a week—Monday & Wednesday." May needed more income as her work for Anzia began to wind down, and in December she wrote, "I shall have to buckle down and get me another job soon. The book went to the agent yesterday. . . . I am worried about money. I had an escapist dream about the bliss of going insane."

May lamented in her diary, "I don't make enough to live on," and the situation had not improved in February. "I must get hold of some money—Have only $15 left." She had "sent out 9 poems," but "all the poems came back but 2 from London." May also persevered with her prose. "One night in the corner library I wrote this thing <u>A Poem Happens to Me</u>. It has very little basis in fact—no it is factual—enough—but treated superficially." (Published posthumously in 1998, this essay is one of May's better known works of prose.) When none of her attempts to publish panned out, May, becoming desperate, wrote "an extortion letter to Plat."

May formed a scheme to trick Plat, her financial lifeline, into giving her money. She wrote to him on February 27, 1938, claiming that she had found someone interested in his play, but the potential producer wanted to see it rewritten in screenplay form. May explained to Plat that she would need to purchase expensive books to accomplish the task. Plat agreed to send her money to purchase the books. Relieved, May confided in her diary, "Now I must take the plot one step farther. I am digging for $100." She continued recording the saga the following day.

I wrote a 6 p. letter to P, tieing the final knot. Wrote a card to the P.O. Box [i.e., Plat's] pretending to give requested info about screenwriting books. It looks like a push-over. I don't see how it can miss. In a week I ought to be on my feet.

But Plat sent her nothing ("Have had no word from Plat. Can't imagine why"). Plat was a successful self-made businessman and no rube. He was shrewder than May realized and was not to be taken advantage of. Her desperation to survive financially, tempered only by pride, is almost palpable in her diary entry of March 13.

Had a 20¢ breakfast . . . all out of anything to read—had to re-move my reserve dollar from the lending library. Rent nearly a week overdue. Typewriter overdue. . . . Tomorrow shall go up to 4th ave see if I can run down a lousy $15 dollar week job. Don't think I'll make it. That other day I tried to get that letter-shop job, and my hands without gloves were so cold couldn't control the keys. The Jewish girl said contemptuously: "you're too slow." "Give me another chance—my hands are cold." I made the mis-take of begging. "go on! you're too slow. I wouldn't give you an-other chance for a million."

Despite May's easy and affectionate interactions with Jews, she occa-sionally displayed jarring anti-Semitism, as in her comment above.

With little else to do, May began participating in antiwar demon-strations with a new friend, Doris Smith. They rallied in Times Square on Saturday, March 19, 1938, to protest Hitler's invasion and annex-ation of Austria the week before.[22] "I was a Red for a night," wrote May. "Leering pedestrians on the side-line—the cops swinging their clubs with vicious eyes—Doris' coat was torn—a club caught me in the mouth. We scrambled over the bumpers of the stalled honking taxis, crowded around the effigy of Hitler—Stop Hitler! Hitler is a murderer! It was big, it was booming, & the newsmen's flashlamps startling here and there." After the police broke up the demonstration, May and Doris "tramped home along 7th avenue."

During this period, the relationship between May and Arnold was temporarily cool. A month earlier, on February 15, 1938, May wrote in her diary that Arnold had come to her apartment to talk and that they had "had it out" with each other about their future together. Arnold told May that she "was the one person who had caused him seriously to think of marriage." May balked, explaining that she had no interest in being married. The "ceremony itself, the ring, the vow, etc." held no appeal for her. He accused her of "shallowness"; she thought he was "naïve." They shook hands and he left. The next morning, Arnold took her to breakfast at Schrafft's in Times Square. "He said when we parted: I'll get in touch with you," May wrote. Apparently he did not; there is no record of her seeing Arnold socially during the next several weeks.

On March 13 May noted that "Anzia let it out one day that he [Arnold] is going with Dorothy Farrell, ex-wife of James Farrell!" (The author of the *Studs Lonigan* trilogy, James Farrell, had married Dorothy Butler in 1931; they divorced soon thereafter, only to remarry in 1955.) May and Arnold's on-again-off-again relationship survived his brief interlude with Dorothy, but by the time she and Arnold were back together, May's financial situation had declined precipitously.

May's overriding hope was to work for the Federal Writers' Project, as Anzia had done. With that goal in mind, in late March 1938, May went to an FWP symposium conducted by Richard Wright. "He is memorable," she wrote. "I would have spoken to him, but was ashamed of my appearance." Her shoes had holes in them and her dress was shabby. Two weeks later, however, Anzia unexpectedly provided another opportunity for May to meet Wright. With Robert Frost's advice still lingering in her mind, she wrote in her diary:

> In this underground world the two are strangely mixed. Love and need? get them together. There is for instance Richard Wright. He was up to Anzia's house day before yesterday. A communist— an artist. I am remembering his voice with softness & mystery behind it. I wish—

May began her "pilgrimage to the poor house," by which she meant completing paperwork to enroll for welfare payments through the Workers Alliance of America (WAA), a conglomerate of relief associations for the unemployed. Being on relief was a prerequisite for employment in WPA programs, May's ultimate goal.

To qualify for financial assistance, May realized that she would have to prove that she was unemployed, destitute, and without family to support her. She had already filed preliminary papers in which she declared, untruthfully, that her parents were deceased and that she had no means of financial support from her family. On February 28 she wrote, "The investigator was just here. I am an orphan." Now, in mid-March, she returned to the WAA offices to complete her application process.

May endured several grueling days of traveling from downtown offices to uptown offices in the pouring rain and on an empty stomach to submit her paperwork. Finally, she was deemed an "emergency case" and given a slip of paper entitling her to eat at St. Barnabas House on Mulberry Street ("Boy, that butterless bread, gravyless potatoes, hashed turnips & salt-less meatloaf tasted swell!"). Having already been served an eviction notice, she moved in with her fellow protester, Doris Smith.

On April 15 she wrote, "The gov. is going to furnish me a wardrobe—$15. . . . Dad sent me $25 in a check—'birthday present.' I sent it back. In the letter were violets from the West slope—and honeysuckle." After weeks of no contact, Arnold called ten days later to invite her for dinner at a Chinese restaurant. "We were both embarrassed," she wrote. "We kissed. Arnold left me & I wept into the pillow—but I don't know why. He gave me a silver bracelet brought home from Trinidad."

With the fifteen dollars (about three hundred dollars today) provided by the government, May shopped for clothes at S. Klein's department store at Union Square. ("Jesus!" she wrote, in disbelief of her situation.) Anzia, whose manuscripts were being rejected by her publishers, was not faring well either ("She's living on despair"). May vowed to "get a job someway and get out of this," and she redoubled her effort to assemble her poems in the hope of publication. One poem that surfaced as she reviewed her past work was "In Spoonfuls," composed in 1936 in Salt Lake City. Its message, the seeming impossibility of overcoming obstacles in the path to success, strong then, resonated even more now.

The opening of the poem evokes a folktale in which "the mistress charged of her ambitious lover, / that he go with a teaspoon to empty the sea." May sees similarities to herself in both the mistress and the lover when she demands of herself: "You must write these poems." Her self-love, "unreasonable" as it is, compels her to go to the water's edge "to dip up the sea in spoonfuls."

As the summer months passed without prospects, Arnold lifted May's spirits and shielded her from destitution. He treated her to dinner during the week, and sometimes to the movies or the theater. On weekends, they once again took long drives or went horseback riding. Encouraged by Arnold, at the end of July, May placed ads in the *Times* and in the *Tribune*. She found some short-term, low-paying typing jobs. Although she enjoyed intimacy with Arnold ("Last Sat. it rained so A. & I spent all day f—ing in his apt."), she remained as ambivalent about making a commitment to him as he did to her. She couldn't figure him out (Arnold "exists layers down—only in the subconscious. So far I've not seen him in the flesh"). And she couldn't bear to lose her independence ("I belong to no one—yet").

May's "yet" is telling. She was not averse to belonging. She had desperately wanted Helen Richards to belong to her, for them to belong to each other. Edith Welch's sudden marriage had put an end to the possibility of May's and Edith's mutual belonging. In relationships with women, May saw no threat to her ability to grow, flourish, and remain her own person, but she knew that commitment to Arnold would almost certainly result in financial dependence. It would also raise the question of children. The eldest of ten, May knew firsthand the demands of raising children, and she wanted none of it. As much as she loved and respected her parents, May's mother, consumed with household chores, church work, and children, was not a model May wished to emulate. She loved Arnold and enjoyed him sexually, but he offered a conventional life that could never satisfy her. At this critical juncture, only financial independence would enable her to break from him.

Finally, on August 4, 1938, above a pencil sketch she drew in her diary of a building flying an oversized flag bearing the outline of a heart surrounding the initials WPA intertwined with her own, MS, May wrote boldly and triumphantly:

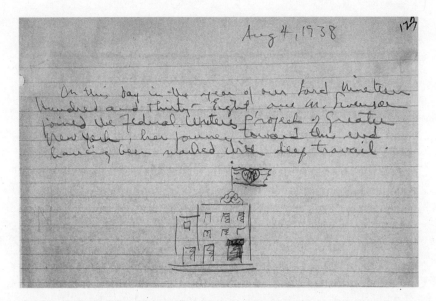

FIGURE 12. In this diary entry from May 4, 1938, May celebrates her acceptance into the Federal Writers' Project. *Literary Estate of May Swenson.*

On this day in the year of our Lord Nineteen Hundred and Thirty-Eight, one M. Swenson joined the Federal Writers Project of Greater New York, her journey toward this end having been marked with deep travail.

CHAPTER 5

I Have Yet to Find My Love

THE FWP'S BEST-KNOWN PROJECT is the publication of the American Guide Series, comprehensive guidebooks for each of the forty-eight states, the District of Columbia, the territories of Alaska and Puerto Rico, and approximately thirty major cities and twenty regions. As conceived by "Project idealists," the mission was to portray the nation "in such an honest and effective way that it would help create a more noble standard of social behavior."[1] Part travel guide, part almanac, each book in the series contained illustrations, photographs, and maps and other information for both real tourists and armchair travelers.

This immense project, which was threatened first by criticism of the writers' Communist leanings and then by the onset of the Second World War, was rushed to completion in the early 1940s. Nothing of this depth and scope had ever been attempted before, and, remarkably, a unified American national identity emerged from the myriad distinct cultures identified in the series. John Steinbeck praised the WPA guides as "the most comprehensive account of the United States ever got together," and social critic Lewis Mumford hailed them as "the first attempt, on a comprehensive scale, to make the country itself worthily known to Americans."[2]

By the time May enlisted as a foot soldier in the FWP's national army of some 6,500 writers, the massive two-volume guide to New York City, begun in 1935, was nearly complete. The first volume, *New York Panorama*, was a compendium of twenty-six lengthy essays on a wide range of topics. Included were articles entitled "Nationalities—New World Symphony," "The Negroes of Harlem" (written by Richard Wright), and "Speech—The Local Vernacular." To continue employing New York City writers, the WPA administration developed eighteen new projects treating such ambitious subjects as "a marine history of New York City, a motion picture bibliography, studies of the major ethnic groups in the city, and a series of books dealing with wildlife."[3]

May was assigned to the Living Lore Unit. She and twenty-six fellow fieldworkers, who were to collaborate with the Social–Ethnic Studies Unit, were charged with collecting first-person narratives, raw material for unspecified future use. They interviewed native-born Americans as well as immigrants from Jamaica, Ireland, Italy, Serbia, Croatia, Russia, Hungary, and Czechoslovakia. Their subjects were construction workers, longshoremen, taxi drivers, garment workers, salespeople, and factory workers, and all of them were willing to share stories about their jobs, their neighborhoods, and their lives in New York or in their home country.[4] Interviewers did not employ tape re-corders. Instead, they took copious notes, preserving as best they could the idiosyncratic speech patterns and pronunciation of their interview-ees ("informants" in WPA parlance). According to Ann Banks, author of *First-Person America* (2013), "Federal Writers were encouraged to arrange interviews through community or work-related organizations, but that suggestion was often ignored in favor of chance contacts. Some writers interviewed their relatives; many more talked to friends or casual acquaintances."[5]

It was the fieldworker's responsibility to gain an informant's con-fidence by creating a friendly and comfortable environment during the interview. As one federal writer explained, "You can't just barge in and start asking questions of people who don't know who you are and how you feel as a person. You have to pass the time of day with them until you reach the point where you feel a warm relationship so that you can talk, so that *they* can talk."[6]

The ability to make others feel at ease around her did not come naturally to a self-absorbed person such as May Swenson. Being a fieldworker for the FWP must have posed challenges, but this work would enable her to foster her career. However contrary to her na-ture, interviewing people promised May a steady income but, more important, free time to pursue her own writing. As one historian of the WPA observed, "The simple act of providing writers and would-be writers with jobs that gave them a livelihood without unduly taxing their energies turned out to be the most effective measure that could have been taken to nurture the future of American letters."[7] Among the twenty-seven members of May's Living Lore Unit, for example, were the novelist Ralph Ellison, future author of *Invisible Man*; the musician and songwriter John Hermann; the playwright and author Saul Levitt; and the leftist poet Herman Spector.[8]

May was employed by the FWP from August 1938 until September 1939. During that time, she spoke with immigrant and native-born American radio and telegraph operators, factory workers, drugstore employees, department store salespeople, and even a tramp poet. They told her about occupations, travel, labor unions, seafaring, military service, and their social lives. As her thirty-three cataloged interviews attest, May established rapport with her informants and successfully captured the stories of their lives as well as their linguistic idiosyncrasies.[9]

The FWP was under continual suspicion of pro-Communist sympathies, and by the late 1930s its critics were able to defund and demolish it. In 1941 thousands of unpublished life-history interviews gathered by Living Lore Unit fieldworkers in New York City and by their colleagues across the country were hastily deposited in the Library of Congress. Because they were destined for projects that were never completed or perhaps never begun, relatively few of these reports have seen the light of day. But the digitization of the American Memories Collection by the Library of Congress gradually made accessible this trove of some ten thousand occupational, ethnographic, folkloric, and linguistic first-person narratives. In her preface to the digital version of *First-Person America*, author Banks wrote about her analog selection process for the eighty narratives in her book, among them May's interview with a resourceful individual named Irving Fajans:

> Sifting through 150,000 pages of material, I was looking to fall in love. And I did— . . . I fell in love with . . . Irving Faj[a]ns, who, while trying to organize his fellow workers at Macy's, hit upon the idea of secretly distributing the union literature via the toilet-paper dispensers.

The narratives in the Library of Congress have been available online since 1996. They often include the FWP forms that fieldworkers submitted with each completed interview. Form A ("Circumstances of Interview") asked for the name and address of the interviewer, where and when the interview took place, and a description of the setting. Form B

("Personal History of Informant") asked for the interviewee's name and address, ancestry, date of birth, education, occupation, community and religious activities, and physical description. The interview itself was written or typed on Form C ("Text of Interview—Unedited"). An optional Form D ("Extra") encouraged the interviewer to add any other comments. These forms provide information about May's informants but also about May and her whereabouts during her time at the FWP. Although she did not always supply all the requested information on these forms, she almost always included her own address on Form A.

May's first day of work was Thursday, August 4. Three days later, she conducted an interview at the Bronx home of a sixty-five-year-old woman of German descent. May recorded the woman's childhood memories of a band of petty thieves, the Frog Hollow Gang, who terrorized her Bronx neighborhood in the 1880s. Eleven days later, May submitted her personal information on Form A along with her completed interview. She listed her address as 228 West 22nd Street.[10]

May subsequently tracked down informants in Manhattan, the Bronx, and Brooklyn, turning in a steady stream of about one interview a week. On August 31 she interviewed a thirty-three-year-old Czechoslovakian immigrant at her apartment at 509 East 79th Street, in Manhattan. This informant spoke freely and comfortably. She had so much information to impart about Czechoslovakia and Hungary and about her work experience in America that May scheduled several follow-up interviews. The two women saw each other socially and developed a friendship. When they met for another formal interview on October 27, May listed her own address on Form A as 509 East 79th Street. She had moved uptown and into the apartment of her new friend, Anca Vrbovska.

Anca Vrbovska Saitta was a Jew, a Communist, and a poet who also worked for the FWP and was, at thirty-three, eight years older than May. Anca's name appears as a "Junior Clerk" on the rolls of the FWP, but the exact nature of her work is unclear.[11] The American Memories Collection has cataloged no interviews conducted by Anca alone, although she was a co-interviewer with May for two life histories, and an informant for four of May's interviews. It was not uncommon for interviewers to interview their friends, acquaintances, and coworkers and to collaborate on projects.

Anca (pronounced AHN-cha and sometimes written with a dia-
critical mark over the *c*: Anča), also known as Anna, emigrated from
Czechoslovakia when she was fourteen. In New York, she worked in
a factory packing Uneeda biscuits for the National Biscuit Company,
and she wrote poetry. If the chronology that May provided in her
diary is reliable, Anca had married Joe Saitta, a baker, in 1929. Their
marriage was not a success, and they separated years before Anca
and May met, but they remained friendly and never divorced. Alfred
Dorn, in his preface to *The Gate beyond the Sun*, a collection of Anca's
poetry published in 1970, identified her as the "first Slovak poet to
write poetry in English."[12]

May recorded two Czechoslovakian folktales, as retold by Anca,
in October 1938, and when submitting her write-up, she added com-
ments about Anca's speech on Form D:

> I was interested in noting the mixture of modern and old-
> world idioms informant used in telling these two stories. She
> used slang phrases such as these: . . . "hurried to prepare some
> eats." . . . "Now come the real juicy part of the story!"
>
> Side by side, are idioms frequently seen in standardized
> myths, fairy stories and folk tales: "No sooner was he gone,
> than . . . " and "Tis true indeed that . . . "
>
> Informant pronounces the word "this" as thees; the word "a"
> as ay and says "reyard" for "reward." Uses such internal phrases
> as: "What shall I say?" and "You see that?"[13]

May's love affair with Anca in the fall of 1938 was as sudden as it was
intense. In early August, Arnold Kates was still the most important
romantic figure in May's life, although she was also seeing a young
man named Bob, whose last name is not known. On August 7 she
recorded in her diary a conversation she had had with Bob about
Arnold.

> I told him about Arnold—"Last night I slept with a guy—If Ar-
> nold weren't there I'd very likely love you—And your being here
> makes me see I will never have Arnold. Life is complicated and
> interlocking and puzzling."

FIGURE 13. Anca Vrbovska (*left*) and May at Arthur's Tavern in Greenwich Village. *Literary Estate of May Swenson.*

"I understand" he said. He looked pale and worn not looking at me. He was tired with emotion and I too. When he kissed me I responded—I felt almost like crying and I almost loved him then. . . . "It isn't you or A[rnold]" I said. "It's neither. I have yet—"

May did not need to complete the refrain she frequently repeated in her diaries since her Salt Lake City days. The first three words were enough: "I have yet . . . to find my love."

May at age twenty-five was enjoying the excitement and the challenge of engaging with two male lovers, yet she wondered whether she could ultimately love either—and she questioned the nature of love itself. On August 17 she wrote:

Today hiking in the wilds of the Bronx following up my Project assignment. . . . When I got home there was a note from Arnold saying—I love you—he sometimes says it in writing—scarcely ever in words aloud. I guess I love him too. Is love a guessing matter? . . .

I'll be spending next weekend with Bob where he's staying up-state in the country. He's arranging a room at a boarding house for me. I wonder—will I give in to him?

On Monday, August 22, now back in New York after her week-end with Bob in Croton-on-Hudson, May metaphorically and aptly described life with two lovers: "Shuttling from one to the other sta-tion, neither of which is a destination." She recapped her weekend. On Sunday, she and Bob hiked "thru pasture and over hill . . . and in the long curly grass under an apple tree overlooking the Hudson had a picnic." They "lay in the grass like children and went to sleep," then read for a while before trudging back to Bob's cabin, where inevitable lovemaking began.

> We went inside. I was in my shorts and bandeau. We lay on the bunk. Bob kissed my breasts and pleaded with me. And so plead-ing half sobbing and I pleading against him, our voices broken agonized murmurs . . . (the night before I had said to Arnold: I haven't belonged to anyone but you since you wrote that first letter to me). I belong to no one—yet. I didn't do it with Bob. But where is the line "Forbidden" drawn?
>
> Bob loves me. He's a sweet kid. Arnold needs me—he hasn't much more time, Arnold, to find love. Life is harsh.

Five weeks later, on September 30, 1938, Anca made her debut in May's diary, a month after May first interviewed her.

> Anca Vrbovska—"a mind like the Devil Himself"—astonishing how the most unlikely appearing people can be recepticles for such enigmas—Evenings of unease—but fascination—coming towards me on the river's edge with such proud shoulders for one so slight—and dark spun halo of hair in the river breeze—or me-dusa tendrils in a radius about a pale smile—a queer curved yet charming smile.

In the same entry, May described how things were progressing with Bob and Arnold.

Bob—it is getting frictional—He's really losing sleep and
weight—There was a berserk Sunday at his new apartment on
2nd St. Fried chicken which made me acutely sick—and a dis-
satisfying & grotesque interval of mutual masturbation. I don't
like the look of him—his thing is so little & sharp-tipped like an
over-anxious little dog—and he is—or tries to be—so decent to
me it gets on my nerves.

  Arnold & I—last weekend he said [to me] as we were walking
up Broadway after seeing "Grand Illusion": "Once you said long
ago that you loved me—and you failed to live up to it." . . . I [re-
plied]: "And you said 'Well, I don't love you!'" . . . [W]e decided
mutually that we <u>weren't</u> in love after all. But that night we <u>made</u>
love in a most meaningful manner.

Two weeks later, however, May's physical attraction to Anca had in-
tensified and reawakened her longing for a female relationship. On
October 13 May wrote:

Anca—this is the prologue to—? Now I think of it, I wonder how
it could ever have happened—E[dith] and I—that was the thing
carried farthest. And now again the thing electric and dreadful
and unwillingly desired—but desired. I have never really loved
any man. She knows me—she guessed much under-surface—and
how does she know? That which is also in her, recognizes me.
Then again I consider the other—Either is love is Love—yes. I
have found myself. Who are you?

May's acknowledgment of her enduring attraction to women and
the choice now before her brought to the surface memories of past
loves. She had pined for Helen Richards and suffered in chaste silence.
She had enjoyed a sexual relationship with Edith Welch, but Edith,
perhaps too conventional, perhaps not passionate enough about May,
had married Floyd Morgan shortly after her graduation. In Salt Lake
City, May dated several men but found none appealing. She would
willingly have had an affair with Gladys Hobbs, but Glad gave her no
encouragement beyond friendship. In New York, May had fancifully
convinced herself that Plat was an appealing man of mystery instead

of a philanderer mostly interested in relieving May of her virginity. Arnold Kates was another story. Arnold and May were genuinely attracted to each other, mentally and physically. Both were ambitious, passionate, and sensitive to art and literature. But May prized her independence too much to enter into a conventional marriage with Arnold.

May and Anca had decided to live together, ostensibly to save money, but surely they sensed other possibilities. On Friday, October 21, May moved in, planning to stay until they found a place together downtown.

May had intended to spend that same weekend of October 21–23 with Arnold, but she never showed up. In a letter dated only "Monday," probably October 24, 1938, May wrote:

Dear Arnold:

As you will have concluded, I found it impossible to meet you Friday and spend the weekend I had so looked forward to.

I have moved, temporarily, to 509 East 79th Street, Apt. 21. My landlord wants more rent for "steam heat" in my cozy coffin of a room. So I cleared out.

I mentioned to you that Anca Vrbovska and I have planned to take an apartment together. She offered [to let] me room with her till November 1st—(her rent is paid up until then)— and as soon as we find a suitable place, we shall get permnently settled.

I want to see you. Won't you please let me know as soon as you can—or will—grant me an evening? I await your reply.

Truely,
May
509 E. 79th
(There is no phone)[14]

If they met soon afterward, no record survives. May began a new diary three days after she moved in with Anca, which was the same day she wrote to Arnold. This, her third surviving diary, is markedly different from her previous two. She wrote much less frequently in it, and her entries concentrated more on her inner thoughts and her life at home with Anca than on day-to-day activities in the city. The next mention of Arnold occurs in her entry on December 5. "I answered A[rnold]'s letters and today got a reply: don't be ridiculous May. He says he loves me and wants me as a wife." Four days later, May and Arnold met in Washington Square.

It was cold in the almost deserted Square—the wind harried the leaves in the empty bowl of the fountain. He came at last out of one of those lighted streets to the dark Square. We got only part way round the fountain and I told him. His hold loosened on my arm—but his voice remained unchanged as we walked jauntily to a bench. It was cold. We lit cigarettes. When he stopped talking, I told him again, looking away, making my words as hard as I could. Then there was a silence. Only his face did not change. But a small sigh—like a spirit slipping free—unnoticed the spirit slipped away—And a small movement of the ankle as if struggling against its sudden chain. After that we understood each other. It was cold and sad in the Square—a few people went by— their steps harsh upon the walk. Soon we arose and he took my cold hand, and I went. When I came home the light was warm and yellow in our house, where she sat waiting.

By December 1938 Anca and May were living at 29½ Morton Street, in the West Village. Shortly after they settled in, May described her new apartment and her new lover, then entered random thoughts.

Sunshine strikes upon the bare floor. Snow is gathered upon the window ledge & the panes are gray with rain. The clock ticks; my little porcelain horse bends his nostrils over a green-backed book "Trial"—Kafka. The house is still. She is in the room, or in the other room; if not she will come. She is on the way—coming toward me forever.

I learned that she is a Jewess. In Czechoslovakia her peo-
ple live in danger. She is 31 years old [Anca was thirty-three].
The other day I tried to pull, one by one, the grey strands from
her black hair—but there are many hidden ones. She has been
married for nine years to a patient cloddish man. She is short in
stature.

We play chess and make love. She is better than I at the for-
mer. She once told me: you have an intelligent body. I have felt
her weight upon me. . . .

My brother George was in New York three days before sailing
to Sweden on a mission.

Grant [Redford] wrote not long ago saying he might come
East.

I have not written to Glad although I owe her a letter.

Some think we will have Fascism in America.

The Writers Project is threatened with cuts.

I have an ultimate dream—all else must be subordinate—
especially my love.

I think Death is our only true lover.

May and Anca spent their first Christmas and New Year's Eve to-
gether quietly. "Christmas came and went," May wrote. "My mother
sent cakes. We bought 3 gallons of wine. I gave F. a ring—a square
signet ring." (For some reason, May called Anca "Frankie" and often
abbreviated her name as "F." in her diaries.) On New Year's Eve 1938,
after browsing in Village bookshops, May and Anca walked home in
the gathering darkness through Washington Square, "where a mourn-
ful-ringed moon wheeled through the grey blue clouds—seen through
the stark twigged tree branches," and spent the evening alone. "It is a
crisp night—with a powdering of snow. They are tooting tin horns in
the street. Each day we make love in the face of pending pink slips and
Czechoslovakia is burning."

Three months earlier, on September 30, 1938, in a fruitless effort to
stave off Germany's war of aggression, the leaders of England, France,
and Italy met with Adolf Hitler to sign the Munich Pact. This agree-
ment sanctioned Hitler's annexation of the Sudetenland, a border
region of Czechoslovakia with an ethnic German majority, in exchange

for Hitler's pledge of peace. This sealed Czechoslovakia's fate and paved the way for the total surrender of Czechoslovakia to Germany on March 15, 1939. Anca was profoundly concerned about the safety of her Jewish family, to whom for years she had been sending money and supplies. Now, when their need was greatest, Anca's livelihood was seriously threatened. Anti-Communists in Washington, led by Congressman Martin Dies, were systematically undermining Federal One, the division of the WPA that oversaw the Federal Writers' Project.

Anca was an ardent Communist. May sympathized with the cause and had participated in demonstrations and marches in support of communism, but she refused to become a card-carrying member of the party. "Everyone I know is trying to make me 'join,'" she complained. But in the present climate, guilt by association was a dangerous reality, and as waves of dismissals circulated at work, both women feared the loss of their incomes. On January 28, 1939, May and Anca marched with members of the Workers Alliance to protest the issuance of pink slips by the FWP.

Tension on Morton Street ran high in January 1939, and keeping their feelings for each other on an even keel was a challenge for two strong-willed women. Anca had written in her diary, "May loves me—so she says and says. I must believe her."[15] But Anca was not reassured by May's repeated avowals of love, and perhaps rightly so. Arnold was still on May's mind. "Arnold keeps writing letters—he impinges on my thoughts," May noted in her diary. Although she wrestled with ambivalence about her new love for Anca, May's nightly lovemaking brought her great satisfaction and helped to alleviate her apprehension. "[H]er body is well explored by me," she wrote. "[S]he is soft and satiable and full of need [and] the touch of her loins is sweeter than kisses." Yet by morning the compliant, tender, and responsive Anca often transformed herself into an evil twin: "In daytime she is fierce and strange sometimes she leaps out at me—her voice is a snarl her face settles into ugliness the corners are acrid with hate. . . . She is there in the other room. When I go in and say—will you have lunch?—she will snarl at me."

May's work for the FWP offered her a break from the mounting stress she felt at home. On January 11, 1939, she submitted a fifty-one-page interview entitled "Tramp Poet." Her subject, Harry Kemp, was a local eccentric and fellow FWP employee who made headlines ("Poet Gets Job!") when he began his tenure with the WPA.[16] It is not clear how May came to interview the then fifty-five-year-old Kemp, but she apparently spent many hours listening to a rambling version of his life, including his early adventures as a railroad hobo and a stowaway on steamships to the Far East. Kemp had settled in the Village in 1912 and published the first of several books of poems shortly thereafter. He eschewed modernism, a surprising decision for such a free spirit, and his poetry took a decided turn toward Romanticism and neoclassicism. May included several of Kemp's poems in her write-up. Although she espoused experimentation and modernism in her own poetry, May was remarkably open-minded and evenhanded in her assessment of Kemp's work:

> But tramp-poetry one might not unnaturally expect to be the unkempt rhymings, probably in vers libre of some half-educated pretender, with far more tramp in it than poetry. Curiously enough, the exact reverse is true; for Harry Kemp's serious work is highly wrought and polished, and in the direct tradition of the noblest, classic English song.[17]

May particularly admired Kemp's ability to be true to both his personal and his poetic ideal.

> Harry Kemp today, living alone in his large, barn-like, Greenwich Village studio, has the look of a man who has achieved that rare transmutation, the fusion of spirit with flesh. . . . He is man of action, and man of imagination: The Tramp and The Poet.[18]

For the title of her interview, May selected "The Tramp Poet," perhaps an homage to Robert Frost's "Two Tramps in Mud Time." "Get your love and your need together" had indeed become a mantra for May, and in her opinion Harry Kemp had achieved what May herself had yet to accomplish.

The Kemp interview might have given May the nudge she needed. In early January 1939, shortly before she had submitted the interview, May wrote in her diary: "I find I am unable & unwilling to write—Art is

[a] substitute for living—and now I live, I do not write. But I want to. ('the well' is dry.)" A month later, however, May returned to her poetry with new energy. On February 8 she wrote, "I bought a new covered file for my things, and am classifying them and retyping. Finished Mirage . . . F. says it misses the mark."

In the poem, May describes a haunting image of home that returns nightly and "waits for the sleeper like a stage." She sees the "green river" by which she brooded, and clouds "above the blue-cloaked fields," and "windless valleys." She also sees a home, which she cannot enter. Her footsteps are confined "to the shadowy stair / and to the green evasive lanes / that bind a house and one room there."

It had been nearly three years since May left Utah, and try as she might to feel like a New Yorker, her western roots and family ties ran too deep. Two months earlier, May's younger brother George had spent a few days with May on his way to serve an LDS mission in Sweden. How much George's visit stirred her memories of home is hard to assess, but her poem, like her thoughts, was filled with dreamy nostalgia.

May published "Mirage" six years later in *The Raven Anthology*, a publication more impressive than its folksy and ephemeral appearance suggested.[19] At first distributed monthly, later quarterly, *The Raven Anthology* was a single mimeographed folio folded into four pages and sold for ten cents in local Greenwich Village shops. Among the frequent contributors were poets Maxwell Bodenheim and Joe Gould and other eccentric and talented Village fixtures. Although Anca was living on the Upper East Side when May met her, the Village was her milieu. There she socialized with fellow members of the Raven Poetry Circle, an organization she had helped establish in 1933.[20] The several dozen Ravens were a kaleidoscopic assortment of students, free spirits, and semihomeless local characters—all aspiring or published poets. "While there was an air of bohemianism about the group, artistic seriousness was demanded, and dabblers in verse were not welcomed."[21] Through Anca, May was introduced to this vibrant society of quirky and creative Village poets.

The Raven Circle's yearly weeklong spring outdoor poetry exhibit was a much-anticipated event in the Village. Ravens and invited guests posted copies of their poems on a tall, green fence bordering a tennis court at the southeast corner of Washington Square. Prices for

FIGURE 14. Raven Poetry Circle members, with Anca Vrbovska second from left (in plaid dress). *New-York Historical Society.*

original poems ranged from ten cents to a few dollars. Newspapers and magazines, often tongue-in-cheek, promoted the show. In its review on May 2, 1933, the *New York Times* spotlighted Anca: "Mostly the poems brought 25 cents each. Anca Vrbovska, a real Bohemian girl, who writes in both languages, sold four at that price. She spent a lot of time, however, trying to tell people how to pronounce her name."[22] And on June 5, 1937, the *New Yorker* featured the Ravens' exhibit in "Talk of the Town":

> The poets come down from their garrets along about one o'clock (at which time the Village is regarded as officially awake), pin their poems up on the wall, and then sit around on soapboxes hopefully until sundown.
>
> The gentleman in charge of the show, Mr. Francis Lambert McCrudden, . . . [is] a great admirer of the works of Edgar Allan Poe, and keeps a stuffed raven in his room. . . .
>
> It is up to McCrudden . . . to assign sections along the tennis-court wall. . . . The place of honor went this year to Maxwell Bodenheim, who is the only one of the Village poets we seemed

to have heard of before. . . . The Poetry Circle meets once a
month and has between twenty and thirty members. It used to
have more, but of recent years there has been a falling off, a num-
ber of the best poets having gone on WPA and two or three hav-
ing drunk themselves to death.[23]

May enjoyed a brief flurry of poetic activity in the late winter and
spring of 1939, when she assembled her retyped poems into a collec-
tion. "I am preparing a vol. of poems for the Yale Series—The Salty
Things I Taste—deadline May 1," she wrote in her diary on April 5,
1939. The "series" was the Yale Series of Younger Poets. Since 1918,
Yale University has sponsored an annual poetry contest, the Younger
Poets Competition. The eligibility requirements, established in 1920,
stated (rather loosely), "Anyone is eligible provided he (or she) is young
and comparatively unknown. The age limit is understood to be about
thirty."[24] "Comparatively unknown" meant that the contestants had
not yet published a book of poetry. The winner was selected by a single
judge, who served a multiyear term. In 1939 Stephen Vincent Benét,
author of the Pulitzer Prize–winning epic poem "John Brown's Body,"
was the judge. The winning poet's book-length collection of poems
was then published by Yale University Press. Twenty-five-year-old
May entered the competition with high hopes, but considering Benét's
penchant for heroic and conventional narrative verse, her loss was no
surprise.

There were forty-odd poems in May's collection, which included
the eponymous "The Salty Things I Taste" and "Mirage," "Haymaking,"
"The Dancer," "To D. H. Lawrence," "The Bough in Spring," "As the Fal-
con," "Wild Water," and "To F."[25] May wrote this last poem, dedicated
to Anca as "Frankie," during the earliest days of their love affair, while
they were living on East 79th Street.

"To F." is a light and breezy four-stanza poem in an *abcb* rhyme
scheme that sets May's newfound happiness with Anca in the context
of their noisy morning rush-hour commute. They set out together for
the downtown elevated train (the "el") as "sunlight lashes the cobbles."
Their paths diverge when they board different crosstown buses. "Your
bus will stop at Christopher / Mine at Abingdon Square / Your hand . . .

'Good luck' and mine . . . 'So long' / The taxi trumpets blare." The poem ends with May's affirmation that Anca's smile lurks in her thoughts all day and "[p]ricks me like a tune."

After her flurry of activity in preparation for the Younger Poets Competition, May again bemoaned her lack of productivity. On April 30, 1939, she wrote:

> [T]hese days I am strangely apathetic about writing. F. remarks (remarks?—na—complains unmistakably) often about her inability to write since living with me. I think, for my part, that this is too settled an existence—I eat too well, sleep too much, and make too much money ($21.57 weekly)—it's anathema to the imagination. Worries? Oh yes quite as many as before, but they are hers—which I must share—not my own. It wears me down.

But May continued writing. During the spring she turned in a succession of WPA interviews with informants in the labor force: workers at the National Biscuit Company, drugstore employees, postal telegraph workers, radio operators. May was working hard for her meager wages, and her relationship with Anca became increasingly difficult as world events exacerbated Anca's erratic behavior.

In March, Hitler had annexed Czechoslovakia into the Third Reich, which made Anca desperate to help her family escape to America. May asked her father to vouch for Anca's relatives, but his help was to no avail. In April, May wrote in her diary, "The affidavit my father signed may do no good since no one is permitted to leave the country. F. has not heard from her mother in many weeks." The threat to Anca's family was dire. May and Anca had seen the feature-length documentary *Crisis*, about Hitler's annexation of the Sudetenland, and the newly released film, *Concentration Camp*, about the treatment of Communists at Nazi hands. Hearing nothing of her family, Anca became increasingly volatile. May's diary was her confidant, her sounding board, and her comfort.

> She [Anca] has a volcanic temper—and she threw the chess men and broke the head of the white king. Other times she has broken things. In the morning mostly she's cross. And she talks a

great deal—mainly about politics which bores me until I feel like crying.

She is very solicitous and tender—at night especially, holding me. One night she said—I want to give you all the Female Love that you have missed and her small breasts brushed me and her lips were wet and soft-soft. . . .

She combines the extremes of ugliness and beauty in all her various postures. I am thrown from peace to storm, from storm to peace.

On April 15 Anca received a letter from a cousin assuring her that "her people are as yet unharmed," and the news helped alleviate tensions between Anca and May ("We are getting on more smoothly"). In learning how to live with Anca, May recognized that she needed time away from her lover, even within their tiny apartment ("For 2½ hours we have not spoken—she in the large room, I reading [Thomas] Mann in the bedroom—these silences are an important vacation from each other").

In public Anca was less likely to show temper or verbally abuse May, so activities like combing Village bookstores were frequent. "I found a new book, Twice a Year in a bookshop yesterday . . . it had in it Kafka and Rilke and a writer new to me, Ana[ï]s Nin, . . . it was marked $1. on the back, so I took it and walked out no one saw me," wrote May. (May's introduction to Nin was her wrenching story "Birth," about a young woman's delivery of a stillborn child.) The stolen book, a journal dedicated to "Literature, the Arts and Civil Liberties," also featured Dreiser, Cummings, and the photographs of Alfred Stieglitz.

Together May and Anca frequented the Life Cafeteria, formerly Stewart's Cafeteria, a lesbian hangout in the Village. "Sometimes we go to Life Bar—where they are always playing that tune 'Melancholy Baby'—and the Lesbians swagger in, their arms about their girls in ruffles and giggles. The Les girls wear men-style coats with overlapping belts, low shoes, and short haircuts," wrote May.

Stewart's Cafeteria had opened in 1933 at nearby Sheridan Square. Patrons were permitted to linger over their inexpensive fare, and soon Stewart's became a gathering spot and safe space for the Village gay community. The following year, Paul Cadmus captured the flavor of

Stewart's in his painting *Greenwich Village Cafeteria,* now on ex-tended loan to the Museum of Modern Art. A raucous crowd of bod-ies—including gay men, lesbians, and prostitutes—writhes in vividly colored attire around a table, while a man pauses at the restroom door, casting an inviting glance to an undetermined reveler, or to the viewer.

During the mid-1930s, Stewart's was closed down for permit-ting public indecency on the premises. The district attorney's report claimed that "certain persons of the homosexual type and certain persons of the Lesbian type" engaged in "acts of sapphism and divers other lewd, obscene, indecent and disgusting acts." The report also described Stewart's as "a rendezvous point for perverts, degenerates, homosexuals and other evil-disposed persons."[26] Life Cafeteria suc-ceeded Stewart's, but the change was only nominal since the clientele and atmosphere within remained the same. Vincent La Gambina's 1936 painting *Life Cafeteria, Greenwich Village,* in the collection of the Museum of the City of New York, captures the flavor of its lesbian scene, and *The WPA Guide to New York City,* published in 1939, de-scribes the likely atmosphere of the Life Cafeteria.

> Sheridan Square . . . is a center for Villagers who frequent . . . unpretentious saloons, lunch wagons, and cafeterias. A cafeteria, curiously enough, is one of the few obviously Bohemian spots in the Village, and evenings the more conventional occupy tables in one section of the room and watch the "show" of the eccentrics on the other side.[27]

Another hangout was an Irish pub, Talk of the Town, on the cor-ner of Charles Street and West 4th. In recording her visit there, May recoiled at the voyeurism of a tawdry patron.

> We found our way to "talk." Had been there barely 5 minutes when a slot machine vendor plops down at the table and starts giving us the I-can-tell-you-by-your-face line. After [a] while he hauls out some pornographic pictures showing girls sucking each other's cunts and guys fucking each other à la Frenchie. They

were pretty good etchings—artistically, I mean. Then this pa-
looka wanted us to go riding on Riverside with him and a bottle
of scotch. So I spit in his eye a couple of times (figuratively) and
he turned tail.

But F. asked him "What sort of people come in here?" mean-
ing in Talk of the Town. And he said, "Lesbians, mostly"—It
sounded ugly said like that. I guess he thot [thought] we were a
pair—and he might could augment his picture albums.

Charles Street was the original home of the Village Vanguard, the
haunt of poets and jazz musicians who predated the Beats and folk
musicians. Because the club had no liquor license, patrons brought
their own and purchased glasses, ice, and soda. The surrealist art-
ist Oronzo Vito Gasparo waited tables there at night.[28] Whether
Anca and May met Oronzo at the Vanguard, at his art exhibitions, or
through his work for Federal One is unclear. Both women admired
Oronzo's art, and each bought a painting from him. May assessed his
work in her diary:

The portraits he does are not like the models at all—yet one
recognizes them—a matter of extraction of the most salient fea-
tures—one which is characteristic . . . —and at the same time
contains elements which can be translated into beauty. Oronzo
made Joe Gould beautiful—that was a feat! I bought a picture of
his—girl in the red cap. And F. bought a portrait of herself which
he had painted without she being aware of it.

When Oronzo came to collect payment for the pictures, May paid him
the five dollars they had agreed upon, but Anca "had a fight" with him.
May, observing their disagreement, later wrote that "glancing at each
other, they looked like brother and sister—Oronzo, the sister."
Anca's behavior kept May on edge. Having made a commitment to
live with her, May hoped that she had at last found her love and lover.
But, reflecting on her past relationships, May doubted her decision.
During the spring and summer of 1939, concerns about life with Anca
peppered May's diary, although she remained optimistic.

APRIL:

I was very angry—and we rode home separately. We had a big fight . . . I am happy. Happy and confused. . . . She rails at me—and then after says again and again that she loves me. She loves me.

You know, I sometimes feel that I am losing myself altogether—I have little time alone and it is not good for me.

JUNE:

F. likes to fight—and if she's mad at herself or at circumstances she fights with me. In a way that's petty. But again it comes from her nature.

[L]ook at F. and if it seems "not perfect as a book" sometimes it is because life is not like books.

SEPTEMBER:

Do I love her? I will stay with her till I have learned her well and memorized her mind—and found her out utterly. Till then, how can I say I love her. To love her is to know her.

During those same spring and summer months, May and Anca relished time together outdoors. They went to the Cloisters ("We sat under the brow of a vine-whiskered hill of rock near a grove of little pines"), the Bronx Zoo ("saw the snakes! I love snakes—they are beautiful and mysterious"), the Ramapoes ("I loved . . . the woodland paths dappled and winding and the cool green mosses and the cold black springs between the rocks"), Central Park ("it was nice resting in the shade of a willow while the boat drifted against the shore—I rowed"), Bear Mountain ("made love upon a large flat rock"), Pelham Bay ("I have calouses on my hands from rowing against the rough waters and the tides").

Nature was their escape from the threat of war and from the fear of losing their jobs with the WPA. On September 1, 1939, Germany invaded Poland. Two days later, Great Britain and France declared war on Germany. On September 9 May wrote in her diary:

There is war in Europe—and a new word has been coined—Com-munazi. And I still "don't know." I am a fence-sitter as ever. F. ran

afoul of the Party line last week in reference to the Nazi-Soviet
Pact and the sheep all began to baa—"Trotskyite!" There are
plenty of meetings on the corners now—and the crowds are ugly.
We were at one last night . . . on Sheridan Sq.

Job is good till Jan. 30, maybe, but F. will be canned around
the end of November. That means the beginning of hard times. I
love our apartment and our walks in the Village in the evenings.

But everything was about to change. Less than a month later, May
recorded:

On Sept. 22 both F. and I got a PINK SLIP. Reason: "Reduction in
Force." Yesterday our landlord, "Mr. Fool-em" presented us with a
disposess—must clear out of the apartment in 10 days. Got a let-
ter from George—he is on his way back from Sweden—mission
terminated on account of the war. . . .

The weather is sharp for fall—rains all last week. But I have
shoes to my feet this time—and about $50 and $20 in the bank.
I've got to find a job. Tomorrow we're holding a sit-down. . . .
F. has been expecting . . . her separation papers from Joe, which
she needs for the Relief investigation tomorrow.

May was confronted with a familiar reality: poverty and uncertainty.

CHAPTER 6

Dreams and Ashes

MAY AND ANCA WERE PURGED from the payroll of the Workers Alliance and dismissed from the FWP on September 22, 1939, thirteen months after May had been hired. May had mistakenly believed that no one would check the validity of her relief status. She explained in a later letter to her father, however, that the FWP had "made a ruling that recertification for need would be conducted every six months. . . . I was knocked off the Writers Project . . . because I belonged to the Workers Alliance, a WPA union, and they cleaned out the Alliance because it contained a few Communists. They couldn't pin the Communists down, so they burned the whole bed to get rid of the bedbugs."[1] In reality, May had been ousted from the FWP not for suspicion of Communism but for her false claim to the WAA that she was an orphan with no supporting relatives.

On October 1 May and Anca's lease was canceled. Forced to move, they found a barely affordable third-floor walkup at 119 Bank Street. In late October 1939 May wrote in her diary, "We put up clean curtains today. The place looks quite cozy and there's a fireplace—altho the floors slope and the furniture and door jambs lean at an angle so that the walk from the front room through the bedroom and into the narrow kitchen gives you the feeling of traversing a ship's deck when she's riding a gentle swell." The proximity of the new residence to her beloved Hudson River delighted May ("through the night we hear the friendly yet lonely hooting of ships passing on the river, half a block away—like cattle their deep, harsh, bleeting voice").

Soon after their move, May's brother George spent two days with May in her apartment after his LDS mission in Sweden had been cut short by the outbreak of war in Europe. On October 28 May wrote in her diary about her twenty-two-year-old brother's visit, "I found him very naïve—but a good kid—though his religious narrow-mindedness got on my nerves." Anca was apparently less successful than May in masking her disapproval of George's excessive religious zeal. Fifty-five years after his visit, George recalled in a strong, emphatic voice his first impression of his sister's roommate. "I didn't especially like Anca," he said. "I didn't feel any warmth from her."[2]

Shortly before George's arrival, May had immersed herself in a recently published and controversial work of historical fiction about the origin and growth of Mormonism in America. On October 4 she wrote in her diary, "I'm reading Vardis Fisher's book—'Children of God' about the Mormons." Vardis Fisher, a director of Idaho's FWP and a fallen-away Mormon, had written a 769-page Harper Prize–winning historical novel about the LDS Church, beginning with founder Joseph Smith's visions in the 1820s and ending with the Woodruff Manifesto denouncing polygamy in 1890. Early reception was mixed. One *New York Times* reviewer called it a "mildly impressive show,"[3] but three days later, another *Times* reviewer raved that Fisher's work was "brilliant" and a "great long story of an immemorial episode of our American past."[4] May's own opinions seem, unfortunately, not to have been recorded. Although May had been a nonpracticing Mormon for years, she had not removed her name from the rolls of the church in New York, perhaps out of deference to her family's religious convictions. Her decision to read Fisher's book indicates a continuing, if nonreligious, interest in her Mormon heritage.

May and Anca were desperate to find work. "Starting Monday to make the rounds of the agencies," May wrote in her diary in late October 1939. "What with rent, moving, bills etc., I now have only about $2.50 aside from that lousy 20 in the bank. Simply got to land something this week." She began teaching herself shorthand but later wrote to her father that "nothing turned up for more than 12 to 15 dollars a week, and that would have meant moving back to a furnished room and eating in cafeterias."[5]

By mid-December, both women had found jobs. Anca accepted a low-paying position as a "Junior Clerk in a Venereal Clinic in Brooklyn at $13 a week." May, now inexplicably reinstated in both the WAA and the WPA, was assigned to the U.S. Travel Bureau in lower Manhattan. The bureau was under the jurisdiction of the Department of the Interior, and May wrote to her father that it was "quite a presentable establishment" that "hires some WPA people, probably to avoid paying higher wages."[6] May was pleased that she "had a chance to get practical experience in office work" and "was treated like a white man for a change."[7] When it was rumored that the Travel Bureau might become part of the Civil Service, May's spirits rose at the prospect of becoming a permanent civil servant.

Although both were now employed, May and Anca were nevertheless unable to afford the Bank Street apartment on their own. Accordingly, in December 1939 they took in a roommate, Rita Rudolph ("Ukrainian, small, vivacious and practical"), a children's book author working for the WPA. The three women relocated to 89 Bedford Street. Their top-floor apartment had three bedrooms—one for Rita, one for May and Anca, and a guest room—plus a kitchen and bathroom, for forty dollars a month.

May's work, initially as a switchboard operator, then as a secretary at the Travel Bureau Field Office, "turned out to be not so fatiguing." On her way home, she strolled past Trinity Church, which she described in her diary as "black with age, with the dire leaning headstones in the sparse green grass," and she noted the "melancholy chime" of its clock. In December 1939 May wrote "Trinity Place," which was first published in 1943.

In this poem May animated the scene of the churchyard with "bootblacks" who "share the sun" with tombstones, and "pigeons perched in Mary's arms," and a nearby policeman, who "like a shepherd / parts the bleating pack of cars." But she ended her poem in reverential awe with a reminder that bones lie under the "sacred soil," and with the observation that "bootblacks kneel / on bits of chamois."

Despite this poem's promise, May's output the following year was slim. Only four poems written in 1940 were later published. "Portrait of Esther," her tribute to Esther Phillips, a Greenwich Village modernist artist, appeared posthumously in 2002. "Sketch for a Landscape," "This Is What My Love Is Thinking," and "Asleep," all love poems inspired by Anca, were published for the first time in *The Complete Love Poems of May Swenson* in 2003.

In "This Is What My Love Is Thinking," May masked the gender of her beloved, as was her custom in her love poems. Here, she complains that she feels "chained" to her lover and "obliged to stay bound." In the penultimate stanza May states her dilemma clearly: "Still I do not want to be rid of him / I only want to be free."

In 1940 May was also writing prose. Because few of her surviving unpublished prose pieces are dated, it is difficult to assess her productivity in the early 1940s. It appears that several of her pieces were never intended for publication but were stream-of-consciousness, introspective, minimally punctuated commentaries in which she questioned her relationship with Anca. For example, in a one-page, typed piece preserved as "Without having to phrase it," written on February 19, 1940, May observes: "I know you do not love me because anyone who loves another could not possibly commit to sharing an apartment with a third person," and "it was too sudden a thing and that is because i am a very silly incautious easily led person and she saw that too but so is she!"[8] And in another piece, "How can I get it all down," written on June 17, 1940, May contemplates the end of her relationship with Anca: "The only way it can be finished is if someone else does it for me, either from the outside, or if I'm ousted."[9]

May was critical of her prose, writing in her diary on March 10, 1940: "Notice this thing about my writing—what little I do of it—I start a thing—and I make a good start, but I forget to decide where I'm going with it. My prose has style and no purpose." May's prose from 1940 was rambling and mostly free of punctuation. This foreshadowed the style of later diary entries and also of her autobiographical prose piece "The Long Tunnel," dating from June 14, 1948, until March 3, 1949.

During the winter and spring of 1940, May and Anca's financial situation stabilized enough for them to resume cultural activities ("We went up to 57th Street to see an exhibition of Paul Klee"; "Wednesday F. and I are going to the Ballet—seats in the 8th row center"). They entertained friends at home ("Hans [Böhler] . . . came for dinner"), and they went out socially ("Had spaghetti at Joe's. Enough to stuff a mattress with"). And on February 18, 1940, May wrote in her diary, "For a year and four months we have slept in the same bed—eaten at the same table—There has not been a day that we have spent apart." But this was not an affirmation of happiness. In the same entry she listed altercations she had had with Anca that frightened her, including one prompted by Anca's loss to May in a game of chess, and another by May's desire for privacy ("[S]he kept me awake all night raging at me for something quite unrelated and thoroughly absurd—the fact that I bought a file case with a lock on it!"). Perhaps motivated by a perceived feeling of exclusion, Anca began surreptitiously reading May's diary, the same betrayal that had precipitated the end of her relationship with Plat four years earlier. Suspecting Anca's intrusions, as a precaution, May wrote a warning letter to her in her journal on February 25, 1940:

Dear F:

The fact that you read this diary does not worry me; what worries me is that you will misunderstand it. Because in it I am talking to myself and so fully intelligible only to myself, since the mind which interprets is the same which writes and it can therefore make the necessary reservation. Any other reader except myself would assume that the words mean what they say, which indeed they do, but they mean a great deal beside what they say on the page, and since they are at best only symbols for what is in my mind at the time of writing, you cannot actually receive a transcript of my thoughts even here.

It is a different matter with conversation, for even though my speech is inept, there at least I make a conscious attempt at communication—at making my meaning clear. In my diary I need not make that attempt, for it is written for no eyes but my own. It is a means of self-examination and mental-analysis. The moment I should discover for certain that someone else reads it, it would cease to be a diary, and become instead a more or less self-conscious and surreptitious vehicle for making an impression and maintaining a pose.

I write this, dear F., so that should you take advantage of my permission to read my diary, you will not interpret it too literally and narrowly. And, of course, if you do not read it (which I would much prefer to be the case) then no harm is done—and even the above little sermon stands in no danger of being misunderstood!

There is no record of when or under what circumstances May had previously given Anca permission to read her diary. On March 10 her entry appears to indicate that if she had once permitted access to Anca, she had subsequently rescinded it: "I'm sure F. reads my diary—because I had a paperclip placed on the first page and it was gone. So what the hell—" With her diaries much on her mind, May tried to retrieve from her friend Gladys Hobbs an earlier journal that she had given to her for safekeeping in Salt Lake City. "I wrote to Glad enclosing $2 to send me my diary & books left with her in my desk. She's getting married to this punk, Don [Goodall]. Well its her life, but I don't envy her—and I told her so." Glad never returned May's diary or accounted for not doing so.

Despite Anca's continued snooping, May recognized that, for all practical and emotional purposes, she and Anca were as committed to each other as a married couple. Though her diary entry on May 26 sounds lighthearted, May's frustration ran deep.

> This business of being married carries its responsibilities: you gotta be home every evening, on time for supper—no dawdling—and lug the groceries on the way—gotta be up on time to make coffee and pit the grapefruits—gotta call your wife every afternoon to discuss the problems of meals, meetings, "how are you feeling?" "Take it easy now." "What time will you be home?" . . . (Hmm what a beauty! She just called from the kitchen, referring to the Sunday steak—"Come and look at it before I turn it over" "I'll look at it when I eat it." "No—come here—now." "Nuts!" I whisper, but I go into the kitchen just the same—married life!)

For May's twenty-seventh birthday on May 28, 1940, her parents sent a letter enclosing a check for three dollars and pictures of her siblings and the house in Logan. May was particularly charmed by the photo of her freckle-faced youngest sister, eleven-year-old Margaret, nicknamed Muggins. The pictures of the house with its "wealth of lawn and leafy trees—and vistas of the lot & gardens & the new house for renters" made her homesick. It had been four years since May had been among her stable, secure family.

The world, too, was increasingly unsettled. "By the way the Nazis are bombing Paris," May wrote on June 5. "Churchill is talking of moving the empire to Canada & America will be in it in a month they say. (Well, what has it to do with me?)" Denmark, Norway, Belgium, and the Netherlands had fallen, and the Germans held more than a million Allied prisoners. The bombing of Paris had begun the same day that the evacuation of British forces at Dunkirk ended. May's apparent dismissal of the sinister events in Europe seems curious even in the light of her once having mused, "I am . . . fully intelligible only to myself." Surely her "wife," Anca, would have been increasingly anxious about the welfare of her family trapped in Europe.

By September 1940, Rita's departure left May and Anca unable to pay the rent. Since they liked the neighborhood, they sought and found a tiny but affordable one-bedroom with a living room, a kitchenette, and a bathroom just a few buildings away at 39 Bedford Street.

In her last entry for the year 1940, on September 22, May assessed how she fit into the world.

> [T]here is a book out on "modern marriage" yes—there is a lot
> to write about can you live it and explain it no and I am living it
> now I want sometimes to tell about twilight over grey winding
> streets and the bare-legged girls & the white-shirted boys—and
> the dingy backdrop of dusty green trees on a misty day in the
> Square & the bums sleeping on the benches & the neckers & the
> Italian mamas and someone unknown, anonymous, sexless
> walking in the dusk—not like the freaks in Life Bar but they are
> in it too.

None of May's diaries are extant for the years 1941–44; they resume briefly on January 1, 1945. May's letters, prose, poems, Knudson's biographical works, and interviews with May's siblings partially fill the gap.

According to Knudson and Bigelow, "In 1941 May took a sculpture class from Saul Baizerman, a well-established Village artist."[10] May appears also to have studied drawing with him. Among May's papers is a brochure advertising Baizerman's class: "A simple yet complete working course in drawing from the nude correlated with structural anatomy, a method devised by Saul Baizerman." Baizerman also dabbled in poetry. On a surviving page from a 1942 issue of *The Raven Anthology*, under the headline "Croakette" (flanked by two perched ravens), is a list of the fifty-four participants in the Raven Circle's spring poetry event, which includes May, Anca, and Saul Baizerman.[11] May formed a close and enduring friendship with Saul and his wife, Eugenie (née Silverman), a talented abstract impressionist painter.

Born in Russia in 1889, Baizerman was imprisoned as a revolutionary at the age of sixteen, but in 1910 he escaped to America. He trained as a sculptor in New York and Paris and by 1926 had refined his distinctive style of hand-hammering thin sheets of copper on both sides to create large human figures and portrait busts. Years later, on the occasion of the Baizermans' joint show at the Artists' Gallery in 1948, May would write a short article about the couple, capturing the exuberance of Saul's technique—and the disturbance his hammering caused in the neighborhood.

It is a good thing Greenwich Village, in fact as well as legend, is a community that believes in "laissez faire." Otherwise Saul Baizerman, the sculptor, would get into difficulties as a disturber of the peace. For the fifteen years that he and his wife, Eugenie (a painter), have maintained their studio and living quarters in the Village, their neighbors have been bombarded from cock-crow to supper time with the clang-clang-clang of heavy hammer on metal. When any of them, out of curiosity (or just a little animosity) poked their heads through the door, they were surprised to see . . . three narrow high ceilinged rooms in which immense sheets of copper were being transformed into giant male and female forms—or heads, or torsos, or here and there, a golden copper infant. . . .

Saul takes a flat sheet of copper, often 10 or more feet square, and neither reduces nor adds to it, but re-shapes it, by pounding with forceful yet meticulously controlled hammer strokes. The copper, despite its rigidity, is handled like pliable material with no mechanical intervention except the round-bolled hammer which has become virtually an extension of his arm and hand. He is able to transmit through each blow on the metal whatever nuance he desires, as exactly as if he were molding clay with his fingers. The degree of convexity or concavity he achieves from a flat sheet of metal is astonishing. Until we move completely around one of his sculptures, we are unaware that it is merely a projection and not entirely three-dimensional. We also have the illusion of full weight and solidity although inside, the form is actually hollow. . . .

When explaining his work to the uninitiated, Saul is fond of using musical idioms "This is a slow movement," he will say; "this is in staccato tempo." His compositions engage the eye much as a symphony does the ear, and in looking at some of his most sonorous pieces, one has the feeling of being "bowled over" as by consecutive claps of thunder, the reverberation of masses against each other is so strong.[12]

One of May's classmates in her 1941 sculpture class was the poet, editor, and literary critic Alfred Kreymborg, "whose help with publishing May was to seek years later."[13] The New York–born son of immigrants, Kreymborg was an autodidact with a keen aesthetic sense and discerning taste in music and literature.[14] In the early 1910s Kreymborg had been invited by his friend Marsden Hartley to a meeting of Alfred Stieglitz's Round Table, an influential group of modernist artists that included such future luminaries as painters Max Weber, John Marin, Arthur Dove, and the photographer Paul Strand.[15] Kreymborg, the sole literary figure in the group, "gradually learned that the lines of painting and sculpture complemented the lines of music and poetry."[16] He founded two experimental literary magazines, *Glebe* in 1913 and *Others* in 1915.[17] In them, Kreymborg showcased marginalized, new young poets, and he actively sought and cultivated female voices.

By 1941 Kreymborg had nearly forty books to his credit, including novels, collections of his own poems and plays, anthologies of modern poetry, works of literary criticism, and his autobiography. Modernists, like May, still respected his early avant-garde literary magazines. Unsurprisingly, a rapport developed between May and Kreymborg in the relaxed atmosphere of Saul Baizerman's sculpture studio. Fifty-eight-year-old Kreymborg doubtless saw promise and pluck in twenty-seven-year-old May, and May recognized his potential as a patron who could promote her work. Kreymborg's impact on May's career would later be profound.

Wartime travel restraints shortened May's employment at the Travel Bureau. Leaving the shelter of the WPA, she found secretarial work in the private sector with J. Widder & Co., manufacturers of fabric notions and trimmings at 110 Fifth Avenue. In a letter to her brother George on April 4, 1941, May explained that she had been fired after only two weeks. She had "had a row with the boss who is a complete moron" and "got the gate." She assured her brother, however, that she already had "a good job lined up at $25.00 per week and so all's well that ends well."[18] The new job was to begin on June 1.

George had completed his aborted mission to Sweden by working for the LDS Church in New Jersey and was "released" in late April 1941. He planned to stop in New York on May 1 to visit May for a week or so before heading to Detroit to pick up a new car to drive the rest of the way home to Logan. May was between jobs and proposed a plan to George on April 24.[19] "There is a chance I may go [home] with you," she wrote, making it clear that she would have to return to New York by June 1. May acknowledged that her parents were anxious to see her and that she would like to "meet their wishes." She told George, "I am thrilled at the dream of going home, if only for a short visit." May calculated a week to get there, two weeks at home, and a week to return. If her brother agreed to forgo his stay in New York, the plan was possible. May advised him not to mention anything to their parents. She would write to her father, since she needed to ask him for money to finance the trip, but she wanted to surprise her mother. Anticipating George's reply, May added a cautionary postscript: "Don't try to persuade me that I could plan on an indefinite stay at home—I can consider it only on the basis of a month's trip."

May and George traveled to Detroit and drove to Utah in his new car at breakneck speed in order to maximize May's time with her family. George wrote in a letter about their "gloriously happy motor trip." Capturing his sister's quick and playful wit, he added, "At one point we were traveling through Nebraska at approximately 80 miles an hour, and, as we were approaching a small town, May said, 'Gee that's a pretty little town we're coming to, wasn't it?'"[20]

May was overjoyed to see her family. She returned the following year as well, and on her way back from that trip, she sent a postcard to Anca from Chicago on Sunday, September 6, 1942. Hoping to arrive at their Bedford Street apartment three days later, May wrote.

Dear A = Arrived without mishap. Mother & Dad looking swell— All were extravagantly glad to see me! . . . I'm making notes on all my adventures—very modest so far! If I don't see you Tues. morning early—phone me at the office. . . . Love & stuff—May[21]

By the spring of 1943, May was making good progress with her poetry. She had published three poems ("Surrealist," "Tiger's Passion," and "Trinity Place") in *Seventeen and One*, a slim, twenty-seven-page, softcover volume with an even slimmer print run of four hundred that Alfred Kreymborg had helped produce.[22] Kreymborg served as "umpire" in the selection process for the anthology and also wrote the introduction, in which he explained that *Seventeen and One* was the brainchild of a group of "seventeen poets of varied experience" gathered together by Dorothy Hobson, founder and director of the League to Support Poetry.[23] The poets had met weekly for four months to discuss their anonymously submitted poems. When someone suggested that they publish their work themselves, they agreed to "an equal division of expenses and of possible spoils." The seventeen poets chose three editors from within the group, and Hobson asked Kreymborg to oversee the selection process. May earned little or nothing from her contributions to *Seventeen and One*, but it was a start in New York and marked the first time her name was linked professionally to Alfred Kreymborg.

On February 23, 1944, Arnold Kates, who still hoped to be a part of May's life, sent her a postcard from Montreal, where he was skiing and snowshoeing "high up in the snow-covered mountains." He closed his note with, "I hope to see you soon. If you have a home phone I can't find it. I've tried. Arnold."[24]

In late December 1944 or early January 1945, May wrote to her brother George, who was in Europe again, this time as a sergeant in the army. She thanked him for the picture he had sent of himself atop the Eiffel Tower, adding, "I will treasure it as a souvenir of a city I have always longed to see and still hope to visit someday when the Krauts have been kicked off the map of Europe."[25]

May's 1945 diary survives only in five scattered fragments—three entries in January and two in March. On New Year's Day she recorded a flurry of good intentions.

Resolved: To Live. To inhabit my body—the whole of it—to give and to respond with every pore of it—to use the complex tool that is mind—the whole of it—to explore the exterior world with it and all creatures that come under its micro (or macro) scope— to explore the interior world of self—and other selves—to exer- cise the intuitive thing called spirit—and to discover the begin- ning of the path into eternity. . . . Resolved—to find myself and thence to search its relation to its world and all others in it.

On January 4, 1945, May and Anca reluctantly attended a psychol- ogy lecture that did not impress them. According to May, Anca dis- missed psychologists scornfully as "termites of the mind," and May aired her own humorously lucid opinion of the lecturers:

Dr. Fred and Dr. Whosit from Chicago weaved back and forth on the platform like two overinflated dirigibles who, hard as they tried to remain aloft over the lesser bulks of a star-gazing audience (made up largely of middle-aged women in persian lamb coats and imaginative hats, and a sprinkling of bespecta- cled males) plopped to earth and were revealed as merely two bald heads (dome-shaped), two aggressive abdomens, two pairs of shuffling feet and two pairs of arms and hands which fiddled in and out of their pockets with the identical embarassment of high-school debaters.

May recorded one point she remembered from the lecture: "that death may be an alibi—that we use death as a last excuse for inability to function—and that the seeds of immortality lie within ourselves as a power which we have not the courage yet to use."

This entry also contains the earliest surviving mention of a young woman named Sylvia Norman, Saul Baizerman's agent. Sylvia was enthusiastic about the study of psychology and doubtless had prompted May and Anca to accompany her to the lecture. At the conclusion of her entry, May wrote, "Sylvia I still can't make out." This seemingly offhanded remark was to prove prescient. Three years later May would devote an intense nine-month period of her life to trying to understand Sylvia Norman.

Later in January, May provided a poetic description of herself as she returned to her apartment from a trip out of town.

> Walking home from the Wannamaker station—leaning against the wind my little suitcase like ballast in my right hand while my left curved out like a rudder—striding in my square-toed flat-heeled "cowboy shoes," my gray twill coat over my black suit and the red "beanie" on my head—I felt all-of-a-piece and self-sufficient—equal to the weather—my dad's grin on my face—(I could feel how my face looked just like my dad's at that moment) swung down Fifth and then the square with its skeletal winter trees and wet wind-combed grass and the dark wet paths—and reached 39 soon after 7. Anca had gone to supper with Jo and left a note for me in the little piano on the bookshelf.

On March 12 May related an "amusing" story of a man who made friendly advances to her while she was on her lunch break at Whelan's Drug Store. He followed her, insisting that he had no intention of picking her up, that he was "merely following an impulse." He kept asking leading questions, which she flippantly but good-naturedly dodged. When they reached Fifth Avenue, May held out her hand and said, "Nice knowing you. So long." But, still clutching her hand, he offered to walk her back to work. Finally, she tightened her grip on his hand and dragged him toward a policeman. The would-be beau took the hint, tipped his hat, bid her goodbye, and strode away grinning. "That was the persistantest cuss I've ever had to shake off yet," she wrote, clearly having enjoyed the entire incident.

On a more philosophical note, she mused on March 19 about love relationships, concluding, "You can love, but not be loved. Therefore, love thyself, for, having no true means of knowing you, no one else can."

In late July 1945 May received another note from Arnold.

May.
I was mighty happy to get your card. It is good to be remembered
by you as I do have a great deal of affection for you. I consider
myself lucky for having met you—because you contributed a
challenge that started the ball rolling to a richer life. Arnold[26]

Arnold's note may have been a response to a postcard May sent him
from Utah. During the summer of 1945, she had gone back to Logan
for her third visit home in nine years.[27]

With the surrender of Japan on September 2, 1945, the war was
over and May was overjoyed to learn that George would be home by
the end of the year, but in the early fall Anca received devastating news
from Czechoslovakia.[28] In reply to a letter she had written to her sister
Mariska in Trnava about her family's fate, her cousin Margit wrote
from Bratislava, "God alack! Of thy whole family with the exception
of Mariska, Kazimir and Anicka, no one remains." Margit provided a
long list of Anca's siblings and extended family members who had been
"dragged off" in 1942. Some had simply disappeared; others were taken
to the "Maidenak [Majdanek] death camp" and never returned. Anca's
mother had been "deported." Margit's own family had also been sent
to concentration camps and her mother had been "gassed" on October
1, 1944. Margit explained that she and her husband had survived only
because they had been "hidden." They lived for months in fear "that
the Gestapo would close down on us."

Toward the end of her letter, Margit returned to the death of Anca's
mother and other family members:

You ask, what have the Nazi murderers done with thy mother?
The same that they did to mine. She was killed in a gas cham-
ber. Thy sister, Aranka, her daughter. Jozsa, thy niece, Berta, thy
sister-in-law, Hermina, Uncle Moritz's daughter, Ilona—they all
had to do slave labor, then, perhaps, became ill from the inhu-
man labor and died—else were sent at once to the gas chamber.
This bad news, however, cannot be verified, inasmuch as thou-
sands were slaughtered daily, and the Nazi sub-species never
bothered to publish the names of those they had murdered. Alas!

That I cannot write anything cheerful. . . . Now we must try to
forget the horrible tragedies. It is too late to do anything else.

The immediacy of the war's toll was made real to May through
Anca's grief. In 1945 she wrote "War Summer," which was published in
1950. In it, May observed how deceptively chaste the earth appears in
the evening, when moonlight turns bloody waters silver and corpses
lie hidden in the cool woods.

May's diary for the year 1946 does not survive, but a highlight for
May was a visit from her youngest sister Margaret ("Muggins"). Fifty
years later, Margaret spoke at length about her New York experience,
vividly recalling details.[29] Margaret credited May with orchestrating
the trip. Aware of Margaret's interest in fashion, May had persuaded
their father to pay for summer courses for Margaret at the Traphagen
School of Art and Design on Broadway and 53rd Street. May promised
to assume responsibility for eighteen-year-old Margaret's room and
board for the seven weeks that she would spend in New York.[30]

Margaret's visit strengthened the bond with her adored thirty-
three-year-old sister. After a three-day journey by train from Utah,
Margaret arrived at Grand Central Terminal, where May awaited her
and accompanied her to Bedford Street. Like her brother George seven
years earlier, Margaret sensed immediately upon meeting Anca that
she was not welcome. Margaret slept on a couch in the living room and
described her sister's apartment as "modest" but "very attractive, with
lots of books."[31] She recalled a "picture on the wall in the bedroom that
gave me the first clue that May was gay." Though they never spoke of
it, Margaret said that May "knew that I knew."

May took Margaret to the opera, musicals, and the ballet. They rode
the ferry to see the Statue of Liberty and went to the top of the Em-
pire State Building. They cruised up the Hudson and swam at Jones
Beach. May even took Margaret horseback riding, a new experience for
Margaret and a favorite activity for May. Margaret remarked that May
loved animals: she couldn't remember a time when May did not have
a cat, and in 1946 her sister's cat was named Jungle Boy. Margaret
and May ate out often, sampling different cuisines. Margaret partic-
ularly enjoyed Italian and German fare and clams on the half shell
from pushcarts on Bleecker Street.[32] "I learned—I really learned," a

still grateful Margaret said. Margaret also noted that May had barely enough money to buy shoes for herself, but she did not hesitate to purchase two blouses for Margaret to wear with her new suit, which was a present from their father.

Margaret knew that May was enrolled in her friend Saul Baizerman's class and was also "taking a course in analyzing dreams." She commented that May socialized regularly with "a gathering of women—lesbian friends—and they were nice." But she did not share fond memories of Anca, whom she found "not attractive" and with whom May frequently argued "behind the bedroom door."

Margaret was convinced that her seven-week stay was a cause of these disagreements: "May concentrated on me. They could have quarreled because May did not include her [Anca]—it was not a threesome." Yet an incident Margaret witnessed on a city bus made her feel sympathy for Anca. The bus driver did not give Anca her change, and when she asked for it, he muttered, "Damned Jew." Anca was angry, Margaret was shocked. This was the first time she had witnessed anti-Semitism, and Anca explained that she frequently endured such treatment in New York.

Toward the end of her stay, May inexplicably gave her sister a folder filled with love poems to take back to Utah. "I made a terrible mistake when I got home," Margaret said. "I was so excited and wanted to share them—they were generic—could be heterosexual. When she [May] came home [to Logan] and found out that George had read them, she took it [the folder] away from me. Nothing was ever said." Margaret thought that May was protecting her parents. She never wanted them to read her love poetry for fear that they might surmise that she was gay.

May wrote fifty poems during the decade she spent with Anca, from 1938 until 1948.[33] Of these poems, about twenty-six have been published, more than half of which are about love. Some capture the pure joy of love, like "Neither Wanting More," written in 1944 ("To feel your breast / rise with my sigh / To hold you mirrored / in my eye / Neither wanting more / Neither asking why"). Others explore the pain of

FIGURE 15. May at the Empire State Building, in a 1946 snapshot taken by her sister Margaret. *Literary Estate of May Swenson.*

lost love, like "Dreams and Ashes," written in 1946 ("Only in sleep or solitude / where fancy's fountain plashes / will my dead love rise to swim / The rest is dreams and ashes"). Anca was no doubt the inspiration for most of May's love poems during this period. But May also returned to other familiar themes in her poems: nature, death, nostalgia, and New York, to name a few.

Since 1942 May had been working for the Federal Wholesale Druggists' Association.[34] Hired as a typist, she gradually expanded her duties to include editing trade publications, writing press releases, and writing speeches for the executive secretary of the association. By 1947 her salary was seventy-five dollars a week, the most she had ever earned, and it enabled her to set money aside on a regular basis.

May's goal was to save one thousand dollars in order to stop working for a time and write.

In the early fall of 1947, Anca returned to Czechoslovakia and planned to stay until at least the spring. In October and November she wrote frequently to May, complaining that a hostile feeling against Jews persisted. She reported that her sister Mariska was despondent, suffered from delusions, and was prone to unreasonable outbursts.[35] Anca begged May to write, and on November 5, distressed by May's continued silence, she asked, "Do you want to live with me?" But May had gone to Utah directly after Anca's departure for Czechoslovakia, and she received none of Anca's correspondence until her return to New York in November. On November 12 May replied to the stack of Anca's unanswered letters.

Dearest Anca:

. . . Thanks for your generosity in writing. Now that I am back and beginning to settle into the groove again I will write a long and comprehensive letter. . . .

I had a wonderful visit with my family in Logan, enjoyed every moment of it, and was glad to find everyone well and fairly well- off. Although Dad is nearing 70 now and Mother 60 they both seem full of energy. . . . Dad is financially under a strain because he either rents free to . . . members of the family or charges them a fraction of usual rental. . . . Muggins and Paul of course are also living at home. . . . I couldn't help feeling that my brothers and sisters are bleeding their parents a good deal—but if Mother and Dad are satisfied, it's not my place to object. The weather was perfect most of the time I was there, and I spent all day outdoors in the lot helping Dad or hiking or riding in the silent colorful canyon a half hours distance from our home.

May also drove to Los Angeles with several members of her family to visit her sister Grace. Grace, a professional chanteuse who accom- panied herself on the piano, performed in supper clubs in Hollywood.

Grace's stage name was Miss Michael Raine, and she informally adopted her professional first name in her private life.

Michael has gone very Hollywood—her hair blonder, dressed to the teeth, has developed a manner and a way with people that gets her whatever she wants. She is beautiful, she has charm—at the same time she has not hardened or become shallow. I liked her very much . . . but of course Mother was a little disturbed—she is no longer fit for a good clean Mormon boy to marry. Hollywood is a curious place—not what I expected. . . . [Y]ou have a feeling of laziness of mind, disinclination to seriousness, escapism. I would like to live there for the climate—it is pleasant, relaxing, but the people would irritate me—they are infants politically that is plain. . . .

I had booked a plane reservation from Los Angeles . . . to Chicago. . . . [I] took the train to Toledo. . . . Spent a pleasant three days with Gladys and Don and their little girl, Brooks. However, I became rather bored with their company after a while—they are slipping into the bourgeois rut. Saturday morning, took off in a smaller plane for New York . . .

I was glad to see Bedford Street again. . . . How small, dingy and cramped the apartment looked when I unlocked the door—the ceiling so low, the walls so narrow. After the wide vistas of the West, the height, the brilliant pure sky, New York is like a dark, damp underground crevice, morose, unfriendly. But I am getting used to it again—it's slipping back into focus. I gathered some unforgettable impressions on my vacation—of the country and of the people, which I will use in my next creative attempt—have put them down in notes. . . .

It is tragic that you do not find peace and goodwill at home in Trnava. . . . As an experiment, be sweet, gentle, yielding and see if she [Mariska] will not do a turnabout toward extreme generosity—once you have won her trust through kindness (in spite of her outbursts) then you can bring her impulses into balance. . . .

FIGURE 16. Miss Michael Raine (stage name of May's sister Grace) performing with a jazz ensemble. *Courtesy Lisa Turetsky.*

Honey, I know what you are going through, and I can only hope that your Mother's spirit will be with you and within you—do as she would do, be brave and good as she, despite every trial. It is lives such as hers that contribute to human greatness.

With love,
May[36]

May's letter is polite, informative, and compassionate but emotionally perfunctory. She was beginning the process of extricating herself from her love affair with Anca.

A badly torn and only partially legible note in Anca's handwriting survives among May's papers. It is undated but was written before Anca's departure for Czechoslovakia in the early fall of 1947 and suggests the probable reason for May's resolve to end her relationship with Anca.

I love you.—What you write about <u>me</u>, is more a part of <u>you</u>, therefore, <u>yours</u>, and [I] was <u>unpardonably</u> in <u>the wrong</u> of <u>tearing up the visible sym[bol]</u> of <u>your thoughts</u>. I promise, it sha[ll] not happen again! Whatever happens in the future days—whatever you might do—I always love you for having been <u>once my friend</u>, and for having brought love in[to] my dreary existence in this stone metropolis—NY . . . often have I behaved like a raging mani[ac.] Anger, uncontrollable, suspicsion, and unbelief dating back to my childhood fixed on you its hope, belief, joy.[37]

Anca had violated May's diary again. This time she committed the unpardonable offense of destroying the pages that had enraged her.

On December 1, 1947, May wrote to Anca in Czechoslovakia for the last time. On January 15, 1948, in a new diary, she analyzed the situation.

Here is what came into my mind the other night—such a shameful thought that it must be the truth: that if she were younger, healthier and good looking (by my own standards) this would outweigh her tantrums, her dictatorship, her jelousy, all the personality shortcomings—that it is not really her treatment of me that I can no longer bear as much as the fact that I can no longer match her in hardly any particular with a prescribed image of "the lover."

When Anca realized that May was distancing herself, she felt isolated and vulnerable, and she panicked. On January 7, 1948, she wrote to May and implored her to respond to the three previous letters she had sent, noting how long it took her to "trudge to the post" each time.

Anca had planned to stay with her family until the spring, but, afraid of losing May, she left Czechoslovakia in late January. On February 1 she sent May a postcard from London, announcing that she would be sailing from Southampton three days later.[38] The next day, she wrote May a brief postcard mentioning the weather.[39] On the following day, Anca sent a telegram to remind May of her imminent arrival.[40]

On February 29, 1948, May typed a page and inserted it into her diary:

A[nca]. came back on the Queen Elizabeth the 9th of Feb. I had it staged—the apt. cleaned, the tulips with the long limp leaves hiding the empty nails where my pipes had hung over the book-shelf. A basket of fruit on the table on the clean cloth and the square envelope. All was clean. . . .

In that square envelope was likely May's farewell letter to her lover of ten years.

CHAPTER 7

I Can Live Free Inside

MAY HAD SLIPPED STEALTHILY AWAY from the apartment on Bedford Street before Anca's return. But she did not abandon Anca entirely. Her diary entry of February 29, 1948, continues:

> That night when I rang the bell, she was there like a gypsy among her wares. Russian cologne the odor of her hair dyed a dark red-brown she looked extraordinarily well. We embraced. She didn't take it anyway I had imagined. She was calm, smiling. . . .
>
> At first I didn't belong anywhere it was like splitting in two but now all has fallen into place. Of course there is the dark and light side of the moon as always. Weekends I go around to 39 [Bedford Street] for my rations on bed and table. It is filling but scarcely has any taste—still one must be nourished. (No one sees this diary now but me—lovely!)

May's oblique phrasing meant that although she and Anca were not living together, she returned regularly to their old apartment for meals and sex with Anca.

> How will the future be? It will be. That is all. Did I do wrong? No, except in letting it go on so long. The coward who finally had the guts to close his eyes and turn his back on the piercing stare of the sorcerer—his enslavement being in exact proportion to his weakness as much as to the domination of the "master" who ruled with fear, because of fear.
>
> Can I retrieve those ten years, or need I? Can I start from Now? . . . Now I've got to wash my hair and go to bed.

Anca's surprisingly calm and resigned acceptance of May's depar-ture from Bedford Street proved an unexpected boon for May and

enabled the two women to remain friendly. Anca's husband, Joe, had
returned to live with his wife, but his work and social habits kept him
from home much of the time, and May found ample opportunity to
be alone with Anca on her own terms.

On October 19, 1948, May wrote,

> back on the platform of my affection again that is F She's a good
> lover that must be granted. . . . Visualizing her having a child it
> seemed a wonderful idea I wish it could happen to her and Joe
> for maybe that would make her happy return her to the pride
> she has squandered. . . . It was lovely making love in the firelight
> very relaxing and balancing and everything falls into place after-
> ward so that tiny barbs don't look like daggers any more and the
> bedrock of what is important emerges and you feel secure. . . . It
> takes a long time to learn to love beautifully.

For her part, Anca regretted the waning of their relationship, and
despite her rapprochement with her husband, she continued to love
May deeply. In *The Other Selves*, a collection of poems self-published
by Anca in 1951, there is little doubt that May inspired the affecting
poem "Song."

> My tears turned into pearls last night
> to a song my weeping;
> the sky was bright with soft moonlight
> while all the world was sleeping.
>
> Again love's old forgotten dreams
> were in my heart awakening;
> I kissed a rose instead of you
> to keep my heart from breaking.

And in a later collection of poetry, *The Gate beyond the Sun* (1970),
Anca dedicated her poem "Sanguine Sea" "To May Swenson."

✳

May was now living in a nearby two-bedroom, second-floor walk-up that she shared with a woman named Trudy Lubitsch. She rejoiced in her newfound freedom and wrote in her diary in June 1948: "It is thrilling to come home to Perry St. to see the green twilight, reflected from the green trees in the garden, caught in the rectangle of my own window." May enjoyed sunbathing nude behind green curtains on the "shabby little terrace" that overlooked the lush back garden of St. John's Episcopal Church on West 11th Street. Her apartment house at 23 Perry Street was one of several buildings in St. John's Colony, a cluster of rental properties owned by the church. May's landlord was Father Charles Graf, the rector of St. John's. To offset some of the financial losses suffered by the parish during the Depression, Graf severely curtailed maintenance of the apartments, often refusing to provide basic services like painting and plumbing repairs. May and Father Graf argued frequently about maintenance expenses during her years on Perry Street.

However, the church garden was always manicured and provided endless delight for May and her next-door neighbor, Mary Cantwell. Mary was a copywriter for *Mademoiselle* magazine, a feature writer for *Vogue*, and a columnist for the *New York Times*. In her memoir of life in Manhattan during the 1950s and '60s, Cantwell remembered May as "a stocky woman" with hair "cropped short over her bullet head," who often gazed into the garden.[1] Cantwell described St. John's garden as "perhaps the most secret of all the Village's secret gardens. It was very large, with two fountains, a small stone altar, private sitting areas."[2] She also recalled "a towering catalpa tree which in spring had a haunting, peppery scent, rose of Sharon bushes and spirea." Fauna included a community of box turtles and even some peacocks.

From her terrace, May sometimes observed Father Graf's young wife walking in the garden with her newborn daughter. May's 1951 poem, "The Garden at St. John's," describes the rector's wife strolling "where the wrinkling tinkling fountain / laps at the granite head of a monk." She imagines the new mother's wonder as she gazes at her infant daughter, and she cleverly jabs at her landlord in the process ("A miracle surely the young wife thinks / from such a hard husband a tender child"). In the final stanza, May places the garden oasis in the context of the all-encompassing city:

A miracle surely this child and this garden
of succulent green in the broil of the city
she thinks as setting the bird-cries apart
she hears from beneath the dark spirals of ivy
under the wall of St. John's in the city
the rectal rush and belch of the subway
roiling the corrugate bowels of the city

Delighted as she was with her new life and pleasant surroundings, May soon began to yearn for a like-minded partner. She worked as a typist in a typing pool, and having painfully little in common with her colleagues, she desired more appropriate companionship for herself. On June 15, 1948, she wrote:

I sit at table with my "girl friends." They talk of boyfriends, of marriage of having six kids. I feel as out of place yet as superior as a purcelaine weed in a tulip patch. . . . I, the sprawling weed, know myself, delight in myself, but how lonely I am! . . . If one exists (myself) there is another somewhere. No living thing is so rare as to be matchless. But the chance of pa[i]ring is slender, the possibility of fulfillment remote.

May cared little about making new friends, but her need to love and be loved was potent. She had missed the mark in her one-sided desire for, first, Helen Richards, then Edith Welch, then Gladys Hobbs. She came closer to intimacy with Arnold Kates, who loved her more than she could love him. She had found what she needed in Anca Vrbovska, but Anca's volatility made it impossible to sustain the relationship. Fifteen months after her breakup with Anca, May did find a long-term female partner, but first came a brief but intense attachment to the beautiful, young Sylvia Norman, Saul Baizerman's agent and factotum.

May and Sylvia had met four years earlier in Baizerman's sculpture class. Decades later, reflecting on the important loves of her life, May would write that from the moment they met she was drawn to Sylvia, enticed by her smile and her piercing blue eyes. May remained smitten by Sylvia, younger by ten years, but she waited until she was free from Anca to pursue a new love. May now approached Sylvia cautiously but with the firm intent to win her. Her first step was to allure the virginal Sylvia, the second to ensure that their love be reciprocal. Both proved inordinately difficult.

Sylvia at first seemed interested in entering into a love affair with May, but she responded ambivalently when May made overtures. The stalemate left May frustrated, angry, confused—and all the more determined to succeed. The few letters that May and Sylvia exchanged provide some insight into their relationship, but "The Long Tunnel" exposes the impact on May of her all-consuming preoccupation with Sylvia.

In September 1948, after several months of aborted attempts at romance, Sylvia apologized in a rambling letter for her erratic behavior and revealed her conflicted feelings about May.[3]

Sylvia had spent years in psychoanalysis and continued to attend regular therapy sessions. May had become interested in psychiatry as a result of her association with Sylvia and would have been familiar with Sylvia's practice of gaining self-awareness by engaging with her unconscious through verbal free association in her sessions. Yet, although May was curious about identifying her own repressed fantasies by tapping into her unconscious, the "talking cure" held no real attraction. May had rejected Sylvia's frequent encouragement to undergo psychiatric analysis and confided in "The Long Tunnel" that her "reluctance to speak about [herself]" was the "real reason" for her refusal. Now May was willing to attempt another route to her unconscious. Instead of disclosing her thoughts in a therapy session, she could write about them to herself. This was the genesis of "The Long Tunnel," an autobiographical work unlike May's diaries.

May described "The Long Tunnel" as both a "novelette" and a "conduit into the unconscious." In addition to recording "surface events," the everyday activities of her life, May plunged into the deeper dimension of her unconscious thoughts. Her method was to record whatever came to mind, letting the unfiltered words flow. The result was random, shapeless, and unpunctuated passages from which the nature of May's obsession with Sylvia emerged. "The Long Tunnel" is a dizzying and haphazard descent into the whirlpool of May's innermost thoughts.

May composed this experiment while working at her job as a typist. To alleviate the daily routine of mindless monotony and boredom, she feigned work while typing her heady novelette. The first entry, on June 14, 1948, begins with May's complex vision of the convergence of time:

Leading into or leading out of, the long tunnel of time is a subterranean conduit between past and future. Above it the two merge into one landscape. Because we are constantly traversing the covered tunnel of the present we think they are separate regions, but they are one.

Immediately following this, May wrote: "Today. I arranged to take riding lessons in an indoor ring on E. 22 St." and added other "surface events" in her life before reverting once again to the abstract: "The trouble with choosing your own ideal is that you thereby diminish your chances of attaining it." And so "The Long Tunnel" continues, weaving circuitously through May's disconnected thoughts. After the summer of 1948 passed without success in seducing Sylvia, on October 13 and 14, May recorded thoughts typical of the overall tenor of this unusual piece of writing:

so what is it I want don't stop to think I want to sleep with her what does that mean one night one good night lots of night how many nights and what about when she goes away that song that says does she love me its too soon (late) to tell But don't forget other things such as writing . . . don't stop till the boss comes back not even for a cigarette but this isn't helping because what I want is to reassure myself reassert myself Im a coward Because of my cowardice and your blindness four years passed in a fruitless dance but is that it and how does she really feel probably indifferent what is the thing with our difference in age. . . . Dont stop just go on till your fingers get tired james joyce and Melville and the sea and Conrad and the others Baudelaire and Rimbaud Rimbaudelaire. . . . I want to look good to her thats what it is do I want her to love me to envy me to make love to me Only if only if then what to say goodby . . .

When May abandoned her search for unconscious thoughts in favor of recording the "surface events" of her life, she provided interesting personal insights. In the fall of 1948, for example, May couldn't settle on a "look"—was it better to please herself or Sylvia? In November she wrote, "The problem of Fem or Butch—wanting to be both at once—excruciating conflict. Alternate sister, alternate." She deferred to Sylvia on some things ("Does she think of me as girlish or boyish I alternate my hair is long and she liked it that way and its softness I want to make her happy forever"). But, though her hair was "girlish," May rejected other traditional manifestations of femininity. She described how she and Sylvia chose to dress for a fall picnic together. "She [Sylvia] wore a skirt and blouse and a girdle to hold up her stockings (my god) and a slip—layers and layers—but a trench coat to spread on the ground and a brown suede jacket. I had on my brother's checked pants and my jodphur boots." May's "look" was clearly in flux in the late 1940s as she navigated her way from "Fem" to "Butch" in the changing landscape of Greenwich Village.

Toward the end of November, May's lengthy cat-and-mouse game with Sylvia at last culminated in conquest. Her memory of bedding Sylvia remained vivid in 1985 when she recorded it in "The Bad Luck Diary." She and Sylvia had gone together to the Baizermans' house to water their plants and feed the cat while they were away. May recalled that she and Sylvia went upstairs and lay together on a cot in a dimly lit room, where they made love for the first and only time.

May's enchantment with Sylvia, so long pursued, was short-lived, for by January 1949 Sylvia had left May for another girlfriend. May was disappointed and exhausted by their breakup, but Sylvia remained an important figure in May's life and work. May privately identified Sylvia as the muse of a group of twenty love poems titled "That Never Told Can Be" and of her frequently anthologized poem "The Key to Everything."[4] May composed the "Sylvia" poems in the late 1940s, and though they were never published as a group, individual poems such as "Neither Wanting More," "In Love Made Visible," and "Dreams and Ashes" were published posthumously.[5]

May vowed to find a new lover: "I am looking out for another and better fitting bedfellow. . . . I will find him-her the one who will rec-ognize me simultaneously with my recognition of her-him. Or else? I will love myself and celebrate myself." Perhaps her open-mindedness with respect to gender was triggered by warm and lingering memories of Arnold Kates, who only weeks before had sent her a Christmas card with a touching message.

To May
a bursting bud of beauty—
upon whose petals the
anguished have found
nectar and the proud its thorns
    Best
    Arnold[6]

In one of her last entries in "The Long Tunnel," a still dejected but resigned May wrote: "Sliver [May's nickname for Sylvia] called we have so little to say to each other. . . . She is not herself. . . . And I am not the same either." On March 3, 1949, a few weeks after her breakup with Sylvia, May put aside "The Long Tunnel" and began a new diary.

May was now thirty-five. Although whether to have children was not a question for her, it was a recurring topic in conversations with her coworkers and her friends of childbearing age ("Hilda called and asked if I knew an abortionist"; "Gladys wrote says she's 'pregnunt' and she hates everything about the idea poor kid"). At the same time, engagement with her older friends, like the Baizermans and Alfred Kreymborg, heightened May's awareness of aging and its attendant onset of bodily decline and illness. In January 1949 May noted sympathetically of the Baizermans, "Saul wrote about nursing [his wife] Genie in the Arizona sun. . . . I should realize my good fortune I'm neither pregnant old or ill."

May had maintained contact with the sixty-five-year-old literary critic Kreymborg, her friend from Saul Baizerman's class. Kreymborg met weekly with her to discuss her work, to play chess, and on occasion to flirt. However, she felt little sympathy for him, as she had expressed trenchantly a few months earlier:

Today Kreymborg by the fire with a yellow cane he gained the
top of the two flights out of breath the fold below his right
eye twitching like a horse's hide plagued with a persistent fly,
and pushed out his mouth to be kissed. Don't be afraid of <u>me</u>
he said . . . impressed his moist mouth beneath bristled gray on

FIGURE 17. Alfred Kreymborg, photographed by Alfred Stieglitz.
National Gallery of Art, Washington, Alfred Stieglitz Collection.

mine a number of times during the session. . . . I hope he will
furnish a passport to publication for me.

May was having little success promoting her work and was discour-
aged by the eight rejection letters she received from Howard Moss,
poetry editor of the *New Yorker*. She had, of course, submitted her
work to other journals, most of which she did not mention by name.
Although May found Kreymborg decrepit and repulsive even when he
wasn't making crude sexual advances toward her, she understood that
he could be useful for her career. Kreymborg had convinced his friend
William Rose Benét to publish May's "Haymaking" in the *Saturday
Review of Literature* in 1949. This was May's first poem to appear in a

national literary magazine. In that same year, Kreymborg submitted poems of his own to James Laughlin, publisher of the avant-garde New Directions press, and alerted Laughlin to May's work. Laughlin wrote a brief but kind rejection letter to Kreymborg, adding a note of encouragement about May's poetry: "I always wish, however, to be hospitable to young poets, and it occurs to me that we might be able to use some of the poems of May Swenson in the next number of our NEW DIRECTIONS annual." Laughlin asked Kreymborg to select "six or eight" of May's outstanding poems and to send them to him in July for consideration.[7]

James Laughlin was a well-respected poet in his own right, but his literary achievements paled compared to his accomplishments as a publisher whose personal wealth allowed him to be guided by his instincts, not by his pocketbook.[8] Under Laughlin's leadership, New Directions published and promoted new voices in modern literature.

Laughlin's interest in May's poems came at an ideal time. She had been systematically reviewing and reassessing her body of work in preparation for writing more new poems. On January 24, 1949, May wrote in her diary, "All mornin spent with recapitulation, reading past creative attempts, notes, going over former territory. This seems necessary before laying out new lot, planning the new road— want to find out why the crops of former seasons were so meagre why they failed, why the land went fallow—scientific farming from now on."

May wanted to break away from Kreymborg, but she continued to follow his instructions. On February 8, 1949, she recorded that she sent poems "to three magazines as per AK list," although she remained wary of

FIGURE 18. James Laughlin, founder of New Directions Publishing and May's employer. *Copyright © 2024 by Leila Laughlin Javitch, Amelia Laughlin, and Walker Laughlin. Reprinted by permission of New Directions Publishing Corp.*

his motives, noting, "[H]e wants me for a symbol of his lost youth." Commenting in her diary about a two-hour Thursday session with Kreymborg, she complained that he offered "the same old stuff." His compliments no longer meant anything to her. "He would say good if I wrote shitshitshit," she wrote.

During this fruitful period, most of May's poetry was like her prose: free-flowing and unpunctuated, although not exclusively so. Among several new poems, she described one titled "Rededication" as "in the old rigid style—but honest in intent at least." May also wrote prose with an eye toward publication. She sent a piece called "The Inmost Circle" to Kreymborg, who praised it rapturously.

March 15, 1949

Dear MS:

I have just finished reading your MS, The Inmost Circle, in one dramatic sitting. It is simply magnificent, a little masterpiece (little in length only). When I told Bill Benet you had "a streak of genius," I thought I might have been reckless, but now I'm certain that "streak" was too mild an expression. There are a number of stylistic flaws I'd like to discuss when you next have time. Don't bother to answer this: I'll phone you on Thursday.

Everyone will claim this thing must have been written by a man and the more fools they. Others will cry, What a pessimistic tale, and they'll be wrong too. It is bold and truthful, that's all, and imaginative. And timely as well, all-timely. How in hell do you do it?

In haste,
AK.[9]

This story, which May seems never to have submitted for publication, takes place in the course of a day in Central Park. A World War II veteran named John has recently returned to New York after a tour of duty in the Pacific theater. His past is revealed through flashbacks as he carries out careful preparations to commit suicide in the park at nightfall. There are parallels with J. D. Salinger's "A Perfect Day for Bananafish" (1948).

Two months later, in May 1949, May shifted from prose back to poetry and from pessimism to optimism. She had found a new muse in Pearl Schwartz, the petite, dark-haired, olive-skinned woman who would be her committed partner for the next seventeen years. Pearl worked as an attendant at the Willard Parker Hospital on East 16th Street, which specialized in treating contagious diseases, especially polio. She cared for chronic female stroke patients and male "tuberculins." She also prepared dead bodies for the morgue. Pearl would later work as a secretary while earning a degree in social work by taking night classes at Hunter College.

The two women had passed each other on the street one evening in the Village, each taking note of the other, and by chance they met again later that night at the home of a mutual friend. The attraction between May and Pearl was instantaneous and strong. Within two weeks May had purchased twin rings. On the card accompanying her gift to Pearl she wrote, "To my darling J. J., Love, Miken, 6/13/49."[10] May was inspired to write several poems for her new lover, including "To a Dark Girl," "Mornings Innocent," and "Love Is," all written within weeks of their meeting.

In "To a Dark Girl," a sensuous poem that begins "Lie still and let me love you," May's title plays on Pearl's surname: Schwartz means "black" in German and, in a variant form, in Yiddish. The name fit. Privately and affectionately, May called Pearl "Blackie" or "Jay" (often shortened to "J." or sometimes "J. J."). Pearl called May "Miken," a nickname derived from the Swedish "Maj" (pronounced "my"). "Jay" and "Miken," Pearl later explained to May's brother Paul, were also code names, intended to blur gender.[11]

Although May's diary for the fall of 1949 and the winter of 1950 is missing, the volume beginning in March 1950 indicates that May had returned from a visit with her family more than a month previously.

In all likelihood, she had quit her job in December 1949 and spent Christmas in Utah, returning to New York in late January or early February 1950.

It is not clear from her diary entries whether May had quit her job solely to spend time with her parents, or whether she had planned to live on her savings and leave free time to write for a while after she returned. Now back in New York, she was reluctant to begin a new job search, and she rued her generosity in having lent Sylvia four hundred dollars. By adding that money to the five hundred dollars already in her savings account, she could have covered her living expenses for a year and had more time to write. She considered asking for a loan from Plat but decided instead to find a job, fearing that she would not accomplish enough to justify the lack of an income ("I seem unable to tackle any long-standing project—tend only toward the sporadic").

May's parents were concerned about her, and on March 9 her father urged her to come home permanently. "I have been worried about how you may be getting along in as much as you returned to New York with very little money and without a job. . . . Why don't you quit Old N.Y. and come out west where at least we have plenty to eat?"[12]

May felt deep affection for her parents and her family and periodically wrote heartfelt paeans to them in her diaries. On March 11, 1950, for example, she praised her father's discovery in his garden of a new type of flower. He had pressed one for her and enclosed it in a letter. "[M]y Dad," she wrote, "over 70, discovers in his familiar garden, nourished so meticulously by him many years, a new anonymous bloom—the ability to see the tiny deviation—to notice newness, to maintain an eye for even the minutest birth—to such a man life never stales no matter how close creeping tentacles of age wrap him."

It weighed heavily on May that she was approaching her thirty-eighth birthday without having accomplished her goal of supporting herself as a poet—of getting her love and her need together. She admired her father's ability to triumph over the effects of aging by finding joy, excitement, and renewal in nature. Thoughts of her father prompted May to consider her own bout with time's "creeping tentacles." Like her father, May delighted in discovering newness, but for May newness often came from reaching within herself for deeper levels of self-discovery.

FIGURE 19. Swenson family photograph taken during May's 1949 visit to Utah. Back row (*left to right*): Roy, Ruth, George, Grace, Dan H. Front row: Margaret, Paul, Greta, Dan A., Beth, May. *Courtesy Lisa Turetsky.*

Dan Swenson had encouraged May to record her thoughts when she was a child. To triumph over the transience of time and its oblivion, May now resolved to commit her newest discoveries about herself to words and to preserve them, like her father's pressed flower, in the pages of her diaries.

> Our constant surprise at the behavior & effects of time—this is what causes me to return to writing my diary—the urge to keep track of the passing days—the foolish impulse to leave a mark—a record—something to stand instead of me when I pass. This is foolish. . . . The mark should be left in objective creative work. But there is a place for the personal record—and it has a therapeutic function for the one who keeps it—it is a way of keeping track & checking back—a way of preserving the instants of revelation the moments of sharper consciousness, of deeper realization of reality as it flows by us, around us.

May's attitude toward her diary had changed dramatically. Gone was unbridled rage at the thought of someone snooping without permission. She now viewed her diary as her "personal record," as a way for posterity to understand who she was and what she thought. Violation of her diaries years earlier had precipitated breaks with Plat and with Anca. She now gave Pearl open access to her journals, and Pearl occasionally surprised and delighted May by adding her own comments to May's entries.

As May approached her first anniversary with Pearl, she reflected on her happiness.

> Suppose one were to record each day the most enjoyable thing that occurred? Today it was being in bed naked with my beloved. Sex play is all-absorbing—to quite an extent self-absorbing. . . . It is a year now she occupies me still body & brain.

Pearl, professing her love for May as "Miken," wrote a gushing response below May's entry in her diary.

Despite their deepening love and frequent intimacy at the Perry Street apartment, May and Pearl were not living together. May had Trudy Lubitsch as a roommate, while Pearl rented an apartment a ten-minute walk away on Leroy Street. May recognized that Pearl was uncomfortable with this situation ("Today I suddenly understood clearly how she feels about staying here constantly with me and Trudy. How it's like being an outsider, being subject to Trudy's disguised jibes—being in the position of a guest where I'm concerned simply because its my & T's apt"). Sometime after May 1950, a year after Pearl and May met, Pearl moved into the apartment with May and Trudy.[13]

In April 1950 May wrote that she was again looking for a job, and two weeks later she found another secretarial position that proved as boring as the previous ones: "Yes, I have a job—Multi-Process house 120 Broadway, 36th floor—begin at 1 pm continue till dismissed. . . . Cut stencils and collate mostly . . . may give me some duplicating machine experience. Earned $42. . . . Can work fulltime & earn $60 if I want but what a grind!"

Work and poetry were obstacles to May's journal writing. On May 19, 1950, she wrote, "Been wanting to write in my diary for days—

FIGURE 20. Pearl Schwartz. *Literary
Estate of May Swenson.*

never get around to it." Pearl missed May's updates too: "J. said last
night—'Your little book is dusty—you never write in it any more—I
used to get your picture of us from it.'"

On June 4 May reported that her wages had been cut and that she
had to start work an hour earlier "to make enuf money," and also that
Pearl, who had taken a course in stenography, had gone "job-hunting"
and would "compete with all the other would-be stenos in their high
heels and hairdo's—a bunch of nothing-but-females hoping to marry
their future bosses." Three days later, May learned from an entry in
her diary in Pearl's handwriting that Pearl had found a job.

May described her office as a "squirrel cage." She railed against the
injustice of the system: "[I]f you kill yourself to get a job out perfect &
do it in half the expected time they just take it for granted & without
a word of approval moreover, expect you to increase the pace. At this
rate, the transmission belt they've got me on, since I'm paid by the

hour, the faster I work the less money I make (because I run out of work) and if I slow down I'm not worth the rate! . . . God for a union in a place like that." May was acutely aware of gender inequality and had no sympathy or patience with those who perpetuated it, male or female.

> After work stood in Nassau St. smoking & watched the Wall
> Str. herd stampede by—well-dressed good looking girls—well
> dressed fat ugly or sick looking bosses, the former hoofing for
> the subway, the latter to their cars—all the money the girls earn
> on their backs or in their impeccable hair-do's—the money the
> boss bastards make in the bank—or on their wives' backs. What
> a life—those stone cliffs down the[re] are really manufacturing
> humanoids—reminds me of what Thomas Mann said in the Past
> last night—"What the world needs is humanistic communism"—
> What it needs is Humanism. . . . why am I so pessimistic—I don't
> know except that my experience indicates business people are
> almost invariably cruel, stupid, narrow, exploitive, half-human.
> Business is cannibalism—competition is a destructive thing.

May spent much of the summer of 1950 tanning herself on her terrace ("spreadeagled in the sun eating cherries;" "getting brown as an Indian") while hopping from one job to another ("Worked for a lingerie Sales Office, a Patent Attorneys Office, a Fabric House & now Bloomingdale's Statistical") and reading ("May Sarton book beautiful in spots. She has suffered and tries terribly bravely to create beauty & surety and calm out of pain";[14] "read Feuchtwanger's huge novel 'Success.' . . . He has a stunning understanding of human character").[15] Her adoration of Pearl deepened ("My beloved I love you—I do love you more than anything else—more than I have ever loved. More than myself? I don't know if I am capable of selfless love—but I do know that I cannot be happy unless you are—that your joy is mine").

May continued to meet with Alfred Kreymborg and to follow his advice about where to submit her work. At his suggestion, she applied to attend the writers' colony at Yaddo in Saratoga Springs, New York. Kreymborg had paved the way by writing to the executive director, Elizabeth Ames. He praised May's poetry, calling it "bold and healthy."[16] Ames, who was still grateful to Kreymborg for his recommendation of the composer Aaron Copland more than two decades earlier, offered May a residency for the fall of 1950.

Relying further on Kreymborg's connections, May entered the Yale Series of Younger Poets competition, eleven years after her first attempt. The prize was publication of the winning poet's first book, and, according to May, Kreymborg intended to write the introduction if she won. May "balk[ed] at the idea of being his 'discovery'" but was pleased to have been selected as a finalist this time. "I forgot the best thing that happened," May wrote in her diary on June 26; "Yale Press wrote me that my book 'The Green Moment' has gone to Auden in Italy for him to judge. Months in which to wait before its rejection."

Yale did ultimately reject May's submission, but she was able to use her finalist status in the Younger Poets competition and her upcoming residency at Yaddo "as a wedge" in letters accompanying new submissions both to James Laughlin and to her college friend Ray West, editor of the *Western Review*. West accepted two poems, "An Unknown Island" and "Each Day of Summer," and she placed other poems in various literary magazines and in the *Dallas Times-Herald*. Thanks to her own persistence and Kreymborg's support, May's career was beginning to gain traction.

During the summer of 1950, Kreymborg was in residence at the MacDowell Colony in Peterborough, New Hampshire. May was delighted to be free of her mentor. It was "a relief to be deprived of his 9 o'clock phone calls," she wrote. "I'm afraid he's really senile—the way he plays chess (the most abject defensiveness) and his mewling puling mannerisms—he's pitiful—and disgusting. How can you even feel sorry for anyone who smells like that—of dirty underwear and stale cigars. Yet he made the first crack in the door for me with publication (because Benét—another senile poet happens to be his crony and of his generation)."

May's assessment of Kreymborg was harsh but honest. At sixty-three, he was a fading legend who viewed May as a protégée who would burnish his own reputation. She remained polite and deferential to him in conversation and in letters, but in the privacy of her diary she complained that she felt manipulated.

May was excited by the prospect of spending time at Yaddo, an interdisciplinary rural retreat for creative individuals such as painters, musicians, and writers. She worked overtime to save money ("Hope to get together enuf advance rent to go away Sept–Oct"). On July 4, 1950, she mused, "I wonder what Yaddo will be like—Hope I can do more work there. It will be lonely away from Jay. Don't like that prospect. I want to start another poem. The Kiss perhaps."

Yaddo's executive director, Elizabeth Ames, single-handedly shaped the community there.[17] For years she had forged personal relationships with prominent creative people and academics, and she relied on them to recommend those who would benefit from a stay at Yaddo and whose presence would, in turn, enhance Yaddo's reputation. Ames became skilled at identifying rising stars and encouraging them to apply for a residency. "Elizabeth Ames was Yaddo," poet and literary critic Malcolm Cowley once declared.[18]

May arrived at Yaddo on September 4, 1950, and immersed herself in her work. There are no entries in her diary until October 8, when she wrote:

> I am at the halfway point—a month more at Yaddo—in New York for this weekend—My beloved is asleep on the bed. Things are as they should be with me. I have more than I have earned. . . . Life shines in the heaving straining muscular waves of the never-subsiding sea. Not in the scum-covered lake—not in the seduction of inertia.

Earlier in her stay, May had received a warm reply from James Laughlin about the new poems she had submitted to him. Clearly their relationship was blossoming. Laughlin opened his letter by recalling a recent evening he and May had spent together when they "wandered around and all the bars were closing."[19] He apologized for his delay in reading her poems but assured her that "this was worth waiting for" and that she was "really whacking it right on the nose." Compliments flowed: "You're really cutting through to your own idiom and saying strong things." He told May that he had selected a group of poems for the annual *New Directions* publication, which he hoped would be out by Christmas, and he closed cheerfully, saying, "[W]ith or without a bar, we must meet again soon."

While at Yaddo, May wrote both poetry and prose. She composed several short stories, including one titled "Appearances," which was set in a writers' colony. The story unfolds in a rustic cabin where three people—the narrator, a doctor, and an artist—are gathered. The artist recounts in detail his recent walk in the dense and unfamiliar woods on campus. The events that unfold, and his interpretation of them, serve as the basis for exchanges between the doctor and the artist about human nature. May, in the voice of the narrator, vividly portrays the artist as "a dark-skinned man": "His dark hair was the color of tobacco ash, his hazel eyes so intensely white around their irises that they gave off a bluish sheen. As he talked, his nostrils, eye shaped and almost as large as his eyes, widened and narrowed above his beveled mahogany lips."[20] That artist was based on the fifty-year-old painter Beauford Delaney, a fellow resident at Yaddo with whom May would form a lifelong friendship. During their stay at Yaddo in 1950, Delaney drew a pensive pastel portrait of a young May with short, curled hair, gazing intently at the viewer as she clutches a lit cigarette. Delaney's portrait is now in the permanent collection of the National Portrait Gallery of the Smithsonian Institution. James Laughlin published "Appearances" in 1951.[21]

"Appearances" takes place in September, and the narrator mentions that "[a]t this time of year there were few guests at the mansion."[22] May drew on her own experience at Yaddo, when the other residents included the poets Jane Mayhall and Elizabeth Bishop, who had been a guest at Yaddo the previous year as well. A poet on the rise, Bishop had gained recognition for winning the highly competitive Houghton Mifflin Fellowship Award and had published her first book, *North & South*, in 1946. She was awarded a Guggenheim Fellowship the following year and in between her two residencies at Yaddo had served as Poetry Consultant (an earlier version of Poet Laureate) at the Library of Congress. Bishop was achieving what May was striving for, and May took note. Their fortuitous meeting at Yaddo was the start of a rich and revealing personal and literary dialogue that evolved over the next three decades until Elizabeth's death in 1979.

In a letter to her friend Robert Lowell, Elizabeth, who extended her stay at Yaddo until March 1951, shared her first impression of May.

I have a suite in East house—very nice and plain and sunny.
At first I shared the house with a rather elderly Negro painter [Beauford Delaney] whom I liked very much, but he's left now.

FIGURE 21. May Swenson (*left*) with Beauford Delaney
and Elizabeth Bishop on the grounds of Yaddo, 1950.
Photo by Pearl Schwartz, Literary Estate of May Swenson.

There was a little poet, May Swenson, not bad, & a nice girl, and
Alfred Kazin—both gone now, too.[23]

May wrote to Pearl in great detail about Elizabeth.

My Dearest One: Well at last I am getting to know Elizabeth
Bishop. She wears skirts with back pockets, has very tiny feet . . .
wears knee-length woolen ribbed sox, spent her childhood in
Nova Scotia, wears no rings on her fingers, is fond of Tennyson's
"In Memoriam," is two years older than I am . . . likes to drink
beer, and can't hold her water. . . . She's about my height, kind of

square shaped, rather chunky in chest and shoulders compared
to her hips—the buttocks look square, the effect heightened by
narrow pelvic bones and a wide waist—nice adolescent legs. Her
eyes are round and brown, half scared, half bold, and her tone of
voice no matter what she's talking about is spoofing.[24]

May was intrigued and inspired by Elizabeth's poetry and success.
While working at another boring New York secretarial job, she wrote
in her diary in mid-December: "[W]hat really irks me is that the Gugg
should be in by now and the Hought Miff too but wonder where I'll be
this time next year." Hoping for greater recognition after Yaddo and
the upcoming publication of her poems in *New Directions*, May again
applied for a Guggenheim Fellowship and was pursuing the Houghton
Mifflin Poetry Prize, honors that Elizabeth had won.

Elizabeth visited New York City briefly on Saturday, February 10,
1951, and May, reluctant and on short notice, planned a party for her.
Typing from her desk at work, she wrote about the event in her diary
on the following Monday.

I will record all about the past weekend. Elizabeth of course
because on Saturday morning when I was still in bed the phone
rang and although I jumped up and sounded glad really I didn't
relish it the fact that she was apparently in town, and perhaps
because of this I thought at first she was in Saratoga, or Con-
necticut and made a fool of myself. . . . Well so the weekend
was a long and hectic one—I borrowed $10 from Trudy and
bought blackberry brandy (E. said she shouldn't drink hard
liquor) and rye and invited Jean [Garrigue], Jane [Mayhall],
Leslie [Katz, Jane's husband], Beauf [Delaney], Elaine (who
couldn't come because her little girl was ill), and Crawley came
and E. brought a man named was it Walling, Warning, Warren,
Waning [Thomas Edward Wanning]—that's it—a man in gray
with a softish gray face and eyes that didn't seem to be looking
at you when they focussed at you behind their glasses. Later we
went to Beauford's and Jay danced to that Kai-ah record (Haitian
I think) and she was like a spiral her hips in one direction her
torso in the opposite. . . .

Oh many things were said—I wonder what impressions
E. got. I wonder why I gave the party why I wrote to her why?
Was it because she kissed me on the cheek when I left Yaddo on
the bus? Why? I make tentative gestures toward meeting, merg-
ing and then stand apart or aside, don't carry through . . .

Appraising well-bred and accomplished Elizabeth made May feel
socially inept and caused her to devalue her own work.

I finished the poem The School of Desire—not at all sure of it, is
it too obvious, too lush? Elizabeth's poetry has magic and mys-
tery and is not sentimental not "colorful"—Henry James the way
he writes—without color, with a slow plunger to the gray marrow
of things so that you feel weight, rather than surface—I am too
concerned with the skin of things the shining skin—the shape
not the substance.

In "The School of Desire," published in 1955, May ruminates on
the progression of a sexual encounter through the metaphorical lens
of horse ("you cantered . . . with forelock curled") and rider ("I stand
alone in the hoof-torn ring"). At first the lovers are on a par ("Our
discipline was mutual and the art that spun our dual beauty"), but
gradually the rider gains control ("I . . . held the . . . lariat"), until the
situation was reversed ("But you have bridled me"). In the final stanza
of the poem, the rider, perhaps having lost interest or perhaps in an
effort to regain a sense of control, ends the relationship ("I will cut the
whip . . . put away the broken ring, and shut the school of my desire").
     May concluded her diary entry with an account of her attempt to
purchase one of Beauford Delaney's paintings:

I want to buy Be[a]uford's painting of the greenhouse—I told
him a rich friend was interested, to make him name a fair price,
but he won't name one. Four minutes now [at work] and i can go
home.

Two months later, in April 1951, May again saw Elizabeth Bishop
in New York. They had earlier spoken on the phone at a time when

Bishop, disturbed by the recent death of her longtime psychiatrist, had been drinking heavily. On this occasion she was more buoyant.

E. Bishop had dinner with us at Leo's Sat. She was very amusing, told her best stories. What a contrast to the night she kept me on the phone an hour just talking about anything, as if she just had to have someone to talk to—and Armstrong on the radio in the background, very noisy. There would be a pause—i wouldn't think of something to say right away, and then she or I would start off again—saying just anything, laughing tonelessly, chattering about trivialities. Was she drunk, depressed or what? No sign of this when she met us on Saturday. She told me she'd seen an analyst [Ruth Foster] for three years, who died last fall of cancer. "That's why I was so depressed at first at Yaddo," she remarked.

May spent her post-Yaddo months reading. She recorded passim: "The Summing Up by Maugh[a]m reading it peacemeal on the toilet and wherever"; "Virginia Woolf's book Orlando is one of the most delicious books I have ever read. . . . I must get a book on her life"; "Reading Oscar Wild[e] essays. Randall Jarrel[l]'s article on Obscurity in Poetry splendid"; "reading Rose MacCauley's [Macaulay's] book on E. M. Forster"). May calculated how she could carve out more time for writing: "[I]f I work through the year (and get bonuses after 6 months) I can save $1000 this year. If I work to end of Aug. and go to Yaddo can't save." And she continued to endure Kreymborg in the hope that he could still open doors for her.

Kreymborg came at 8:30. Embarassed me and made me feel stiff and slimy somehow reading me the letter he had written to me—some phrases in them good—mostly stuffing and boring. He is really the victim of a hopeless passion—a dry, frenetic passion so dressed in illusion that it's astonishing—but an intensity about it that causes him to compose a striking phrase now and then. He didn't look well, his eyes were slitted as if in pain—looked like a gaunt mothy foul with rather greasy feathers, huddled up stubbornly determined to resist old age. . . . I gave him a red and blue tye as a Christmas gift. He left the wrappings there and

stuffed it into his pocket (just as he stuffed the manuscript in
his tiny shaking handwriting away) so that his wife would not
see it—poor old vulture—well he can use me for a hanger for his
illusions as much as he wants as long as he doesn't take too much
of my time—I can't stand his smell, his trembling self his inter-
minable dribble of talk (always about himself) for very long at a
time.

Oblivious to his effect on May, Kreymborg continued to work on
her behalf as well as his. On April 13, 1951, he promoted her poetry to
literary critic Van Wyck Brooks, then chair of the grants committee
for the National Institute of Arts and Letters. He sent May a copy of
his letter along with a note.

Mr. Van Wyck Brooks
Chairman, Committee on Grants for Literature
National Institute of Arts and Letters
633 West 155th Street, New York 32.

Dear Van Wyck:

For one of our Grants this year, I should like to recommend Miss
May Swenson, 2[3] Perry Street, New York. Having consulted
with her on her poetry from time to time, I consider her one of
the outstanding "finds" in my entire career as a poet and editor.
Her work is healthy, bold, forthright, and remarkably brilliant
as well as sound and original. In short, she is much more than
merely promising and has been published, during the past two
years, in about twenty magazines, including New Directions an-
thologies. And is not a coterie poet, God forbid!

Unhappily, thanks to commercial publishers who refuse to gam-
ble on verse, Miss Swenson has not published a book, although
she has a full length volume to submit in case the Committee
is interested. Moreover, a Grant would give her some necessary
economic encouragement.

With continued warm regards.
                    As ever your old friend
                    Alfred Kreymborg

Dear May—
Thought you might like to see this. Keep your fingers cross-eyed.
Will try to ring you this weekend
In haste—AK.[25]

A response came six days later, and Kreymborg promptly informed
May:

Have just received an urgent note from Felicia Geffen, Sec'y of
National Institute, beginning:
    "By all means the Committee would like to see the poetry of
Miss Swenson."
    This must mean that Van Wyck Brooks rescinded the ruling
against unpublished books. I must see you at once—no delay. . . .
    You are not supposed to know, Miss Geffen advises, that you
are up for a Grant. I'm supposed to get the script and turn it in
myself. . . . Phone as soon as you get home. Postpone all dates. . . .
They must not be kept waiting. Nor I, your sponsor![26]

Thanks to May's dogged determination and Kreymborg's relentless
promotion, May's career was moving forward. But she still needed to
balance her time between work at mindless secretarial jobs and writ-
ing ("I can exist in this 8-hour-a-day confinement where I must turn
myself into a mechanism outwardly, but can live free inside").
    Perhaps smug from her success, on April 17, 1951, May typed a letter
left for her on the Dictaphone at her place of employment: Peter A.
Frasse Company, purveyors of alloy, stainless and cold-finished carbon
steels, bars, tubes, sheets, strip, and wire, located at 17 Grand Street.
Employing the skills she had honed as an interviewer in the Folklore
Department of the Federal Writers' Project, May reproduced exactly
what she heard:

Write the Amehican Meteh Cumpny Sject O'der A 116 48 We aw
in receipt uv yer replace o'der un we ah ranging to-eh ship-eh
thee replace uv tree qutteh Odee qut inch wall fum ow fildelfye
bwanch . . .

Thus was a bit of Newyorkese of the 1950s preserved by a skilled
speed-typist with an extraordinary ear for sound play and the cheerful
snark of an ambitious artist finally gaining recognition.

CHAPTER 8

I Am One of Those to Whom Miracles Happen

IT WAS A WONDERFUL WEEKEND. Played tennis Saturday and Sunday [in Central Park]. . . . I was so angry at my ineptitude on the court (we got a clay court) that I was particularly lousy. . . . I feel like such a fool trying to play, I'm so ridiculously punk, but I enjoy it anyway. Too bad J [Pearl] hasn't someone her match to play with. . . . We lay on a slope of grass in our shorts in the sun beside the bridle path, J reading Wm. Carlos Wms. and I watching the riders and mentally criticizing them . . . wished I had a horse of my own. . . . When we go out West . . . we'll . . . really learn to ride well.

May and Pearl celebrated the second anniversary of their love affair on May 6, 1951, a few weeks before May turned thirty-eight. Later that month, May learned that recent cataract surgery had left her seventy-year-old father temporarily blind. Concerned, she wrote to him:

It does make me wish I could be there to read to you and talk to you. I want you to know that if you should really need me at any time, I would come immediately if you asked me to.[1]

Although May had left home fifteen years earlier, her parents still hoped that she would abandon New York and return to Utah and to the LDS Church. They took some comfort in knowing that May had not removed her name from the rolls of LDS members in the Manhattan ward, even though she was listed as "inactive."[2] But May never seriously considered a permanent return to Utah and was too deeply dissatisfied with the Mormon position on women to reengage with the church. In the spring of 1951 she wrote in her diary:

The Mormon religion gives, of course, more importance to the male than the female—the latter being designated as his "help-meet," and the wife of a Mormon is expected to "take her glory from her husband's glory" (something I obviously resent).

A few months later, two female Mormon missionaries, hoping to bring May back into the fold, knocked on her door while she and Pearl were having dinner. One missionary was an ex-Catholic of Italian heritage "with shiny black fanatical eyes," and the other was a "very poised and oratorical . . . assistant buyer of women's hats for Lord & Taylor." May and Pearl continued with their dinner of "heart" but listened politely as the visitors called "skittish attention to the Next World."

The missionaries' opening gambit was familiar to May from Sunday School days: "As man is, so God once was; as God is, so man may become." Seeming to take the bait, May asked, "If God was once like man, there must have been many more than One of Him. . . . Why, then, do we worship just this one particular God which you speak of?" When the missionaries "reasonably pointed out" that mortals worship Him because they "owe everything to God," May's seemingly guileless response was:

> Well, then, if . . . God, as you say, was once like man, he must "owe everything" to His creator, so we must assume that God worships His God—or rather the Gods worship their GrandGod—Is that it? And if this is so, our God is not all-virtuous, all-just, and all-everything which it is necessary for us to think He is in order to <u>worship</u> him; He is only <u>relatively</u> so, in your scheme of progression. And that would mean he can make mistakes, or

Here May's diary entry ends abruptly, possibly because she was typing at work and a supervisor was near. We are left to imagine the missionaries' hasty retreat.

On May 29, the day after her birthday, May sent her parents a copy of a poem she had recently published, and she enclosed thoughts, addressed to her father, about the meaning of art.

I often wonder, and have doubts about whether what I write has any significance for you. I don't imagine it does—for your life is so full and active that you have no need for the playthings of art. Your creative urge is spent directly in living—and shaping people through your influence, in cultivating growing things—not in trying to capture sensations through the medium of art. The word "art" is contained in the word "artificial," the opposite of natural. Well, it is that—it is a sort of opposite of life—a sort of rebellion against life perhaps, or an attempt to control or equal it with a synthetic creation of one's own, rather than riding with art, giving in to it, immersing oneself in it, and resigning oneself to being but a particle in a process. Art grows out of individual arrogance, I suppose.[3]

May seemingly felt more comfortable philosophizing with her father than with Alfred Kreymborg, her usual interlocutor on matters poetic. Kreymborg had arranged May's first residency at Yaddo, and she had been invited to return in the fall. She planned to use her second visit to produce a "definitive volume" of poems to "determinedly circulate" for publication. With an eye toward Kreymborg's usefulness, she sent him a flattering letter.[4] "I deeply value your comment and criticism," she wrote, "and your advice as to publication of a volume would, of course, be especially appreciated."[5] But May was also casting a wider net by seeking guidance from her new friend Elizabeth Bishop.

May and Elizabeth were close in age and poetic sensibility, but they came from very different backgrounds. Elizabeth's father had been a successful builder who died when Elizabeth was eight months old, and her mother was institutionalized for mental illness by the time Elizabeth was five. Elizabeth, an only child, was shuffled back and forth from Nova Scotia to Massachusetts to live with an assortment of relatives. Although there were periods of contentment and stability, these were interrupted by periods of debilitating loneliness and uncertainty until she was placed in Walnut Hill, a college preparatory school for girls in Natick, Massachusetts. A comforting routine replaced the disorder of her childhood, and she made close friends with whom she spent vacations and holidays. Elizabeth's teachers nourished her intellect and creativity, and by graduation she had produced an impressive array of short stories, plays, and poetry. At nineteen Elizabeth entered Vassar College, where her social circle included the writers Mary Mc-Carthy and Eleanor Clark, and where she was introduced by the Vassar librarian to her lifelong friend and early promoter, the modernist poet Marianne Moore.

Elizabeth and May, both drawn to modern literature and poetry, had graduated from college as English majors in 1934. Elizabeth was financially secure and left Vassar with a polished education and advantageous social and literary connections. Poor and constrained by the Depression, May left Utah State Agricultural College with an only adequate education and with no one except herself to promote her literary career.

In a letter to Elizabeth years later, May mentioned her lack of scholarly training in poetry and explained unapologetically that poems just happened to her.

> From the very beginning I came at poetry backwards. I never studied prosody; I never acquired a background in what had already been done by others. In the few cases where I've approached the traditional in my work it's happened accidentally. . . . [M]y approach to writing, since the beginning, has been sort of irresponsible—playful, not scholarly—I have excused my ignorances, I've been lazy and easy on myself, never trying very hard. The poems that I think are worth something (a few) that I've done have come to me, from somewhere—it hardly feels as though I made them. I tooled them, of course, but not very strenuously. And I've not found how to make good ones come.[6]

The Swenson archive in St. Louis contains about 275 items of correspondence between May and Elizabeth, beginning on December 12, 1950. May had returned to New York from Yaddo a month earlier, while Elizabeth remained until March. In her first letter, Elizabeth declined May's invitation to spend Christmas with her. The final item is a postcard from Elizabeth in Boston to May in Los Angeles and dated April 12, 1979, six months before Elizabeth's death. This remarkable two-way testament to the poets' mutual respect and admiration survives because May saved Elizabeth's letters and also preserved carbon copies of her letters to Elizabeth.

During the early years of their correspondence, Elizabeth lived in Brazil, near Petrópolis, a mountain town about fifty miles north of Rio de Janeiro. Having received a Bryn Mawr traveling fellowship of $2,500 in the spring of 1951, she planned to spend a year circumnavigating South America. However, upon arriving in Rio in the fall, she bit into a cashew fruit and suffered a severe and sustained allergic reaction. The resulting prolonged recuperation turned out to be the unlikely beginning of a fifteen-year stay in Brazil.

Four years earlier, Elizabeth had met Maria Carlota ("Lota") Costallat de Macedo Soares and Mary Morse in New York, and she was instantly attracted to Mary. Elizabeth had arranged to stay in the apartment Lota and Mary shared in Rio while the couple was at their mountain retreat near Petrópolis. But after Elizabeth ate the fateful fruit, it was Lota who nursed her back to health, and after separating from Mary, Lota became Elizabeth's lover. Elizabeth and Lota then divided their time between the Rio apartment and Lota's extravagant and sleekly modern house then under construction on land she had inherited from her mother. Lota's land was part of a large tract called Samambaia, but over time she and Elizabeth would speak of being "at Samambaia."

The Swenson–Bishop correspondence supplements May's increasingly sporadic diaries and becomes a substitute for them after 1959. Isolated in South America, Elizabeth was hungry for the latest news about people, poetry, and literature, all of which May was well positioned to provide. For her part, May had access to a kindred poetic spirit with whom to discuss poetry and to seek career guidance. Their letters were at first formal and reserved, although always affectionate in closing, but the tone warmed as May gained confidence in her own writing and as Elizabeth realized that May was more than a worshipful acolyte.

In the second letter of the correspondence, written by May at Yaddo to Elizabeth on October 11, 1951, May told Elizabeth: "It's a dreary, rainy day here—and I am quite unable to write when it rains. It has been raining quite a bit the last two weeks so my 'output' has been meager. However, I have written 6 new poems (3 good I think, 3 awful I'm sure)."[7] Next, May gave Elizabeth her impression of the Yaddo guests. She singled out the painter Hyde Solomon as a particularly congenial companion, "a non-objective painter (whose non-objects I have learned to like, having had the time to enter in to them). He stutters, but this doesn't stop him from talking more than any of us and he's a wonderful comedian, keeps us laughing all the time." May played tennis with Solomon, although "[h]e had never played before and hit every ball over the fence, mostly in to the patch of stinging nettles, so that in recovering them we got a rash on our legs that still hurts when you take a bath."

May wrote about residents playing chess, ping-pong, Chinese checkers, anagrams, and charades, and she described a masquerade party she attended, dressed as a unicorn. Her letters to Elizabeth from Yaddo reveal a congenial, social, and fully engaged poet thriving in the company of outgoing and stimulating fellow residents.

May asked Elizabeth to sponsor her for a Guggenheim Foundation fellowship, and she also solicited support from Malcolm Cowley, James Laughlin, Alfred Kreymborg, Elizabeth Ames, and others. In this way, May cautiously opened the door for dialogue with Elizabeth about her poetry. "Actually, I know, you don't know my work very well, and so will you mind if I send you a copy of the stuff I'm preparing for the Committee so that you can have some background on which to base an opinion?" she wrote. "And, if after reading it you decide not to stick your neck out, just forget about it. . . . I won't be mad."

Elizabeth, herself a Guggenheim recipient, agreed to recommend May without waiting for her poems to arrive. She also volunteered suggestions for strengthening May's application. May thanked her by return mail, closing with, "I'll be leaving here Nov. 2 & back to the dictaphone the following Monday."[8]

Once back in New York, May wasted no time arranging her next escape to a writers' retreat. She was invited to spend the months of June and July 1952 at the MacDowell Colony in New Hampshire and to return for a third stay at Yaddo in September and November. For her previous visit to Yaddo, May had obtained a leave from her typing job but at the cost of losing her bonus benefits, and two more approved leaves within a year would be unlikely.

In the spring of 1952 May assessed her long-range financial situation. She had recently been diagnosed with cervical cysts and feared she could not afford both the operation to remove them and time away from work. Sylvia Norman still owed May four hundred dollars from an earlier loan. On April 14 May adroitly broached the subject of repayment in a letter to Sylvia. After reporting that their mutual friend Saul Baizerman had been awarded a Guggenheim worth "something like $3,000," she noted that the grant would make him "secure financially for a couple of years."[9] May then revealed her own rejection for the same grant, which she "didn't expect to get" but had hoped for and even daydreamed about so she could wire Sylvia to say: "Forget debt. I'm in the money!"

May told Sylvia that she needed to pay for apartment upkeep and deferred medical expenses. "If you could possibly send me $300 by May 15, I could swing both of these projects—the operation, so I could quit worrying about that—and this chance to do some creative work and make some writing contacts."[10]

A week later May received a check from Sylvia, who had taken out a loan to repay her in full. A relieved May replied, "I don't see how you managed with such immediacy. . . . [It] does make me feel completely secure now, in quitting my job to go to New Hampshire, and having enough to fill in the gap before I get another job when I get back."[11] In closing, May told Sylvia that she was sending her "two songs Howard Swanson composed, and a little note from the Times about him. . . . I think you've read the two poems before—they are quite early ones. Interesting that he should have picked these two lugubrious ones. He did have more cheerful ones to choose from."[12]

May had met Howard Swanson, who was another recipient of a Guggenheim in 1952, at Yaddo. She described him to Sylvia as "a very talented Negro composer who's had a rough time and only now beginning to get the recognition he deserves."[13] At that time, Swanson set two of May's poems to music, "I Will Lie Down" and "Why We Die" (which he titled "Saw a Grave upon a Hill"), and in 1955 he would set another, "White Mood," which he renamed "Snowdunes." May's poems were to be the last of Swanson's seventeen poem-songs, which had included works by Langston Hughes, T. S. Eliot, Vachel Lindsay, and Carl Sandburg. According to the critic Orin Moe, May's poems matched those of Hughes and Sandburg in strength and variety of verbal rhythm. Moe also noted that, compared to the men, hers were more "introverted" and "saturated with imagery of the physical world."[14]

At about the same time, the composer Otto Luening wrote music for May's poem "The Tiger's Ghost." Over the years that followed, May's poems were set to music by more than forty composers, including Pulitzer Prize winners William Bolcom and Aaron Jay Kernis, as well as Ricky Ian Gordon, composer of art songs, opera, and musical theater. (Swanson's musical adaptation of May's poem "I Will Lie Down" was sung by May's sister, Grace Turetsky, at May's funeral service in Logan in 1989.)

After her residency at MacDowell in June and July and at Yaddo in September and October of 1952, May calculated that her savings would support her for only a few more months. In December, feeling restless, unproductive, and nostalgic, she wrote in her diary of her need to "get a job again—save money." To foster a sense of productivity, May made lists of her daily activities. Accomplishments for the months of December and January included:

> Phoned K[reymborg]. He talked 20 minutes.
> I weigh 124 pounds
> reading Nation & [Wallace] Stevens' poetry
> Crossword puzzle
> Typed two poems for Thing & Image
> Fixed B[lackie, i.e., Pearl]'s black shirt
> I spent morning & part of p.m. with Cecil [Hemley, of Noonday
>   Press]
> Walked away from Noonday in a beginning snow-storm

And she wrote regularly to Elizabeth Bishop. On March 10, 1953, she explained to Elizabeth what "Thing and Image" was:

> I've assembled a book, or rather three. I guess when I wrote you it was one big one, "Another Animal," but all the poems didn't fit together sensibly in one, so made three smaller vols. of 30–40 each. "Thing and Image" and "Sky-Acquainted" are the other titles.[15]

May added that she had submitted all three collections to Twayne Press, which had been founded in 1949 by Jacob Steinberg, whose original intent was to publish translations of Chinese classics. However, when John Ciardi joined the staff, Steinberg's interest shifted to poetry. He had assured May that he would send her submission on to Ciardi, who would respond in two weeks. May also told Elizabeth that she was doing some typing for the poet Cecil Hemley, the founder of Noonday Press.

In early February 1953 May had sent Elizabeth a batch of recent poems. Elizabeth pounced on them. "I like the egg poem ['At Breakfast'] so much that of course I can't keep my hands off it and want to make suggestions and ask questions—please don't mind, will you."[16] May was overjoyed by the praise, but she trusted her own instincts and ignored Elizabeth's suggestions. Her forty-six-line "egg poem" was anthologized in 1955 in *Discovery No. 5*. May included it in four later collections of poems, including *Poems to Solve* in 1966. The delightfully accessible and playful ode to an egg, a few lines of which are excerpted here, is one of her early riddle poems:

What's inside?
A sun?
Off with its head
though it hasn't any
or is all head no body
a
One

In subsequent correspondence, both poets show professional forthrightness and thoughtful criticism. May and Elizabeth regularly discussed current trends in poetry, the latest gossip about prominent literary figures, and sometimes the highs and lows of their personal lives.

Elizabeth was concerned about May's financial situation and often asked for updates on her employment. In the spring of 1953 May reported, "I had a job for 4 days, and couldn't stand it, it was so awful it literally made me ill, so I had to quit but as an antidote I wrote about it and got well immediately. It's a very funny piece (I hope) about an IBM machine (electric typewriter)."[17]

"Mutterings of a Middlewoman" is a poignantly humorous short story. The protagonist (a thinly disguised May) reports for her first day at a new office job. She is expected to type on a futuristic machine, the "Atom-atic," which anticipates and types the intended key before the operator's finger actually strikes it and sets the pace of typing at an ever-increasing speed. Stress and anxiety drive the protagonist to delirium. In 1955 May published the piece in *Discovery*, a short-lived magazine featuring avant-garde prose. In 1973 Howard Moss, poetry editor of the *New Yorker*, included it in *The Poet's Story*, a volume of short stories by poets.

May regarded prospective publishers as no better than office supervisors. She vented to Elizabeth about James Laughlin, whom she viewed as a shameless pretender.

> Laughlin did something quite disgusting—he wrote me when I was at MacDowell in the summer and invited me to contribute to his anthology again. Six months passed without acknowledgement of poems sent; ND 14 appeared without them and I still haven't received them back—then he writes me the other day as though nothing had happened and suggests I send something as he is now helping to edit "Perspectives U.S.A." He's just full of crap.[18]

And she was disillusioned with Howard Moss's editing of the first poem of hers that he had accepted. Moss had changed her title, "By Morning," to "Snow by Morning." May agreed reluctantly to his addition of punctuation and to his new title, but she aired her complaints to Elizabeth. The punctuation was "alright," May wrote (her version had none), but the inclusion of the word "snow" in the title, she felt, spoiled the poem. Moss had removed the playfulness and cleverness of her riddle.[19] But May wanted the prestige of publishing in the *New Yorker*, and she needed money.

"Do they pay on publication or acceptance, I wonder?" she mused to Elizabeth. "I felt it would be too ungrateful to ask him," adding, "I haven't a job yet, but must have in next two weeks, as my savings are about gone—it will probably be another dictaphone job."[20]

Elizabeth reassured May, pointing out that editors at the *New Yorker* "like to over-punctuate" and, regarding the title change, that "they just <u>have</u> to be obvious—& when it appears in book form you can always change it again."[21] And she told May that she would be paid on acceptance.

"Snow by Morning" appeared in the *New Yorker* of January 30, 1954. Later that year, May published her twenty-two-line poem her way—unpunctuated and with its original title restored—in her first collection of poems, *Another Animal,* and then in four subsequent collections, including *Poems to Solve* in 1966.

By Morning

Some for everyone
    plenty . . .

Transparent at first
    each faint slice
    slow   soundlessly tumbling . . .

Streets will be   fields
    cars be   fumbling sheep . . .

By morning we'll be   children
    feeding on manna

    a new loaf on every doorsill

In Moss's version, the end of nearly every line was punctuated with a dash, a comma, or a semicolon, and all lines were left justified. Moss also removed May's extra spaces between words, evocative of snowdrifts. And of course the new title eliminated the surprise and enjoyment of guessing the subject.

Elizabeth worried that May was living too close to the edge financially, and she pressed her about it. "I'd like to know what you are doing right now for bread & butter," she wrote on July 27, 1953, and offered

May a job.[22] Elizabeth planned to assemble a manuscript of about a dozen of her prose pieces for publication. "I just can't face typing them over again after all these years. I'd pay you whatever the best MMS copiers are getting these days, and for the paper, carbon, etc.—Would it interest you at all? . . . I thought you might want to earn a little extra." May accepted eagerly, and their friendship warmed further when Elizabeth sent May a copy of her poem "The Shampoo." "It has been turned down both by The New Yorker and Poetry, and although I don't think it's world-shaking, I can't quite figure out why—it seems perfectly clear to me, and rather pretty. So please tell me exactly what you think."[23]

Undoubtedly pleased to have earned Elizabeth's respect as a poet, May sent her reaction:

THE SHAMPOO I like very much—after many re-readings. Especially now, as I just read it, it sort of gently assembled itself for me. It feels right, but I would have a deuce of a time saying why. It's not intellectual, and at first I tried to bite too hard into it and worry a meaning out. I felt I didn't quite get it. Well, I still don't specifically— . . . I'm willing to accept "precipitate and pragmatical" now which annoyed me at first reading, as a hippity-hop in the rhythm, and sort of inconsistent with the affectionate tone of the rest. I find it's alright read aloud, though, and "precipitate" has an important double meaning, I guess. Then I like "pragmatical" and "happened" near each other—the sounds. In a way I don't care to figure out what it "means"—One enjoys the way it's put together—the unexpectedness that the images as well as the rhythm have. It's pretty tightly organized and regularly rhymed, which comes as a surprise because it sounds so casual, spontaneous, unpretentious. I'm dead sure it's a good poem. . . . I like "flocking" in the last stanza echoing "rocks" and—"shocks" in the first—and the way the poem comes round at the end—satisfying. In sound it's very agreeable, and I like the dependable construction, which isn't stiff—still maintains a naturalness.[24]

Bishop's "The Shampoo," a meditation on nature and time, is also an avowal of the poet's love for her partner ("dear friend"), a love undiminished, indeed strengthened by the passage of time, which has been "amenable." The poet transforms the act of washing her lover's graying hair ("shooting stars in your black hair") into an intimate celebration of aging. Elizabeth had sent "The Shampoo" to the poet Marianne Moore, her friend, in 1952. It was first published in the *New Republic* in 1955 and in the same year appeared in Bishop's *Poems: North & South—A Cold Spring*.

In October 1953 May spent three days with her parents and her eighteen-year-old brother Paul, who were en route to Sweden to serve a three-year mission. She took them to St. Patrick's Cathedral, whose interior "awed and appalled them."[25] Generous as always, May also treated them to a Broadway show. To Paul's great delight, the World Series was in progress, and May bought tickets for the sixth and final game, a Yankees victory over the Brooklyn Dodgers.

May did not mention any interactions between her family and Pearl, but by then Pearl had moved into the two-bedroom apartment on Perry Street that May shared with Trudy Lubitsch.

May sent Elizabeth a portion of the manuscript she was typing for her by airmail, explaining that the delay was due to her parents' visit. Elizabeth promptly paid May for her work and reimbursed her for the postage. Although May could be somewhat casual in financial dealings with other people, she was scrupulous with Elizabeth and replied:

> Thanks ever so much for the check, which came just in time to pay my delinquent State Taxes for 1951. They finally caught up with me and I had to pay a $2 fine as well. I can't remember why I didn't pay it that year—probably decided to test if I'd get away with it. You need not have reimbursed for the air mail postage, and please deduct $2 from next payment, because those stamps were stolen for me from her office by Pearl, who regularly keeps us in postage, and her wealthy boss is none the wiser. Also, folders, paper, envelopes, etc., I get from my office so there is no outlay on my part for these things.[26]

Elizabeth was fascinated to learn that May was raised as a Mormon and asked about the Mormon practice of baptism. May replied with details of her religious past.

> The Mormons not only believe in it for the living, but for the dead, who missed it due to having departed this world before the advent of Joseph Smith and the Latter Day Saints. A "born Mormon" such as I was, is baptized for himself at 8, then takes on the job of "being born again by immersion" for all dead relatives that can be traced through genealogy. . . . In a long white dress and white sox, I had to go under for what seemed the population of most of the graveyards in Sweden. The baptismal font was oval, of marble, and mounted on 12 gold oxen (wood carved and painted gold) and you walked up a golden ladder to get into it, and after each dunking you sat streaming in a white metal chair while the Elder who pushed you under now put hands on your head and said a prayer mentioning the name of the one whose sins you were washing away by proxy. The water was pleasantly warm, a milky blue, reflecting the ceiling of the Temple. You could be baptized only for the dead of your own sex, I don't know why—so many more female souls got liberated than male, since boys weren't as interested in doing the baptisms as girls.[27]

Elizabeth commented, "Mormonism must be very strange—I had known about saving dead souls, but I didn't realize you actually were baptized over and over again for them—poor little May—no wonder you still look so clean."[28]

Both women expressed their shock at the death of the poet Dylan Thomas, in November 1953, at the age of thirty-nine. "I can't believe it—I suppose they must be right—I just can't," Elizabeth wrote. "Even if those who knew him felt it was coming, as I did even after the first time or two I met him. It is a tragedy. I wonder what on earth happened to him—and can't bear to think what might have," wrote Elizabeth.[29] To which May responded:

> Dylan Thomas died in St. Vincents [Vincent's] of a cerebral-something which was the end result of drinking. I hadn't

seen him since he read "Under Milkwood" in the Spring. The
following is rumorous so I don't know how far to credit it—but
it is said he collapsed in the apartment of a girl. . . . I know her
slightly—in fact, she lives just across the square from us on
Charles St. She got panicky, being afraid of a scandal, and instead
of immediately calling a doctor or an ambulance, she wasted
time by phoning all her friends and asking what to do and still
keep it quiet. . . . When he finally did get into hospital, they gave
him morphine although he had alcohol in his blood, and this is
supposed to have hastened his death. I don't know how true all
this is. It was uncanny, though, hearing his voice on the radio a
night or two later, reciting: "Death Shall Have No Dominion."[30]

In January 1954 May shared with Elizabeth news about the publi-
cation of her first book:

Do you know either of two poets named Harry Duncan and Mur-
ray Noss? Well, they are going to be my bookmates. The book
will probably be called Three New American Poets Today and
will come out from Scribners in September. It is to be the first of
a series of such volumes, of three full-length volumes in one. If a
smaller house were doing it I'd think it a shabby idea, but since
[John] Wheelock tells me they intend to promote it well and
make a "distinguished" volume out of it maybe it will turn out
o.k. and open the way for a second volume of my own later on. I
hope so.[31]

The book was not May's only success. In 1954 she wrote eighteen
new poems. "Oh, bits and pieces of notice and evidence that my poems
are flying around by themselves; they are actually live birds in the air
now!" she observed in her diary.

In May 1954, shortly after her forty-first birthday, May wrote to her
parents, still in Sweden:

Thanks so much for your wonderful birthday letter to me. It
came on my birthday and was the nicest present I received. If I
were to collect all the birthday letters you've written me through

the years (and I do have them all saved in my file case) it just occurred to me I'd have a <u>book</u> that would illustrate the wonderful love of a pair of parents for their firstborn child.

You will no doubt be puzzled, at first, to find the enclosed check. It represents a little part of an unexpected piece of luck for me. I sold a story the other day (to the same publication in which my five poems appeared—"Discovery") and they paid me $250! This is the most money I've gotten so far in one chunk for any piece of writing, so I have to brag a bit and present the evidence. I hope you won't have trouble turning it into Swedish money, and that you both will accept it as a small contribution to your mission.[32]

Although May lived frugally, she spent "extra" money generously on her family and friends. In interviews conducted decades later, May's siblings shared warm memories of the thoughtful Christmas gifts she lavished on them each year from a big box that arrived in Logan marked "Do not open until Christmas."

When May's sister Ruth was thirteen, May gave her "a silk bra and satin panties." Ruth admitted she "had nothing to put in the bra," but it was so special to her because "it said that May knew that [she] was growing up."[33] May's sister Margaret remembered "a little bunny fur muff with a tortoise shell bracelet on it. Here was I, wearing hand-me-down clothes. . . . She cared about me and I knew it—even though I didn't know her too well." Margaret added, "May came home about every third year," and on one summer visit, when their father was "getting elderly," May gave him a check for a thousand dollars.[34] Another sister, Beth, had similar memories of May's generosity. "She always had something special for us. I can remember some gifts. In fact, I have one on my finger. She gave me this pretty little ring . . . and a pretty little purse with a 'B' for Beth. . . . She chose gifts that just suited."[35]

On September 14, 1954, May's first book, *Another Animal*, was published in Poets of Today by Scribner's with a print run of 1,500 copies, of which 500 were sold by November. Elizabeth received her copy in mid-October. "What strikes one first of course is the array of forms and the willingness to try something different every time," she wrote, "and the appearance of *energy*—Thank you so much for sending it."[36]

On the strength of *Another Animal*, May applied a third time for a Guggenheim. The book's publication had raised her profile among literary luminaries. She was sponsored by poet and critic Mark Van Doren; Malcolm Cowley; poet John Wheelock; James Laughlin; John Ciardi; poet Elizabeth Sergeant; poet, critic, and anthologist Louis Untermeyer; and, of course, Elizabeth Bishop. May was invited to parties where she met both new and established writers who were as eager to meet her as she was to meet them. May's diaries and her letters to Elizabeth throughout the mid- to late 1950s are filled with impressions of new acquaintances. About John Ciardi, who favorably reviewed *Another Animal* in the *New York Times*, May noted that she was "a little suspicious of his chronic enthusiasm for my work." But on December 5, 1954, she added, "I'm most grateful to him. I met him a week or so ago when he invited me to a P.E.N. meeting where he spoke, and we had a drink afterward at the Blue Ribbon on 45th St. I was glad to find that I liked him very much—he's vital and stimulating as well as sensitive, I thought (tall, dark and nearly handsome, too)."[37]

On February 1, 1955, May wrote in her diary: "Tomorrow, to dinner at U[ntermeyer]s' on 72nd St. where [poet and novelist] Conrad Aiken and [poet] M[uriel] Rukeyser are to be met, and U.'s third, or is it 4th, wife, and I have to find a blouse today at Macy's I hope to wear with the black swishy skirt." Two of May's poems, "Feel Like a Bird" and "Evolution," had been accepted by Louis Untermeyer, "a great talker, and jokester," for publication in his *Treasury of Great Poems*. The evening, as May wrote to Elizabeth, "turned out to be a punning contest between Louis and Conrad," but "the roast beef was good."[38] In her diary, May described Aiken as "subtle and quiet, a British look; I liked the way his clothes hung on his roundness, a little slouchy." May was, however, surprised to find Rukeyser "quiet, almost humble in temperament," and not what she expected from her poetry. Like May, Rukeyser appeared in Untermeyer's revised anthology, along with Elizabeth Bishop, Robert Lowell, Richard Wilbur, Henry Reed, Karl Shapiro, and Theodore Roethke.

Three weeks later, on February 20, May was invited to the home of poet Babette Deutsch. "I was so glad to find her thin—all the authors I've met recently have been fat (except U)," May wrote in her diary.

Deutsch was then teaching at Columbia, where, in the late 1940s, poet
Lawrence Ferlinghetti had been among her students.

During the spring of 1955, May awaited decisions about fellowships
and grants. Besides the Guggenheim, there was a travel grant from
Bryn Mawr College and another from the Writers' Workshop at the
University of Iowa, funded by the Rockefeller Foundation. In addition,
Another Animal had been named one of twelve finalists for the Na-
tional Book Award. As the days passed with no word, May grew less
confident. On May 2 she wrote in her diary:

> I am in a very bad slump, which has lasted all the week. Seven
> gray days—the sky and my "innards"— . . . Will there come the
> upswing again? Does one swing as high as one dips low? It
> doesn't seem so; the dips get deeper, the rises less high, less fre-
> quent. That's a scary prophesy and I take it back. . . . No Mail—
> not a piece of mail for 7 days—and none today. All my ships are
> lost, it seems.

A few days earlier, May had a chance meeting with her close friend
and former lover Arnold Kates. May's spirit did not rise.

> On Friday after B. [Pearl] and I had Smorgasbord at The Ugly
> Duckling on 3rd St. and were walking home on M[a]cDougal—
> who but Arnold should appear? Looking <u>old</u>—his head on side
> in a self-pitying manner—his voice slow & meandering—he's
> become philosophical-talking—his false teeth didn't fit right. He
> evidently thought B. was Anca! Said he enjoyed my book—and
> approved of the typography—Well, he sounded very sincere
> about the book. Shadows of the past—the shadows multiply &
> lengthen with time's accumulation. Yet, so far, I have little sensa-
> tion of the downhill way—<u>gradualness</u>—time's trickery—but we
> should be grateful for it.

By the end of the month, May had received rejections from the
Guggenheim Foundation and the National Book Award committee,
and Bryn Mawr had notified her that no grant would be awarded
that year. Only the Rockefeller remained possible, and May was not

hopeful, but on June 5, 1955, "The Rockefeller came through," she wrote triumphantly in her diary. "I am one of those to whom miracles happen—outside of the general—a person in a tale." She sent a hasty postcard to Elizabeth informing her of the good news. "Last ship came in, laden with moola," she wrote and followed that up with a letter in which she explained, "[S]ometime this summer I'm to receive $2,000 tax-free, through Iowa U. I don't have to be a resident at Iowa and can spend it where I please; chances are I'll stay right here, and just get rid of the job I now have, and try to complete a second vol. of verse—stories, too."[39] And a week later May was informed that she had been awarded a two-week fellowship in August to Bread Loaf, the writers' colony in Vermont, for which John Ciardi had nominated her.

Elizabeth delighted in May's success, but Pearl was less enthusiastic.[40] With writers' retreats and literary parties occupying more of May's time, Pearl felt neglected. Further complicating matters, she was weaning herself from psychological analysis and planned to terminate her sessions completely during the summer of 1955. This decision brought on a new "crop of anxieties." Pearl worked full-time and was taking courses at night toward a degree in social work. Ed Field, one of May's friends, recalled Pearl returning home to Perry Street while gatherings of May's literary friends were in progress. She "would greet people briefly, and retire to a back room," exhausted and uninterested in joining the party.[41]

May was sensitive to Pearl's needs. She told Elizabeth that she hoped to save enough money for Pearl to quit her job and attend day classes. May organized parties for their nonliterary friends and planned a summer vacation with Pearl to Martha's Vineyard. Nevertheless, the relationship began to splinter. As Field observed:

Pearl seemed to have changed, and complained openly that she didn't want to spend the rest of her life with someone who didn't take care of her properly. . . . I began to sense intrigues among the women invited to the parties. Apparently May and Pearl had come to "an arrangement," whereby May accepted Pearl's necessity to search for a partner more sympathetic to her needs. With May's increasing literary reputation, there may also have been an element of competitiveness.[42]

FIGURE 22. May Swenson, 1950s. *Courtesy Lisa Turetsky.*

In 1955 Elizabeth published her second collection, *Poems: North & South—A Cold Spring*, eighteen poems in all, of which ten were "entire surprises" to May. She offered Elizabeth her reaction to this "wonder-full package."

> [T]hey engage something else than the emotions. What is it? Something else, and something more important. They are hard, feelable, as objects—or they give us that sensation—and they are separate from the self that made them, rather than self-effigies as poems easily tend to be.[43]

Elizabeth was thrilled.

> I've been a rosy glow because of your letter for eighteen hours or so and I must answer you right away. I am still in a glow—I imagine my temperature is about 100 Fahrenheit right now. . . . If I had 1,000 readers like you I'd feel life had been worthwhile—

no, that's asking too much—500 would do nicely. No more of that nobody-appreciates-me feeling. . . . But I shall try to make one reader like you do me, and be properly grateful for that.[44]

May and Elizabeth did not engage in idle flattery. A few months later, Elizabeth sent May her reaction to "The Centaur," May's backward glance at childhood, gender identity, and love of nature, animals, and physical activity. "I think THE CENTAUR is extremely nice," wrote Elizabeth, and then she addressed specifics. She didn't think the second mention of the knife was necessary toward the end but approved of May's phrase "ghostly toes," and she liked "spanked my own behind" but thought the parallel expression, "I slapped to his rump," was redundant. Her principal objection was to the poem's length, and she thought it could be trimmed by two or three stanzas. She especially disliked May's use of the regionalisms, "cut me a long" and "filled me a glass," complaining that they sounded colloquial or "Utah-ian," though she acknowledged that perhaps May "had a good reason" for using that construction.[45]

May thanked Elizabeth for her "evaluation" and promised to "try to make it better with your feeling about it in mind."[46] But for May, serious revision was unthinkable. "This was one of those poems that I didn't have much control over while writing; it came very quickly, and it seemed that certain details simply had to go in. I'm sure a Freudian would find all the symbols of an open-and-shut case, but I don't mind," she explained. She told Elizabeth that Howard Moss, to whom she had submitted it, "wanted to chop off the last two stanzas, and I felt sure that wasn't right." May explained to Elizabeth the importance of the poem's western linguistic overtones and the significance of the knife.

[T]he constructions of "cut me a long" and "filled me a glass"—I used them as Westernisms, they came naturally, this being the way we used to talk out there when I was little (they still talk like that in my state.) The knife is there to point up that she's doing something tomboyish, which her mother objects to. I did used to carry around my brother Roy's knife, whenever I could sneak it away from him, to play mumblety-peg with, or cut willow switches.

The Centaur

The summer that I was ten—
Can it be there was only one
summer that I was ten? It must

have been a long one then—
each day I'd go out to choose
a fresh horse from my stable

which was a willow grove
down by the old canal.
I'd go on my two bare feet.

But when, with my brother's jack-knife,
I had cut me a long limber horse
with a good thick knob for a head,

and peeled him slick and clean
except a few leaves for the tail,
and cinched my brother's belt

around his head for a rein,
I'd straddle and canter him fast
up the grass bank to the path,

trot along in the lovely dust
that talcumed over his hoofs,
hiding my toes, and turning

his feet to swift half-moons.
The willow knob with the strap
jouncing between my thighs

was the pommel and yet the poll
of my nickering pony's head.
My head and my neck were mine,

yet they were shaped like a horse.
My hair flopped to the side
like the mane of a horse in the wind.

My forelock swung in my eyes,
my neck arched and I snorted.
I shied and skittered and reared,

stopped and raised my knees,
pawed at the ground and quivered.
My teeth bared as we wheeled

and swished through the dust again.
I was the horse and the rider,
and the leather I slapped to his rump

spanked my own behind.
Doubled, my two hoofs beat
a gallop along the bank,

the wind twanged in my mane,
my mouth squared to the bit.
And yet I sat on my steed

quiet, negligent riding,
my toes standing the stirrups,
my thighs hugging his ribs.

At a walk we drew up to the porch.
I tethered him to a paling.
Dismounting, I smoothed my skirt

and entered the dusky hall.
My feet on the clean linoleum
left ghostly toes in the hall.

Where have you been? said my mother.
Been riding, I said from the sink,
and filled me a glass of water.

What's that in your pocket? she said.
Just my knife. It weighted my pocket
and stretched my dress awry.

Go tie back your hair, said my mother,
and *Why is your mouth all green?*
Rob Roy, he pulled some clover
as we crossed the field, I told her.[47]

By May 1956 May was working part-time at New Directions, a position she described to her parents as "the first job I've ever had that I've liked, because it's in my field."[48] To Elizabeth, however, she revealed frustration. Laughlin "never comes to the office," she wrote, explaining that he spent most of his time traveling in Europe, skiing in Utah, or working at the Ford Foundation.[49] (In 1950 Laughlin had founded International Publications, a subsidiary of the Ford Foundation, which produced *Perspectives USA*, a literary quarterly edited by Laughlin and circulated in Europe.) May worked instead with Bob MacGregor, editor, director, and vice president of the company, whom she described as "very nice on the surface—but doesn't really appear to care much how things run." Despite her misgivings, May would remain at New Directions for twelve years, first as a typist and copyeditor, and then as a manuscript reader. She proved indispensable and was granted leaves of absence whenever she requested them.

In January 1957 May complained to Elizabeth about Laughlin's (and everyone else's) preoccupation with the Beats.

After spending many months selecting the best manuscripts (and some very good ones, I'm sure, among them) for Laughlin to decide about [for publication in *New Directions 16*], he could be bothered reading only about a third of them, and turned around and invited a clique of "wild Willies" on the West Coast to send their stuff, on the advice of [Kenneth] Rexroth and [Lawrence]

Ferlinghetti: Jack Kerouac, Allen Ginsberg, James Purdy—and others—the crew that Eberhart wrote about in the Times Book Section a while back. Ferlinghetti of City Lights Bookshop in San Francisco and Jonathan Williams of <u>Jargon</u> in North Carolina are both publishing them—"Poets of the Beat Generation" they call themselves.[50]

Although May had begun to tentatively accept invitations to read her poetry after the publication of *Another Animal*, primarily to supplement her income, she expressed her insecurity to Elizabeth. On January 6 she was already practicing for a reading at the Poetry Center at the YMHA still three weeks in the future. "I'll be glad when <u>that</u> is over. I also have to find, and buy, something to wear and shoes, because I haven't a dress that will do—and I hate to shop even worse than I hate to read." May would never feel comfortable reading her work in public.

May mentioned to Elizabeth that her second collection of poems had been rejected by Harcourt. Discouraged, she quoted from their letter: "'Everyone who has read it here has been impressed. . . . Your skill is really prodigious. . . . Yet, the sad news is' etc. Well, if I were entirely satisfied with it I'd put it out to some other publisher right away—but I don't feel certain of it."[51]

In 1957 John Ciardi, then-director of the Bread Loaf Writers' Conference, appointed May the Robert Frost Fellow for the summer session. Two decades after having heard Frost read in New York, May met the poet whose "Two Tramps in Mud Time" had so inspired her. At Bread Loaf, May gave her idol a copy of *Another Animal*. Shortly afterward, Frost returned it to her, commented tersely and enigmatically, "It reeks of poetry," and stood up to leave. May was too shy to ask him what that meant.[52]

In September she attended her third session at the MacDowell Colony, where she continued to revise her second collection of poems. In January 1958 May reported to Elizabeth about her progress. "I have just written to ten publishers. . . . There are 66 poems and it would go to about 100 pp.—probably much too big a book, but I did weed out a good many."[53] After a rejection from Harper's a month later, she confided in her diary: "I have been having ski-jumps of mood—one day sailing, the next tumbling. When I get the book settled maybe I will settle."

By March of that year May had received an offer from Rinehart, and she told Elizabeth that *A Cage of Spines* would appear in late September although the financial arrangements were not to her liking:

> The royalty deal with Rinehart is a steal for them: 5% on the first thousand copies and 10% "thereafter." On the advice of people who ought to know ([poet] Louise Bogan for one) I agreed to this. Others said I should grab the chance without any royalties at all—that these days poets, even those with reputations, are entering into share-expense deals with publishers because the latter won't risk it otherwise. Anyway, for good or ill, my contract is now signed.[54]

When May saw the finished product in August, she was disappointed with its appearance. "I think the jacket is in very bad taste and the picture turned out awful. . . . The print is cramped and hard to read—and it's shockingly over-priced," she complained to Elizabeth.[55] The book was priced at $3.75, about $39 today. Because she expected negligible compensation from royalties, May pursued opportunities to earn extra money: "some reviews, critical sessions with 'poetry groups'—The Woman Poets (ugh!) and 'The Craftsmen' (ditto) and judging a high school poetry contest—small fees, and probably foolish considering the time and work involved."[56] She planned to finance a trip with Pearl to Utah and the West Coast by scheduling speaking engagements at two venues in San Francisco and one at her alma mater in Logan.[57] Her college friend Grant Redford, playwright, poet, and professor at the University of Washington in Seattle, had proposed that she read there as well, but the selection committee chose Marianne Moore instead.

Grant Redford, campus rebel at Utah State and May's fellow "Scribbler," remained a close friend. He was an important link to May's college years and her western roots, and he understood her in a way her New York friends could not. Although their correspondence was sporadic, Grant reliably lifted May's spirits and rejoiced in the milestones of her success. "You are your own person, May," he wrote to her after the publication of her first book. "Your mind is tight, sharp, precise. It's a delight to read your stuff. And I congratulate you for keeping at it."[58] In thanking her for a copy of her second book, he said: "Your every promise is being most emphatically and extensively fulfilled. I'm extravagantly proud of you."[59] Perhaps, as May's brother Dan speculated, there had been the additional element of a love interest between Grant and May.[60]

May sent Elizabeth a letter from Sausalito, California, in October 1958 with an update about her trip with Pearl to the West Coast. "We've been here a week. . . . My 'lectures' turned out to be less difficult than I'd expected," she wrote.[61] "It was a pleasure to meet and talk with Josephine Miles at Berkeley. James Broughton and Lawrence Ferlinghetti are two others I'm glad to have met. Spent a typical tourist evening in North Beach last night going from one night spot to the next and taking note of the 'Beatniks.'"

The poet and literary critic Josephine Miles became the first female tenured professor of English at Berkeley and a groundbreaker in the field of digital humanities. She experimented with early punch-card technology and directed the creation of a concordance to the poetry of John Dryden. This first computerized concordance was completed in 1957, the year before Miles and May met. Miles was an ardent proponent of Beat poetry, particularly the work of Allen Ginsberg.

Poet Lawrence Ferlinghetti had printed Ginsberg's *Howl and Other Poems* in 1956, and the following year he was charged with obscenity for selling the book. May met Ferlinghetti less than a year after his acquittal, but she was no fan of the Beats. Her creative sensibilities were likely more aligned with those of the Bay Area modernist James Broughton. A poet, playwright, and experimental filmmaker, Broughton was resident playwright with the Playhouse Repertory Theater in San Francisco in 1958. Six years later, May would write and direct her own experimental play, *The Floor*.

May and Pearl's trip also included a stop in Logan, where May's parents attended her reading at USAC, and in October 1958 May and Pearl returned in good spirits to Perry Street.

On January 2, 1959, May began a third-person account of her life with Pearl titled "Now and Then," an autobiographical experiment she continued for the next six months. She referred to herself as "Miken" and to Pearl as "Purple" or "Pear." "Maybe 'the book' would teach her [Miken] how to write prose," May mused in the margin on January 13.

One of the first episodes in "Now and Then" is an incident of infidelity on Pearl's part. May had rebuffed "overtures" made to her by a woman named Lynda, one of her coworkers at New Directions, whom she described as "young, impulsive and too plump and careless to become involved with." Lynda next made advances to Pearl, with the opposite result. May saw Pearl and Lynda kissing at a social gathering and confessed that she "felt a little bothered that she was not bothered." May affirmed that she was "compulsively loyal" to Pearl, as she had been to former companions, but that Pearl was a "flirt."

May wrote another episode about an evening visit to Perry Street from Richard Wright. With him was novelist James Baldwin, whom Wright introduced to May as "Jimmy." May served them whiskey and explained to them that her roommate had gone to bed early and would be disappointed not to have met them. On cue, Pearl emerged in her bathrobe and said to Baldwin, "I thought 'Go Tell It [on the Mountain]' was 'marvelous.'" May commented that "Pearl was partial to Negroes—in some cases exorbitantly so, . . . and here was the superior and electric compound: Negro-homo-writer in a single package."

The men talked about Baldwin's recent TV interview and about Paris, and Wright passed around pictures of his English wife and young children. May wrote about Baldwin's two books. She referred to *Giovanni's Room* as "an embarrassingly bad book, stage-like, unreal, but he had disclosed himself in it," and she had read it avidly. Unlike Pearl, she had not yet read *Go Tell It on the Mountain*, which she described as "the good one."

May was "magnetized" by Baldwin and described him:

His eye-whites were soiled with yellow . . . and his teeth were not snowy as he parted rich lips on a height with her own. She wondered what he sensed from her narrow Scandinavian eyes, ruddy skin, straight cap of hair and cool hand that clasped his with momentary pressure.

Baldwin and Wright were on their way to a party in the Village and did not stay long. As they left, Baldwin "pressed his address and phone number" into May's hand, "saying he was having 'a brawl' at his apartment on Horatio the next evening." May explained with disappointment that she was previously engaged uptown, but Baldwin did not see that as an obstacle. He replied, "A lot of show people are coming and not, naturally, until after the last curtain drops. It'll go on all night." There is, however, no record of May's attendance.

A week later, May noticed her name in the book review section of the *New York Times* along with six other finalists for the National Book Award in Poetry for *A Cage of Spines*. She did not expect to win but hoped the nomination would increase her book sales. The *New Yorker* had recently offered her "their $100 a year arrangement to have first look at [her] poems."[62] May celebrated by buying a new typewriter with the money. She would go on to publish sixty-one poems in the *New Yorker* during her lifetime.

On February 1, 1959, May wrote about a party at the house of Mary Britton Miller, known also by her pseudonym, Isabel Bolton. According to May, Miller was "tall and old, deep-voiced, slow-enunciating, rheumatic and partly blind." May had read Miller's latest novel, *Many Mansions*, published in 1952 and shortlisted for the National Book Award, but decided to "pretend not to have because it's very bad." Now in her seventies, Miller had produced memoirs, novels, and volumes of poetry, most of which were informed by her tragic past. She was orphaned at the age of four and devastated by the drowning of her twin sister when the girls were fourteen. May wrote:

> Before knowing her [Mary Miller], Miken had been intrigued
> by the veiled content of her books and stories; it was as if Mary
> had been disguising a personal secret in code—the secret of
> inversion—moreover, incestuous inversion. She knew that Mary
> had a twin, a sister with whom she had shared half her life until
> the twin had died.

Seeking to understand the nature of her own sexuality, May had become interested in the theory of inversion: the adoption of the sex role and psychological identity of the opposite sex, and on May 6, 1959, in "Now and Then," she recalled an interaction that had occurred the preceding year at the MacDowell Colony. May had hoped that a fellow resident would confess his "inversion" to her "so that she could confess hers (she longed to, to someone up there at the Colony—she felt so alone and ambiguous among the others, always wondering if <u>any</u> of them were like her . . .)."

May had enjoyed a ten-year relationship with Anca, and had been together with Pearl for nine years. She regularly socialized with gay friends at parties and gay bars but refrained from discussing her sexuality with new establishment literary acquaintances. In 1954 May reported in her diary that at an uptown soiree someone "asked me if I were Lesbian and I casually said yes; this is the first time anyone has asked me this." May came out, to use the contemporary term, guardedly and only gradually within the milieu of her newfound fame. It was at a time when, as a friend of May's explained, "downtown, gays could be open about their sexuality, but uptown, among the more conventional members of the literary set, they felt safer in the closet."[63]

Through Mary Britton Miller, May met a colorful and eccentric painter named Tobias Schneebaum, who in 1955 received a Fulbright to study art in Peru. May described him in "Now and Then" as

> a young Jewish painter whose German last name meant Snow Tree. Had been to Peru and lived in the jungle with Indians that no white man except archaeologists had been among before. Tobias himself went naked in the warm jungle, swam and hunted with his new companions, painted their portraits, although they did not recognize themselves for they had never used mirrors. The tribe was bi-sexual and any and every impulse (even commerce with animals) was common and legitimate among them, and while there was sporadic lesbianism among them, it was only an accidental easy-come-first occurrence, Tobias said.

After seven months Schneebaum emerged from the jungle wearing only body paint.[64] Schneebaum subsequently studied anthropology and lived among other isolated forest-dwelling people in search of new cultural experiences. Among May's notes for her poetry readings is a reference to a poem she would later publish in the *New Yorker*. "Some paintings of the natives of Borneo by Tobias Schneebaum, an artist friend of mine, led to the making of 'Naked in Borneo' a poem that reflects my almost trance-like attraction to a primitive way of life within the embrace of the tropic sun."

Around this time, the poet Edward Field became one of May's closest friends. They met at New Directions, where Field had submitted the manuscript of his poems, *Stand Up, Friend, with Me*.[65] Like many other people, Field found May an attractive person, and his first impressions were vivid:

> When she came walking toward me (at New Directions—she had read my book), I remember her little strides, her perfect gold bangs. She was crisp and focused, her eyes dead center—all May. We loved each other immediately.[66]

After May moved from the Village to Long Island in the mid-1960s, she accepted Field's invitation to use his apartment in the West Village when he and his partner were away and she needed to be in the city. May later paid tribute to her friend's generosity in a poem, "Staying at Ed's Place" (1975), which compared his sunny apartment on Bethune Street to "the Sea—of Tranquillity."

In the spring, May listed "things that happened in [the past] two months." She had written seven new poems. More than six hundred copies of *A Cage of Spines* had been sold. She had completed an article about the painter Milton Avery for *Arts Magazine*. And she was offered an Amy Lowell Traveling Scholarship of two thousand dollars, for which she had to agree to live away from the North American continent for one year, beginning in September. When Pearl announced her unwillingness to leave her job at the Bureau of Child Welfare, May hoped to change her mind by requesting a six-month deferral of the award. Then, as a possible omen of more good fortune, she received a "financial & tax questionnaire" from the Guggenheim Foundation. Reminding herself that it was "just a form," May acknowledged that she had a good "<u>chance</u> of getting a Guggenheim grant ($3600)."

May wrote to Elizabeth about her travel award. As she confessed toward the end of "Now and Then," she hoped for a reply that said, "Come with your $2000 and live with L[ota] & me in our new house above Rio, where the toucans & the black babies are—where it's summer all winter and the stars are different in the sky." May was far more attracted to South America than to Europe, but she feared that transportation costs for herself and Pearl would be prohibitive. Staying with Elizabeth would be a way to economize.

Elizabeth, in fact, did offer Lota's apartment in Rio to May and Pearl or accommodations with her and Lota in Samambaia, but she cautioned that, even if they could afford transportation, they could not live for a year in Brazil on what would remain of the two thousand dollars. She explained also that Portuguese was difficult in comparison with other European languages.[67]

An exultant May replied with more good news on April 21:

> Well, it never pours but it avalanches, and I <u>did</u> get a Guggenheim Fellowship! The announcements were in The Times and Tribune yesterday and I was notified a few days ago. What is so lucky is that I had previously asked for the Amy Lowell grant to start in the Spring of 1960, which they agreed to, and so the two good fortunes won't be running concurrently and I can have both!—the Guggenheim for this year and the other for next. Of course I am walking on the ceiling and feel very strange, with mixed reactions of "Do I deserve it" and can I live up to it?—then "Never mind—I like it—it feels <u>good</u>." So this makes Europe very possible, for both me and Pearl. But we probably won't be going until next spring, and I will take a course in French in the meanwhile, and we will make very careful plans on just where and how to spend a year abroad.[68]

Pearl was now willing to leave her job, and she and May spent the next year preparing for their trip to Spain, France, and Italy. May enrolled in a Berlitz French course; Pearl, who was already conversant in Spanish, studied Italian. After researching cars, they decided on a Simca, which they would pick up in Paris, and they bought camping equipment in New York. May's excitement increased with every letter to Elizabeth. "It is a wonderful feeling this seeming to be <u>rich</u>," she wrote.[69]

May's French improved rapidly, and she practiced on Elizabeth. "I listened to a play in French on the radio yesterday—came into the middle of it—and wished there was a knob (like on the dictaphone) that would turn them to SLOW."[70]

May and Pearl sailed in late March. Three months later, May sent Elizabeth a postcard from their campsite near Nice. May and Pearl had pitched their tent "under two Russian Olive trees, with palms, spruce, cypress all around." Although mosquitoes, spiders, and beetles were plentiful and the washing facilities primitive, "we like it better than bigger, better organized camps."[71]

The year 1960 was "the best year of my life," May later told her college friend Ray West.[72] May kept a careful record of each day's events on postcards, describing her routes and first impressions of Europe. More than two hundred of these cards now reside in the Swenson archive in St. Louis.[73]

May was prolific during her time abroad, producing at least fifteen poems, written on her transatlantic voyage; in the car as they traveled through northern Italy; and in Barcelona, Paris, Aix-en-Provence, Arles, Venice, Florence, and Rome. She published eleven poems between 1961 and 1963, including four in the *New Yorker*: "A Hurricane at Sea," "The Alyscamps at Arles," "Above the Arno," and "Notes Made in the Piazza San Marco." Three others were published posthumously.

May's extraordinary powers of close observation pervade the poems inspired by her European journey. In "The Alyscamps at Arles," she reacts to the ancient Roman necropolis, noticing that "the lizard darts between the thick lips of the hollow-bodied stones" and "[u]nder the broken lids the scorpion lives transfixed." In "A Boy Looking at Big David," she notes that the toenail of Michelangelo's statue in Florence is "wide as my hand." In "Notes Made at the Piazza San Marco," she describes the lips of the four life-size Byzantine horses on the façade of the church as "tugged back into wide loops," further observing, "The bits are absent." And in "The Pantheon, Rome," she discovers that the rain falling inside from the oculus scours the dull colors on the temple's floor.

After May and Pearl returned to New York in the late fall of 1960, they learned that Elizabeth and Lota were considering a European

FIGURE 23. May at Piazza Navona, Rome, 1960. *Washington University in St. Louis, May Swenson Papers.*

adventure. Still glowing from her own experience, May offered practical advice:

> To make the money <u>stretch</u> in Europe, you should camp. It's easy, <u>not</u> rugged—easier and more pleasant than using hotels—as long as you have a car and the weather is warm. We camped from May to October in Spain, France and Italy, except for the month in Aix where we took an apartment, and 10 days in Florence in a pensione. . . .
>
> Pearl . . . kept our budget and did all our buying for camp (as well as the driving—she let me drive a little in Spain where there

was no traffic, I had no license)—so you see I had the easy end
of things. About all I did was to make our "blue cloth house" and
"furnish" it, when we camped, and take it down and pack things
when we moved on.

I must have told you that camping is a common thing in
Europe now—there are plenty of camps to choose from. . . . The
sites are guarded, have washing and toilet facilities, many have
restaurants and stores. The Europeans use them for vacations,
so that one meets people from many countries. . . . The good air,
and peacefulness, and exercise, and nature around you keeps you
relaxed and full of energy all the time. And it's so cheap—average
cost per night about 30¢ apiece! If you make your meals in camp,
of course, that's a big saving compared with eating out, too. Our
practice was to make breakfast, then buy stuff for sandwiches
for lunch which we'd take with us and eat wherever we'd hap-
pen to be; we'd often have dinner out, but sometimes make it in
camp. . . .

They make tents very compact these days and easy to erect.
Nice thing about camping is you don't have to shift luggage in
and out of hotels or tip porters and maids, and you can drive into
a camp without reservations. Also you can dress any way you
like. . . .

We did discover we weren't equipped to camp in very cold
weather. France and Italy had great rains and floods through
September–October, and it got unexpectedly cold. We were stub-
born and decided, when we left Rome Oct. 4, not to use a hotel
until we got to Paris. We took 10 days on the way, stopping 2 days
at Sienna [Siena], a day at Pisa (after spending a day shopping
in Florence). We went to Genoa via the coast and entered France
from the Italian Riviera. A freak cold set in with almost inces-
sant rain as we moved up the Lyon route in France. The camps
were deserted but we used them anyway, sleeping with layers of
clothes on inside our sacks in the car. Water was too cold to wash
in and it was too cold to change clothes. . . .

[I]n a camp run by a farming family near Digne, a cou-
gar came down off the mountain—we heard him scream—he
sounded just across the creek from us where we were sleeping

in the car. Glad we weren't in the tent—he might have come in hoping to get warm. I enjoy telling this—it sounds so wild—but actually camping is tame and safe. I guess you could say it takes the place of motels in the U.S. (but more pleasant). We could not have spent the length of time we did in Europe, on the money we had, or could not have seen as much of it, if we'd used hotels all the time. We did use them in the north of Spain (they were inexpensive there) and in Paris both in the Spring and Fall. . . .

I think you are right to fly. It costs so very little more than a boat, and saves time. I was delighted with the sea on the voyage out, but got quite bored coming back. It took 11 days! . . .

A regret I have is not having gone south in Italy, or into Sicily. We got down to Paestum, which is just below Sorrento. Pompeii was a marvelous experience. All these generalities! I can't begin to describe anything specifically. Pearl kept a day-by-day diary and took many pictures, and I have a big postcard collection with notes on the back. I have so much material—hope some of it will find its way into my work.[74]

Despite May's glowing account, camping held little appeal for Elizabeth.

Your letter was so persuasive that when I read it aloud to Lota she actually, for the space of one minute and a half, maybe, considered camping in Europe—both Mary and I just looked at her, aghast and unbelieving. . . . Of course it passed over soon, but you see the power of the written word, when things are presented well, as you presented them. . . . No, I think it is pensiones for us, even if they get lower and lower class as we go on.[75]

May returned to Yaddo in August 1961, armed with a manuscript of new and old poems to be shaped into her third book. But Yaddo had changed. "There's a poet population explosion—it's time for birth control. Worst is that some of them are good, too, the little bastards," she wrote to Elizabeth. And they are young, "younger than me," a somewhat unnerved forty-eight-year-old May observed.[76]

In the fall of 1961 Elizabeth and Lota came to New York. They stayed for several weeks at 61 Perry Street in the temporarily vacant apartment of Elizabeth's good friends, the artist Loren MacIver and her husband, Lloyd Frankenburg, a literary critic and poet. May was delighted that Elizabeth and Lòta were a two-minute walk from her apartment. A hand-delivered note from Elizabeth suggests the convenience of their get-togethers. "Dear May—Sorry you're out—we went by, to take a little walk—If you & Pearl are home before 10 why don't you come to call on us? Elizabeth."[77] By December, Elizabeth and Lota had returned to Rio.

In the spring May had agreed to publish her third book, *To Mix with Time*, with Holt, and she anticipated a publication date in the fall. But toward the end of May, Holt postponed publication for a year. Furious, May obtained a release from Holt and placed her book with Scribner's, who promised to have it out in the spring of 1963, providing she expand it to include selections from her two previous books.

In September 1962, her deal with Scribner's secure, May flew home to Logan for a two-week visit. All her siblings and their thirty-one children convened to celebrate Dan and Margaret's fiftieth wedding anniversary. This happy occasion was the last time May would see her eighty-two-year-old father alive. In May 1963 Margaret wrote that Dan had suffered a stroke. May's reply to her mother included a message to her father:

> <u>Dearest Dad</u>: I am always with you in my thoughts. Often memories of my childhood come to me, and I wrote this poem about me and you, called "The Seed of my Father." I hope it can convey a little of what you mean to me. I love you both—so much.[78]

Her mother assured May that she had read the poem to her father and that he was touched by it although he could no longer speak.

FIGURE 24. Swenson family photograph taken for Dan and Margaret's fiftieth wedding anniversary, August 21, 1962. Front row, seated (*left to right*): Roy, Greta, Dan A., May. Back row, standing: Margaret Swenson Woodbury, Paul Swenson, Ruth Swenson Eyre, George F. Swenson, Dan H. Swenson, Grace (Michael) Swenson Turetsky, and Beth Swenson Hall. *Courtesy Lisa Turetsky.*

The Seed of My Father

I rode on his shoulder. He showed me the moon.
He told me its name with a kiss in my ear.
"My moon," I said. "Yours," he agreed.
And as we walked, it followed us home.

Hold my hand, he showed me a tree,
and picked a peach, and let me hold it.
I took a bite, then he took a bite.
"Ours?" I asked. "Yes, our tree."
Then with a hoe he made the water flow beside it.

When I was older he showed me the sun.
He made me a wooden wheel on a stick,
of pine wood, raw and bright as the sun.
I used to run and roll it.

A flashing circular saw was the sun,
like the one he made my wheel with.
"This little wheel belongs to me, the big one
to you?" "Yes," he agreed, "just as we
belong to the sun."

He let me plant the corn grains one by one
out of a long hollow slip-box thrust in the ground.
"I who plant seeds for my father,
I am the seed of my father."

And when the corn was tall, it swallowed me up, all,
whispering over my head. "You are the seed of your father."
And when the husks were sere, my father with a rake,
in the cold time of the year, made a bush of gold.

He struck the bush to burning for my sake.
I stood at his shoulder, a little the higher.
I was the seed of my father, my father
outlined by the fire.

He made a garden, and he planted me.
Sun and moon he named and deeded to me.
Water and fire he created, created me,
he named me into being: I am the seed of my father.

His breath he gave me, he gave me night and day.
His universe is in me fashioned from his clay.
I feed on the juice of the peach from his eternal tree.
Each poem I plant is a seedling from that tree.
I plant the seed of my father.

Her father's condition worsened, and May flew to Logan two weeks later, but she arrived two hours after her father's death. She remained with her family for the funeral and returned to New York briefly before beginning a residency at the MacDowell Colony in New Hampshire. She wrote to Elizabeth.

> My mother is a very strong, courageous person and, although she had done all the suffering—for Dad was in a coma—she was the one who comforted us children. She's 73, and all her life has been devoted to her children and to Dad. . . . My family's religion is really curative for them at this time—(the Mormons believe in an afterlife, and that they will meet their loved ones "in their ideal body" in "the next world.") I won't go on about the funeral, and all the things that are still filling my mind . . .
> My birthday was on May 28. . . . It was celebrated, too, even though it was the day after my father's burial. My sister Ruth baked a cake and we had ice cream, and two of my nieces and a nephew put on a program: Sherry, aged 5, sang a song accompanied by Ricky, 16, on the banjo and harmonica, and then Lisa, 8, my sister Grace's girl, played the harp and sang "I wonder as I wander."[79]

May's sister Grace was alternately referred to as Michael, her stage name, throughout her life.

May returned home from MacDowell in early July 1963, just as reviews of her book *To Mix with Time: New and Selected Poems* were beginning to appear. A month before, Anthony Hecht had written a favorable review in the *New York Review of Books*, then in its fourth month of publication. His opening paragraph read:

> One way of indicating the distinction and quality of May Swenson's poetry is to say that she deserves to be compared to Elizabeth Bishop. And indeed there are things in this book, which contains new poems together with selections from two previous volumes, that sound a note of indebtedness. Miss Swenson's "The Totem," for example, about the Empire State Building, may vaguely remind the reader of Miss Bishop's "The Monument."

But if there are points of kinship, the differences are still import-
ant; and May Swenson has an idiom and voice of her own, both
more playful and baroque than Miss Bishop's.[80]

On June 17 Elizabeth graciously broached the topic of the Hecht
piece to May. "I am so pleased with Anthony Hecht's review of your
book. I think it's the first really intelligent review of your poems, so
far. I hope you don't mind his reference to me, which seems a bit
beside the point—to me. 'The Totem' doesn't strike me as being like
my 'Monument' in the slightest. But I think it's a good review and he
notices the right things in the right way—"[81]

May must have been pleased with Hecht's plaudits throughout
the review, but she was bothered by his implication that she imitated
Elizabeth and also by the critical attitude about female poets. "I guess
it's because you endorsed my book that reviewers have decided I'm
following in your tracks—a foolish conclusion to jump to—the other
foolish notion is to lump women poets together, or connect them in
some way. Well, categorizing is the first (and often only) duty of the
reviewer, it seems."[82]

As May's letter progressed, she reconsidered the question of her
indebtedness to Elizabeth and mused about the subtlety and effect of
Elizabeth's poems in comparison to her own, and about why and how
their manner of composition differed:

[T]he fact is I <u>have</u> been influenced by you a lot—not as to
method, but as to attitude. I'd like to be more so. But when I
write I find I can't do just as I intend to—it goes its own way.
I would like to find the casual and absolutely natural tone that
you have in your poems—they are never over-colored or forced
the least little bit—they are very honest, and never call atten-
tion to their effects. Their brilliance is inside, and not on the
surface. And they are subtle—not obvious. I think my greatest
fault is being obvious—and I never know it until the poem's been
printed—quite long after that, and it's too late. I come from a
poor education, and from being a loner, and never letting anyone
else in on what I'm doing—not having the benefit of better judg-
ment than my own.

In September, May's focus shifted temporarily to theater after she
received a grant from the Ford Foundation, which would place her as
a resident playwright in a repertory company. She was likely inspired
to follow this course by James Broughton, the poet, experimental film-
maker, and resident playwright at the Playhouse Repertory Theater
in San Francisco, whom she had met in 1958. She wrote to share the
news with Elizabeth:

> It seems I have won a Ford grant that's tied up with a theatre
> project—it won't come to me until next year, fall of 1964—but
> is $7,500! (I'll have to pay taxes on $3,900.) I'm supposed to be
> located with some repertory theatre group, study their stage in
> action, and write a play. Although I don't absolutely <u>have to</u> write
> a play, they say. I told them I wouldn't go to Texas or Washington
> D.C. San Francisco, O.K.—or anywhere in the New England area.
> Won't know until April where they'll send me. . . . But I've al-
> ready begun to write a play—completely static, and unactable, so
> far . . . that would be the actors' problem, wouldn't it?[83]

In June 1964 May was "assigned" to the Lincoln Center Repertory
Theatre, whose temporary stage was "right on Washington Square."
No longer worried about employment, May left New Directions. "That,
I'm convinced, is a good result of my getting this crazy grant," she wrote
to Elizabeth.[84] May wrote a surrealistic one-act play, *The Floor*, which
was performed at the American Place Theatre in its 1965–66 season.

With a full complement of paid speaking engagements across the
country and invitations to serve with honoraria on major award se-
lection committees, such as the Lamont Award and the National Book
Award, May felt as if she had been "kicked upstairs."[85] Though at times
she longed for her "natural state" and "a big patch of irresponsibility
and anonymity to wade around in," she rejoiced in the recognition
she had earned.[86]

In June 1965 May congratulated Elizabeth for accepting a position
as visiting professor, beginning in January 1966, at the University of

Washington, the home institution of her college friend Grant Red-
ford. She also had some news to share. "I've got a similar, though I'm
sure, lesser problem: Purdue in Indiana wrote me and asked me to
be writer-in-residence for the academic year beginning September
'66—I would have to teach one class of about a dozen piglet-poets.
Don't know what to say. Don't want to teach nobody nuffin, but by that
time I'll very probably be needing moula and they offer $10-thou for
8 months. Is it worth it? I don't know anything about Purdue except
they're big in football, I think. Will have to research the situation and
decide."[87]

May's decision was complicated by her increasingly tense relation-
ship with Pearl, who expressed no interest in joining May in West
Lafayette, Indiana. "Pearl didn't think May valued her enough and
wanted to play the field, and she urged May to find someone at Purdue,"
remembered May's friend Ed Field.[88] May accepted the eight-month
position and wrote to her friend Grant Redford to share the news. She
was oblivious to the poignancy of his reply until months later.

> Well, so you've broken down and are going to teach. Fine. You'll
> be really fine. So you're not a <u>social</u> person, many teachers are
> not. But when they talk about the subject of their interest they
> break through barriers into enlightenment. That's you, as I re-
> member you, and as you emerge from your letters, poems and
> the one story of yours I remember. . . .
>   Well, so long for now. I'm sorry that I'll not be coming along
> your way as planned. But, to quote somebody, it's a long road. . . .
>   Did I tell you that I'm on leave this year? I sold my houseboat
> and have settled in this little cabin for the year.[89]

Three weeks later, Grant Redford took his own life at the age of
fifty-seven. The *Seattle Times* reported that he had been found dead
in his automobile near his cabin, a hose connected from the exhaust to
the car's interior.[90] Unaware of her friend's death, May suggested that
Elizabeth look him up, and referred to Grant as "an old boy friend of
mine."[91] A letter from Grant's wife three months later informed May
of his death. "[T]his was not a sudden decision but something he had
been contemplating for some time," she wrote.[92]

Among May's papers is a draft of an author's bio, dated December 1965, and "almost 300 wds too long," May attests at the bottom of the page. Its intended publication is unidentified, but "I am the first," as it is titled, is a retrospective of May's life and accomplishments at the age of fifty-two.

> I am the first of ten children born to Dan Arthur and Anna Margaret (Hellberg) Swenson in Logan, a mountain town about 80 miles north of Salt Lake City in Utah. My parents were both born in Sweden, and came to America and settled in the Rocky Mountain region as a result of joining the Mormon Church. I was brought up a Mormon, but since the age of thirteen have had the distinction of being the only blacksheep among my living four brothers and four sisters.

As a point of correction, May was not the only "blacksheep" in her family. Her sister Grace, eight years her junior, also left home and Mormonism in her twenties.

> At thirteen . . . I began to write poetry. My father was a teacher in the Mechanical Engineering Department at the Utah State Agricultural College (now Utah State University) in Logan, and it was there, naturally, that I took my Bachelor's—the only degree I have. After graduation I worked as a reporter on my hometown paper and on the Salt Lake City Deseret News. . . .
>   My first national publication did not occur until 1949 . . . [when] The Saturday Review of Literature accepted a poem called "Haymaking." By this time I was living in New York City's Greenwich Village—where I've been "making it" ever since.
>   At the age of twenty-one, I decided not to marry. I also decided to commit suicide by the age of forty to avoid old age, but it's now too late for that.

Although May often wrote about death in her poetry and prose, nowhere in her extant diaries did she express a desire to commit suicide.

> My initial attempts to support myself in New York appear comical at this distance. On failing to get a job on any of the

newspapers, I began answering their want Ads under "Author's Assistant," and so found myself apprenticed to a series of peculiar would-be writers who expected me to execute their generally grandiose plots for novels or scenarios; they had the ideas, I was merely required to furnish the words—at a fraction of a ghost-writer's fee. I soon learned that typing correspondence in business offices, though monotonous, was better paid, and even offered opportunities (if I was careful) of pursuing my own writing "on the boss' time"—also on his stationery inserted into his typewriter. . . .

If asked about my attitude toward politics I would say this: By the same habit of independent thought that makes me label myself a pantheist, I would call myself a "non-patriot" in the sense that I love the world above any nation, and look forward to pledging allegiance to The United Nations—would that it might become, in deed, the nucleus of effective world government in my lifetime. Meanwhile I content myself with being a registered Democrat who usually votes Liberal. . . .

For the academic year 1966–67 I have accepted the post of writer-in-residence at Purdue University in Lafayette, Indiana.[93]

But May did not write that, although money was certainly a motivating factor in her acceptance of Purdue's offer, she also wanted distance from New York and from Pearl, and she needed something new to spark her creativity.

CHAPTER 9

It Is Squaresville Here

MAY WAS UNUSUALLY BUSY in the months before her departure for Purdue University.

After a brief, relaxing vacation with Pearl on St. Thomas in the Caribbean, May worked feverishly to complete the manuscript of *Poems to Solve*, riddles for children, that Scribner's would publish in October 1966. She also honed her next collection for Scribner's, *Half Sun, Half Sleep: New Poems*, in order to meet her July 1 deadline for publication in 1967.[1] And in the late spring of 1966 she oversaw the production and performance of her surrealistic one-act play, *The Floor*.

May's highly unorthodox mise-en-scène featured two actors dressed as clowns, one of whom rented to the other a room that had the singular distinction of having no walls or ceiling, just a floor. In a letter to Elizabeth, an energized May described her debut into the world of theater. "Working on it [*The Floor*] with the director and the actors has got me completely hypnotized—it's almost taking the place of living—and I'm glad it'll soon be over."[2] *The Floor*, which appears to have perplexed audiences, enjoyed a brief run at the American Place Theatre on West 46th Street.

Upon her arrival in West Lafayette, Indiana, in September 1966, May sent letters to the three most important women in her life: her mother, Pearl, and Elizabeth. "What a pleasure to find your letter in my new mailbox," she wrote to her mother on September 18, and she explained that she had no car and was living on the ground floor of a frame house near campus.[3] Her teaching duties included a weekly three-hour seminar for a dozen students.

"Dear B-Cat," she began an upbeat letter to Pearl on October 4,

> I thought the class went well today. . . . I think they are getting to like me and to be scared of me in about equal parts, which is healthy. I am giving them zany assignments along with serious ones—I'm keeping them on the qui vive. There are some hopeless

dumbunnies and some promising ones and one or two that <u>might</u> become something like real writers—so it's all interesting.[4]

For years now, May and Elizabeth had corresponded about poetry, nature, their travels and pets, yet were circumspect about their love lives. May had no way of knowing that Elizabeth's relationship with Lota had been unraveling for some time.[5]

In the early 1960s Lota de Macedo Soares had been asked to supervise a large public works project to convert a landfill in Rio into a park. Lota was talented and well connected but lacked credentials in both architecture and landscape design. Her coworkers and superiors used these shortcomings as an excuse for political machinations, and over time they undermined support for the project. Nevertheless, Lota persevered and was able to create the park, which was inaugurated to public acclaim in April 1965. Elizabeth had remained with Lota in Rio during the turmoil of the park's construction, anticipating that upon its completion they would both return to the relaxing ambience of Samambaia. As it happened, however, Lota refused to relinquish control of the park, and she elected to remain in Rio.

Frustrated by Lota's decision, Elizabeth had reluctantly accepted a lucrative visiting professorship in Seattle. She told May in the spring of 1965, "I have tentatively said I'd go and be one of those prize-pig-poets at the University of Washington next January—for the two terms until June. . . . But I am getting very cold feet about it."[6] Her appointment would provide a respite from the emotional upheaval in Rio while allowing her to reconnect with her growing American audience and also to acquire needed funds.

Before leaving for Seattle, Elizabeth purchased a rundown house in Ouro Preto, an appealing colonial town ninety miles north of Rio, and there she quickly formed a relationship with a woman named Lili Correia de Araújo. Elizabeth evidently considered taking May into her confidence about her new girlfriend but did not, offering in November 1965 only the tantalizing, "I meant to stay two weeks [in Ouro Preto] and ended by staying over two months (I'll tell you all the fascinating reasons in my next)."[7] Elizabeth also hinted at the strain in her relationship with Lota. "Lota is working so hard these days and going through such a hard time—I am not much use to her in Rio, but also felt I'd abandoned her. . . . She finally came and <u>got</u> me in Ouro Preto . . . so I felt she really wanted me back!"

The following month Elizabeth left for Seattle.

Once Elizabeth was settled into her six-month appointment at the University of Washington, May reported to her how much things were changing in the Village. "Beards are disappearing on MacDougal St. now and long hair is in for the boys. Long—very long hair, straight & lank for the girls, together with leather jackets, pointed toe boots, patterned stockings, white lipstick, lots of eye makeup. Please give us the scene in Seattle."[8] May also hoped to receive some encouragement from Elizabeth about her own impending teaching appointment, but none was forthcoming.

May heard nothing from Elizabeth for ten months until in November 1966 she received a cryptic postcard mailed from London and forwarded to her in Indiana from New York. Elizabeth reported that she and Lota were returning to Rio the next day because Lota was not well. She promised to send an explanatory letter soon and asked May to write. Elizabeth signed the card, "With love from us both."[9]

May was eager to reengage with Elizabeth and did not wait for the letter she had promised in her postcard. May replied immediately, telling Elizabeth about, of all things, a power plant.

A big thrill to see your handwriting again, on a card from London which came this morning. . . . I'm in a little old-fashioned house with a peaked roof on a dead-end street near the railroad tracks—can walk to the campus (about 5 blocks north)—have the pavement to myself, since everyone is in cars. There's a big new power house almost across the street, a grassy hill with trees on its property; the power house, especially at night, is the best and most exciting building around here—all of glass, in big squares, which let various colors of light through, pastel colors— gladioli shades, or sweet pea—a big high stack on one side has red blinker lights which flash in alternate rhythm to the airport beam fanning back and forth about a mile to the west. I walk up there quite often before going to bed—to the power house—and sometimes the doors are open (they slide up) and I can see the weird contraptions inside, metal tubular things on platforms,

a balcony with other peculiarly shaped generators, or whatever
they are—this ground floor part in a cold cathode light, a mixture
of hummings heard, smooth sounds not very loud—and not a
human anywhere in there—it seems to work by itself. Well, once
I did see a watchman strolling on the balcony in an olive uni-
form, his hands and face greenish in light.[10]

That building became the subject of May's poem "The Power House,"
whose opening lines formed the shape of "the tall square tower" that
topped it.

> The
> Power
> House
>
> Close to my
> place is the
> power house.
> I knew there
> wouldn't be
> anybody in it.
> It's beauti-
> ful. Like a
> church. It
> works all by
> itself. And
> with almost no
> sound. All glass.
> And a tall square
> tower on it.
> Colored lights
> shine from within.
> They color the
> glass. Pink. Pale
> green. Not stained.
> Not that kind. And
> not fragile. Just
> light. Light weight.

(Two years later Elizabeth spotted the poem in the *New Yorker* but had forgotten May's earlier enchantment with the building. "I think I did write you a card about how much I liked one of yours in the N Yorker—'The Powerhouse' I think it was called—anyway, very mysterious, about a building.")[11]

May also liked "The Power House," one of her early shape poems. She would include it in her sixth book, *Iconographs*, in 1970. The word "iconographs," May later explained, "is a made-up word of mine, which means image writing. After the poems were done—and I wouldn't even know they were going to be shape poems or anything—I would give them typographical arrangement on the page. The shape that you would then see would have something to say about what was being said in the poem."[12]

May described her new surroundings to Elizabeth:

> I can see the studs in Orion's belt on clear nights. About the best thing out here is clear air, smell of grass and evergreen, and all the time now burning leaves. There are juniper bushes around the house and yard and they have a wonderful odor. The house doesn't get dirty—or my nails and hair—and that's nice.
>
> The campus is rather ugly—flat, spread out—it looks like a manufacturing plant—and is. The only building with any grace on the campus is an old Main (not used for that anymore) with a little tower—French style architecture—and they've remodeled the inside so that it's boring inside. Near it is John Lafayette's grave stone, a short thick round-topped slab in the center of an oval hedge enclosure.
>
> My "teaching" is going all right by now. The class meets each Tuesday afternoon for three and a half hours—a break for smoking in the middle. I have 13 students, upper and undergraduate, ranging in age from 19 to about 45—about half men. There are two (mail—I mean male) who may become writers. Some of them are nuts about me—or just plain nuts—and becoming flagrant about it. It is Squaresville here by the Wabash, and gossip is the sport, second only to football. Ladies may not put an elbow on a bar in this town—in fact, to <u>find</u> a bar takes underground connections—but there is a good Negro bar called Al's on the shady outskirts, that's got a juke and a colored TV and

best spareribs I've ever eaten. There's a roadhouse too, where
you can get fried catfish—Friday nights there is a good place for
camping—at least I haven't seen anyone from the English Dept.
there yet.[13]

May informed Elizabeth that she was flying to Texas the following
week to visit friends and to give a reading at the National Council of
Teachers of English convention in Houston; that she was looking for-
ward to Pearl's visit in West Lafayette; and that she would spend the
Christmas holidays with her family in Utah before traveling to New
York in mid-January.

On November 29 Elizabeth wrote the promised explanatory letter
to May, but she made no mention of her new girlfriend in Seattle.

The trip to Holland & England had to be cut short—Lota was
just not up to it—in fact she has had a complete breakdown after
the past six years of overwork, and is in bed in Rio, with a nurse,
etc.—We thought she was getting better and that getting away from
Brazil would be the best idea, but it didn't work that way. . . .
She sleeps most of the time, and the doctor—whom I like
very much, thank heavens,—thought I might as well get away
and attend to business for a few days and get a bit of rest my-
self—since the trip got to be pretty awful before I got us back
here safely—(Please don't mention this if you write.) . . . Now of
course I am very gloomy, and extremely worried about Lota—I
do think she is all right, just exhausted.—I really shouldn't write
you this—I am not writing most friends about it—but feel sure
of your sympathy, etc.[14]

May, for her part, did not inform Elizabeth that she had made a
promising new acquaintance of her own, thirty-four-year-old Rozanne
("Zan") Knudson, a doctoral candidate in English education at Stan-
ford University who had been teaching at Purdue for more than a year
before May arrived.[15] Zan was a native of Washington, DC, and, like
May, the oldest child in a large LDS family. Her mother was from Salt
Lake City, her father from Brigham City, Utah. Zan's parents had
sent her to Brigham Young University in the hope that their outgoing,
sports-crazed daughter would settle down and marry in the Mormon

Church. At BYU, Zan fell in love with reading and majored in English. After graduating in 1954, she received an MA from the University of Georgia and for several years taught high school English in Florida. She then enrolled at Stanford, where she studied under the novelist Wallace Stegner and earned her PhD in 1967.

Zan had read about May's arrival on campus and was eager to meet this prominent poet who had grown up in Utah. Upon learning that May was in effect stranded without an automobile, Zan offered to take May to the grocery store, and May accepted. Weary of the polite small talk of well-meaning colleagues, May welcomed the opportunity simply to stock her kitchen so as to cook for herself. After one of their grocery runs, Zan invited May to a favorite restaurant for fresh catfish. She and May were soon spending evenings together, often at Al's Bar, where they listened to jazz, danced, drank beer, and ate barbecue. May enjoyed these off-campus escapes and her vibrant new younger friend, and in return introduced an eager Zan to birdwatching, which became another of their many shared interests.

When Pearl came to visit in the fall, Zan volunteered to serve as May and Pearl's chauffeur. The visit was not a success. May's friend and fellow poet Ed Field remembers that Pearl had initially wanted a break with May and encouraged her to date others in Indiana. But Pearl, discouraged by her own lack of social success, arrived unenthusiastic about any new friend of May's, especially an attractive young one. Rivalry flared. Vivacious Zan faulted Pearl's lack of spontaneity; reserved Pearl thought Zan frivolous. May must have realized that she would soon have to make a decision.

In early January, May returned from a visit, without Pearl, to Utah and reported to Elizabeth that "Christmas with the family and seeing old friends was happy and funny and devastating emotionally."[16] Christmas without her beloved father was understandably difficult for May, and she and her college friends doubtless shared memories of Grant Redford, their literary classmate who had recently taken his own life. May was, however, heartened to find her mother in good health and reported to Elizabeth that she "[p]rays a lot, and made me be with her on her knees a good deal, so that I was glad for the carpet!" May also revealed that she was leaving for a ten-day trip to New York on January 19 to see the dentist, her tax accountant, and "the people at Scribner's," but she chose not to mention that she was breaking up with Pearl.[17]

A week later, May mentioned Zan to Elizabeth for the first time: "[M]aybe I'll buy a VW belonging to a friend of mine here, Rozanne—she's teaching me to drive it—I was having a driving lesson in the cemetery on Sunday—no traffic there."[18]

Zan drove May from West Lafayette to New York City in late March so May could accept a Rockefeller grant and give a poetry reading at the Guggenheim Museum. After depositing her on Perry Street, Zan left, perhaps for Virginia to visit her family. There is no indication that she spent the night with May or attended her events. On a later memorable occasion, however, May and Zan spent a day at the Coney Island Aquarium, where, by chance, they watched two beluga whales mating. Afterward, they dined in Manhattan and enjoyed a romantic interlude at the Waldorf Astoria. This day was the inspiration for May's poem "Wednesday at the Waldorf," which blends the two events.

FIGURE 25. Rozanne (Zan) Knudson and May Swenson at Purdue University, spring 1967. *Literary Estate of May Swenson.*

>Two white whales have been installed at
>the Waldorf. They are tumbling slowly
>above the tables, butting the chandeliers,
>submerging, and taking soft bites
>out of the red-vested waiters in the
>Peacock Room.

The young, blonde, and blue-eyed athlete Zan was the muse of another playfully erotic poem, "A Trellis for R." May repeatedly arranged vertically the words "rose" and "blue," allusions to Rozanne's name and the color of her eyes, to create a visual latticework of words. Like "The Power House," "A Trellis for R," here excerpted, appeared in *Iconographs*, May's later collection of shape poems.

> When I kiss
>
> your eyes' straight lashes
> down crisp go like doll's
> blond straws. Glazed
> iris R
>   o
>   s
>   e
>   s your lids unclose
> to B
>   l
>   u
>   e ringed targets their dark
> sheen spokes almost green. I sink in
> B
> l
> u
>   e black R
>   o
>   s
>   e heart holes until
> you blink.

Although Pearl accepted Zan as a fixture in May's life, she refused to lose May altogether. They had months before committed to renting a summer house in East Hampton near Amagansett, on the east end of Long Island. But when May confirmed that there would now be three of them in the house, Pearl became progressively melancholy, despondent, and desperate. She made it clear to May that Flo, the woman whom she herself had been dating, could never hold her affection.[19] Attempting to garner May's sympathy and attention, Pearl alluded repeatedly to her own heavy drinking.[20]

On June 18 Elizabeth informed May that she might be in New York "for a little while, so please let me know (Rio) where you are to be."[21] Unaware that she would be in the city alone, May attempted to lure her and Lota to Amagansett. The invitation glowed with a love of nature.

> [P]lease come to see me here. . . . The view is oak trees in the front yard and then a big meadow of pasture grass, on the other side of which the L.I.R.R. tracks run along a wooded ridge—I see the windows of the cars flick through tree leaves on the ridge. Not too far a walk away is a paddock with six horses that I go to to give carrots to and pet their noses. . . . Am working well, most days. The rented house is comfortable—two guest bedrooms. So come, and stay a while.
>
> It was so good to hear from you. I'm so glad both you and Lota are feeling fine now. It would be wonderful to have you both out here for a visit. I could show you pheasants, Bob Whites, orioles, thrashers, flickers, hairy and downy woodpeckers, a big rat rabbit who eats off the tops of the sunflowers the minute they're two inches high, a chipmunk who has a whole maze of tunnels under the lawn—also the bays and beaches including Gosman's Dock where they drag in lobsters bigger than newborn babies. . . . Pearl comes on some weekends. I'll give her your greeting.[22]

Elizabeth did not visit May in Amagansett, nor did she share with May the reason for her trip to New York. Lota's psychiatrist had insisted on a separation between Elizabeth and Lota until at least December. Lota had discovered an incriminating letter from Elizabeth's young Seattle girlfriend, and this had exacerbated Lota's already fragile mental state.[23] While Elizabeth was spending the summer of 1967 in the vacant studio of her artist friend, Loren MacIver, at 61 Perry Street, she learned from Pearl that May and Zan were planning to buy a house together after they left Amagansett.[24] On August 25 Elizabeth wrote to May, "P[earl] tells me you think you've found a nice house in Seacliff? Whenever you come to N.Y. do please call up—I'll be here for some time—until Christmas, probably—and I am much, much better at last. . . . My regards to Roz(x?)anne."[25]

In September, Lota called Elizabeth to announce that, in defiance of her psychiatrist's recommendation, she was flying to New York from Rio, to arrive on September 17. Sometime in the early hours of September 18, Lota overdosed on Valium, collapsed, and remained in a coma at St. Vincent's Hospital until her death on September 25. After arranging to transport Lota's body home, Elizabeth returned to Brazil in November, where she received a cold reception from most of Lota's family and friends.[26] On the very day of Lota's death, unaware of everything that had happened, May had written to Elizabeth.

Dear Elizabeth:

I've tried to phone you several times from here—I guess you've been very busy and out of the house a lot. Rozanne and I were in New York this past weekend. . . . I gave you a call, but didn't catch you. We are hoping to get into the Sea Cliff house (73 [The] Boulevard—Zip Code 11579) before the end of the month. If we don't, I don't know where we'll go, since [we] can't stay in this house beyond that. . . . But when we get over there [in Sea Cliff], and straightened around, we want to come and get you and show you the view from the terrace—it's really on a cliff (up about 40 steps—overlooking Hempstead Bay—) and only an hour from Manhattan by the L.I.R.R.—a bit less by car.

I'm o.k. driving around here, but yesterday tried to drive up 3rd Avenue in Saturday traffic around 1 p.m. and scraped a taxi, putting dents in front and rear right fenders. I'm not ready to drive in New York—maybe never will be.

Hope to see you on our next trip in.

Love, May[27]

CHAPTER 10

If Distinction Comes,
Can Extinction Be Far Behind?

SEA CLIFF, NEW YORK, provided a secure home base for May for the rest of her life. There were many attractions to this charming, quirky little village overlooking Hempstead Harbor on the north shore of Long Island and easily accessible to New York City by both car and the Long Island Railroad. Affordable, cabin-sized houses were plentiful, many with sweeping views of Long Island Sound and proximity to the beach. An abundance of old-growth trees offered a natural habitat for local and migrating birds, a boon for birdwatchers like May and Zan. And Sea Cliff was a magnet for creative New Yorkers, particularly writers.

Zan found a position supervising teachers in a nearby public school district, and May felt confident that the suburban environment would be conducive to her writing. They found a little bungalow high on the cliff directly across from the beach. May appropriately named their new home Kestrel's Nest in honor of the kestrel, a colorful falcon that perches high while searching for its prey. Perhaps May was mindful of her own habit of sitting high in trees during her childhood in Utah, or upon rooftops in her early years in the Village. Now on the heights of a cliff edge on Long Island, May sought the nourishment of poetic inspiration.

May described the cottage to her mother:

It sounds fantastic, but I have bought a house here on the north shore of Long Island Sound, only about 45 minutes from New York by car or train, but with a beautiful view of the water with sail boats riding by and seagulls flying by. I am half owner of the house and small lot—bought it with Rozanne Knudson, with whom I became friends out in Indiana, and she has a good job as school supervisor in Hicksville, a town close by. . . . We have a mortgage on the house but the payments are much less than rent would be in the city. It has an upstairs and downstairs, has a lovely flagstoned terrace, and sits on a little cliff, really, right above Hempstead Harbor, with a beach below. We got it furnished. . . . Has a fine modern kitchen, . . . Bathroom upstairs with stall shower and half a bathroom . . . downstairs. Two good bedrooms, a dining porch glassed in, lovely front room L-shaped, one part of which serves as my studio. Lots of built in shelving for books, and lots of closets. It's heated by electric radiators—that's the one thing that's going to be expensive in the winter, I know—but in the summer this place is a dream. . . . I'm looking at the waves of the bay splashing on the little beach, as I type—can see clear to Connecticut across the water, through the window here.[1]

A month later, May answered her mother's questions about Pearl and Zan, and she volunteered more information about her financial situation.

[Rozanne] teaches two nights a week besides her daytime supervisory job. Yes, Pearl has the apartment at Perry St. . . . She's glad to have it to herself—has many friends—is fine. We are friends—I go there whenever I am in New York (at least once a week I get over there). . . .

I put in half the price of the property in <u>cash</u>—much of which I earned out there in Purdue— . . . I am well off financially—I still have money in the bank and it's earning interest, and I received just the other day a sizeable royalty check from Scribner's on the three of my books which are still in print. <u>Poems to Solve</u> . . . is going into a paperback edition for schools and it will continue to earn me money. I've promised Scribner's a sequel to it, to be called "More Poems to Solve."[2]

May's mother was thrilled to learn that Zan was a member of the LDS Church. She wrote a warm, friendly letter to Zan, expressing the hope that Zan would bring May back into the church.

May's mother surely did not suspect that May and Zan were more than friends. Her delight in Zan's affiliation with the LDS Church might have been tempered had she known more about Zan's own ambiguous relationship with Mormonism. Although Zan embraced the church's

FIGURE 26. May on Sea Cliff beach, early 1970s. *Literary Estate of May Swenson.*

emphasis on family, like May, she found the LDS position on the role of women problematic. Unlike May, however, Zan attended Mormon services when she was in Sea Cliff and even taught Sunday school.

Sea Cliff provided May with an abundance of new experiences to explore in her poems. During the fall of 1967 she wrote "A Subject of the Waves," which begins:

Today, while a steamshovel rooted in the cove,
leveling a parking lot for the new nightclub,
and a plane drilled between clean clouds in the October sky,
and the flags on the yachts tied in the basin flipped in the wind,
I watched my footsteps mark the sand by the tideline.
Some hollow horseshoe crab shells scuttled there,
given motion by the waves. I threw a plank back to the waves
that they'd thrown up, a sun-dried, sea-swollen stave
from a broken dinghy, one end square, one pointed, painted green.
Watching it float, my attention snagged and could not get off
the hook of its experience. I had launched a subject
of the waves I could not leave until completed.

Except for a brief camping trip in Florida, May and Zan stayed in Sea Cliff throughout the winter of 1968, whose severity strained their inadequate electric heaters and played havoc with the plumbing system, leaving them repeatedly with no hot water. Ice and snow accumulated on the forty-four front steps that provided the only access to their cottage, forcing May to sprinkle the stairs with beach sand to provide traction. In March, May wrote to Elizabeth, "It's been unusually cold and the harbor has frozen over to past the middle three times; during those cold snaps our pipes froze but fortunately didn't break."[3] That first bitter-cold spell would drive May and Zan to warmer climates in future winters.

In the same letter to Elizabeth, May wrote, "I have to do four readings in Minneapolis the first week of May and am doing one in NYC in June. Otherwise, I'm just taking care of the house and writing. Have promised to teach in Greensboro, N.C. next year. Have to do a two-week stint at Bryn Mawr in the fall, as they are giving me a fellowship." May's regular pattern for the next several years involved giving readings, teaching for short-term engagements, judging the occasional contest, writing poems to publish in new collections and in literary magazines—and trying to navigate life with boundlessly energetic Zan.

For May's fifty-fifth birthday in 1968, Zan took her to a baseball game at Yankee Stadium. May caught the spirit of the game in her breezy beloved poem, "Analysis of Baseball," which concludes:

> It's about
> the ball,
> the bat,
> the mitt,
> the bases
> and the fans.
> It's done
> on a diamond,
> and for fun.
> It's about
> home, and it's
> about run.

Although their new life together was rewarding, Zan's peripatetic and impulsive behavior at times exasperated May, who preferred being a homebody. May thrived in contemplative solitude; Zan, who was nineteen years younger, flourished in an atmosphere of frenetic activity. In the fall of 1969 May sank into a blue funk.

On October 29 May wrote to Elizabeth, and being unsure of Elizabeth's whereabouts, she mailed two copies, one to Ouro Preto, the other to San Francisco. May was uncharacteristically open about her low spirits but offered no explanation. "I have been so lost, and depressed—consequently so slothful (and confused)—and this is why I haven't answered your two cards."[4] Perhaps difficulties with Zan prompted May's feelings, and perhaps she was also frustrated with her work. In the same letter, May alluded to complications in the production of *Iconographs*. "I've given them [her publishers] a problem with my typographical 'shapes' and 'frames'—I should probably never have done it this way. You'll probably hate it when you see it, but I'll send you a copy anyway."

May's despondency resonated with Elizabeth, who responded from Ouro Preto. "You say 'lost & depressed' and I shall just let that cover my last six months, but mostly the depressed part of it. . . . I have some PILLS to make me happy—they work pretty well until about 3 PM," Elizabeth wrote.[5] Low spirits seemed contagious. Zan learned in March that her contract as supervisor in the Hicksville School District had not been renewed.

The new decade, however, offered all three women reasons for lifted spirits. In January 1970 May told her mother that she had been invited to read at the Library of Congress in Washington, DC, "and I'm to get the highest fee ever offered to me for one reading—$1000. . . . So in token of this good luck, and just to say 'I love you' I'm enclosing a small check. Which, <u>please</u>, spend on yourself, and don't put it in the savings bank."[6] In the spring, May was inducted into the National Institute of Arts and Letters. She planned her outfit for the event carefully and told her mother, "You may not remember a pair of lace stockings you sent me long ago (you got them in Sweden), well, I'm going to wear them—with a yellow lace dress—to that Ceremonial at the National Institute where I'm to be inaugurated next Tuesday."[7] But earlier she had mused in her diary about the implications of being enshrined in the National Institute. "Why am I there? If distinction comes, can extinction be far behind?" After a long adulthood of striving, professional success was proving unexpectedly problematic, even ominous.

Elizabeth's future also brightened. She accepted Robert Lowell's invitation to take his place at Harvard for two years beginning in 1970. And Zan, whose position in the Hicksville School District had never been a good fit, accepted a teaching position at York College, a division of the City University of New York.

Iconographs was published by Scribner's in the summer of 1970 and was hailed as one of the "50 Books of the Year" by the American Institute of Graphic Arts. In celebration, May and Zan enthusiastically set out on a road trip to explore LDS landmarks in Illinois.[8] May knew her mother would be pleased.

> Rozanne and I visited Nauvoo and Carthage, Illinois, and had such an interesting tour of the Church Restoration property. We brought home a reproduction of the Sun Stone (one of those that used to be on the Nauvoo Temple)—it's only a plaster cast, of course, but beautiful, and it's now on our mantle. . . . It was fascinating to go into Brigham Young's house, Joseph Smith's house, and into the Carthage Jail, all of which have been restored just as they were in the 1800's. A guide tells you of all the events of those times, as you are driven around the grounds in a limousine.[9]

After their return, May's health began to decline. A stiffening in her muscles and joints compromised mobility, and at age fifty-seven, her lungs were noticeably affected by decades of heavy smoking. Any apprehension about the onset of old age was doubtless heightened by the contrast with thirty-eight-year-old Zan's exuberance. On August 24, 1970, May wrote to her friend Ed Field, "Zan is scaring the sh_t out of me by going up her 30 ft. aluminum ladder on [a] steep slope to saw off tree limbs that keep the sun off our terrace."[10]

In late October, while Zan was in Wyoming visiting her sister, May wrote from Sea Cliff to Elizabeth at Harvard.

> I just got back from two days in Wappinger's Falls, N.Y. where I did <u>nine</u> readings, or workshops, or whatever they wanted to

call them, for junior & senior high school kids and teachers. I'm
exhausted, have vowed "Never again!" Just before that I'd been
in Kansas City four days and earned some money reading at
their Poetry Center and a college—and was at Hallmark, hired
to tell the greeting card makers "What's Happening Right Now
in American Poetry." Sounds monstrous, doesn't it? But I had
fun really telling them. I brought a sample case of contemporary
poems (by Snodgrass, Auden, Strand, Jim Wright, others) that
shook them a bit, I think.[11]

Exhausted, May vowed, "Never again!" but in the same letter she
mentioned a new and different type of proposal that she was consider-
ing. "Someone wants me to do translations of a Swedish poet, Tomas
Transtr[öm]er. Have you ever heard of him? Maybe I will, if I like his
book—haven't seen it yet—he's getting some prize or other from the
International Poetry Forum in Pittsburgh."

Tomas Tranströmer, a native of Stockholm, was a psychologist by
training and a poet by avocation. By the time May was introduced to his
poetry in 1970, Tranströmer had published five collections of poems in
Swedish, the first in 1954 when he was twenty-two years old. His most
recent collection, *Seeing in the Dark*, had just come out. Tranströmer's
work fell within the modernist and expressionist/surrealist tradition
and was characterized by clarity, simplicity and nature imagery: a
perfect match for May's skills and interests.

The translation and publication of selected poems by Tranströmer
was a joint endeavor of the Scandinavian Foundation and the Inter-
national Poetry Forum. May collaborated on the project with Leif
Sjöberg, editor of the Twayne Press World Author Series on Nordic
Authors, whom May likely knew from previous part-time employment
at Twayne. Sjöberg had worked closely with other poets, most notably
with W. H. Auden and Muriel Rukeyser.

May confidently embraced the challenge of a new form of poetic
expression, and she wrote Tranströmer an enthusiastic letter on Feb-
ruary 17, 1971.

I am finding it quite an adventure to try to translate your poems
into English—an exciting and rewarding one, in that it acquaints

me with your mind and work—but a precarious one, frankly, because I am almost entirely ignorant of Swedish, in spite of being born of Swedish parents. However, I have strong trust in my instincts and intuition (maybe too much so) and I think their genetic roots are somehow operative, in my own poetry and, possibly, for apprehending yours. At least, I sense affinities between us, behind some of the symbols and images of your poems.

Leif Sj[ö]berg who, fortunately, is providing me with literal renderings of your poems, suggested I send on to you the first versions of what we have done so far. I would be grateful to have your advice and clarification wherever, on the pages enclosed, you find that something is not accurate or could be improved.[12]

The project consumed May's time and attention for a full year. On December 2, 1971, she wrote to Elizabeth:

I got the 100-page ms. of the Tranströmer translations in to Pittsburgh Press the other day. However, Tomas now wants to drop some of the poems, so it'll probably be a smaller selection. Such a lot of business and correspondence has been necessary with this, and I've been at the project a whole year. It's about worn me out. The translating itself was enjoyable—but I'll never do it again.[13]

Despite May's frustrations, *Windows & Stones* was well received when it appeared in 1972, and Elizabeth expressed her approval in February 1973. "I do think that translation of Tranströmer is awfully good, even if you have turned a bit against him, and even if I don't know Swedish—I somehow feel you've done very well by him."[14] And when a "startled" May learned the following month that *Windows & Stones* had been nominated for the National Book Award in translation, she suspected Elizabeth's hand in the book's nomination.[15]

While May was laboring over her translations from Swedish, Zan was assembling an anthology of poems about sports. After the publication of *Sports Poems* in 1971, Zan's editor at Laurel Press urged her to write a book about women in sports. Drawing heavily on her own background, Zan launched a successful series of young adult novels featuring girl athletes. Her first, *Zanballer*, was published in 1971 and spawned subsequent titles like *Zanbanger* in 1977 and *Zanboomer* the following year. In addition, Zan published biographies of celebrated women athletes. She left her teaching position at York College to devote herself full-time to her new writing career and ultimately produced more than forty books on sports and fitness.[16]

During the early 1970s, May experienced a serious and worsening sinus condition accompanied by frequent and debilitating headaches. As these "allergies" became more pronounced and troublesome, May sought the healthful benefits of a dry and sunny climate. After a visit with her sister Grace in California in the fall of 1971, May wrote to Elizabeth: "In L.A. I stayed at my sister's house in [the] Hollywood Hills—sunbathed on the patio—and for 10 days was nearly rid of a stuffed-up nose. Now, back here in the rain, it's miserable."[17] The following month she wrote to her mother. "This winter it's been . . . almost constant stuffiness and runny nose—like hayfever, but it's not that."[18] The problem persisted for years and eventually drove May, who had smoked heavily for her entire adult life, finally to quit using tobacco. "This is Day 12 without a cigarette. It's really weird," she wrote to Elizabeth in 1973.[19] She sought help from a series of doctors, each of whom prescribed new medication, but nothing relieved her symptoms or restored her energy.

As she approached sixty, May's recurrent sickness reawakened thoughts of aging and death, and her mother's failing health in the spring of 1972 intensified these anxieties. May flew to Utah in late May in time to be at her mother's deathbed. Margaret Hellberg Swenson died on June 4, 1972. May spoke at her funeral and read from her mother's journal:

> As a eulogy for my mother I want to read two or three pages from her Diary . . . a specimen of her everyday life. It was a life totally bent on helping others: her family, her husband, her friends and relatives and neighbors—and especially in the service of her God. . . . Her own voice—her speaking voice—provides the "style" of writing, because my mother did not try to be literary. She cared only for truth, and that needs no application of art.[20]

✳

From the mid-1970s through the 1980s, May and Zan abandoned Sea Cliff in winter and traveled frequently during the rest of the year. They spent short intervals at "Unsubdued," the Knudson family's beach house on the Delmarva peninsula, and entire winters in Tucson and Tempe, Arizona, and in Los Angeles.

Restless and gregarious, Zan often set out alone to pursue her own adventures, sometimes causing friction with May. But May did not doubt Zan's love for her or hers for Zan. She wrote to Elizabeth praising Zan's literary success in a genre unusual if not groundbreaking for a female author of the time.

> Zan, as you may not know, quit teaching and became a juvenile writer—recently moved from Dell to Harper's (who will publish her fourth novel, about an Apache Indian girl who becomes a runner on the "Uintah College" track team, and winds up in the Olympics (!) Exciting teen-age stuff. But she talks of trying to go back to teaching (has a PhD. in English Ed. from Stanford) because writing is so tough, advances are so small, and her savings are draining away. But I am trying to keep her at it, because she is a superior writer in her genre, and she is also learning things about herself, as she puts herself into her main characters.[21]

In the same letter, May recounted to Elizabeth a drive she and Zan had taken from Tempe, Arizona, to Provo, Utah, in treacherous weather conditions—and the medical challenges both of them were facing.

> The reason I spent some days in Provo (unscheduled for this trip because it's in deep snow country) was that Zan and I stayed at my sister's place while Z. went to Salt Lake City for a series of gastrointestinal tests; had had chronic stomach ache and was finally diagnosed as having inflammation of the duodenum but not yet to the ulcer stage, so she has to take pills and watch her diet. Meaning she should change some extreme eating habits, like eating nothing one day and a bushel of potato chips the next. Well, we drove through a dangerous blizzard between Jacob's

Lake and Kanab, at night, at about 8,000 feet, without snow tires. . . . So, while I'm at it I'll report my operation: the only time I've ever spent even one night in a hospital—I was at The Desert Samaritan here, in Mesa, three nights—having never had even my tonsils out, or had a baby—made it a "big deal" for me. For about three years I've been going to allergists for chronic nasal congestion, rhinitis, post-nasal drip that led into asthma, got worse and worse; scratch tests never located a cause; it took away my energy and most of the time I couldn't do anything but sniffle, cough, hawk and spit, and sound like a frog when I talked. It was terrible. I quit smoking, but nothing helped. Well, a surgeon here whom I located in the Yellow Pages took an X-ray of my head—No other doctor had thought to do so—and saw a completely puss—no, pus-filled, maxillary sinus. So, operation. And since then, a month ago, I can breathe through my nose, most symptoms are gone (except slight asthma if I breathe cold air)—and my sense of smell is returning.

Despite her optimism in the immediate aftermath of her operation, May's sinus condition returned, which sapped her energy again and dampened her spirits. She bemoaned the depletion of her creativity. There would be an eight-year gap between the publication of *Iconographs* in 1970 and the publication by Little, Brown in 1978 of her eighth volume of poetry, *New & Selected Things Taking Place*. May was uncertain about the future of her career and sought Elizabeth as her sounding board on December 2, 1978:

Scribner's kept me dangling about a new one while letting the others go out of print. Little, Brown took almost two years to produce my New & Selected after asking for the manuscript. All of this was discouraging. Also, for certain personal reasons my powers went into hibernation. But they are warming now—they are coming back. I'm working. I've never had enough chutzba to push for attention. Maybe this book will win a prize, and I'll win back my identity. And maybe not. Doesn't matter. I know who I am. "I'm the one who'll be with me for the rest of my life." That's a quote from [a] poem now in the works.[22]

FIGURE 27. May in Arizona, 1974. *Literary Estate of May Swenson.*

May had, in reality, been more productive in the 1970s than she admitted. She had produced a second volume of her popular riddle poems, *More Poems to Solve*, in 1971, and *Windows & Stones* in 1972. Moreover, to complete her option obligations with Scribner's before leaving them for Little, Brown, in 1976 she published *The Guess and Spell Coloring Book*, a book for children based on riddle poems. Although May hoped for a comeback with her new book, the poem in progress that she quoted to Elizabeth did not project a new burst of confidence but rather resignation to a quiet and solitary old age.

The Rest of My Life

I'm the one
who'll be with me
for the rest of my life.

I'm the one
who'll enjoy myself,
take care of myself,
be loveable, so as to love
myself for the rest
of my life.

Arms, be strong to hold me.
Eyes, be with me.
Will you be with me
for the rest of my life?

I'm the one,
the only one,
the one who won't leave me
for the rest of my life.

Elizabeth responded to May's despondency by working behind the scenes to promote her interests. The following year (1979), May received a longed-for jolt to her career: induction as a Fellow of the Academy of American Poets. Sounding like the enthusiastic May of former days, she wrote to Elizabeth:

It's wonderful luck for me that I've been made a Fellow of the Academy and gifted with $10,000! I know that you had much to do with it. If only I could make you feel my joy and thanks. Although I have other friends among the Chancellors—bless them— your influence is most immense, and without your nod I'm sure this luck could not have happened. Please know that I love you— always will. The money means a lot to me just at this time. The honor just as much—a spur to my work and to my self-belief.[23]

Elizabeth did not deny her role in May's award, admitting in her reply, "I had a hand in that, of course."[24]

Less than a month later, on April 12, 1979, Elizabeth sent May a postcard—a thank-you note for May's gift of a jigsaw puzzle. "This is a rather gloomy card, considering it's almost Easter and that today we have sunshine—yesterday, too, after at least 2 weeks of rain, sleet, snow, winds—& mixtures of all," she began.[25] This was the last May would hear from her old friend. Six months later, on October 6, 1979, Elizabeth Bishop died in her Boston apartment of a cerebral aneurysm. She was sixty-eight years old. May was in Delaware at Unsubdued and did not learn of Elizabeth's death until days later. Rather than entrust her feelings to her diary, May turned to poetry:

In the Bodies of Words
For Elizabeth Bishop (1911–1979)

Tips of the reeds silver in sunlight. A cold wind
sways them, it hisses through quills of the pines.
Sky is clearest blue because so cold. Birds drop down
in the dappled yard: white breast of nuthatch, slate
catbird, cardinal the color of blood.

Until today in Delaware, Elizabeth, I didn't know
you died in Boston a week ago. How can it be
you went from the world without my knowing?
Your body turned to ash before I knew. Why was there
no tremor of the ground or air? No lightning flick
between our nerves? How can I believe? How grieve?

I walk the shore. Scraped hard as a floor by wind.
Screams of terns. Smash of heavy waves. Wind rips
the corners of my eyes. Salty streams freeze on my face.
A life is little as a dropped feather. Or split shell
tossed ashore, lost under sand. . . . But vision lives!
Vision, potent, regenerative, lives in bodies of words.
Your vision lives, Elizabeth, your words
from lip to lip perpetuated.

Two days have passed. Enough time, I think, for death
to be over. As if your death were not *before* my knowing.
For a moment I jump back to when all was well and ordinary.
Today I could phone to Boston, say Hello. . . . Oh, no!
Time's tape runs forward only. There is no replay.

Light hurts. Yet the sky is dull today. I walk the shore.
I meet a red retriever, young, eager, galloping
out of the surf. At first I do not notice his impairment.
His right hind leg is missing. Omens. . . .
I thought I saw a rabbit in the yard this morning.
It was a squirrel, its tail torn off. Distortions. . . .

Ocean is gray again today, old and creased aluminum
without sheen. Nothing to see on that expanse.
Except, far out, low over sluggish waves, a long
clotted black string of cormorants trails south.
Fog-gray rags of foam swell in scallops up the beach,
their outlines traced by a troupe of pipers—
your pipers, Elizabeth!—their racing legs like spokes
of tiny wire wheels.

Faintly the flying string can still be seen.
It swerves, lowers, touching the farthest tips of waves.
Now it veers, appears to shorten, points straight out.
It slips behind the horizon. Vanished.

But vision lives, Elizabeth. Your vision multiplies,
is magnified in the bodies of words.
Not vanished, your vision lives from eye to eye,
your words from lip to lip perpetuated.

Bethany, Delaware October 13–15, 1979

Elizabeth Bishop had been May's correspondent for nearly thirty
years and the person most in tune with her poetic and literary sen-
sibilities. The shock of her death and May's delayed knowledge of

it complicated her emotions ("How can I believe? How grieve?") and reminded May that death was the great equalizer ("A life is little as a dropped feather"). May entered the 1980s with renewed dedication to the cause of poetry. She capped her career with honors and achievements that she and Elizabeth would have delighted in celebrating together.

In 1980 May was invited to participate in First Lady Rosalyn Carter's Salute to Poetry and American Poets at the White House. That same year, she was elevated to Chancellor of the American Academy of Poets, a position she held until her death. In 1981 May received Yale's prestigious Bollingen Prize, awarded every two years to one or more living American poets. She was commended for her "clarity of vision" and her "accessible language." Elizabeth Bishop, had she lived, might have been a co-recipient. As it happened, the committee issued a special citation, a poignant addendum to May's award: "We wish to recognize and acknowledge the debt of American letters to the late Elizabeth Bishop."[26]

In January 1982 May composed "Some Quadrangles," which she read as the guest poet at the Phi Beta Kappa Literary Exercises, a traditional part of Harvard's graduation ceremonies since the eighteenth century. And in 1987 she received the jewel in her crown, a MacArthur Foundation Fellowship in the astonishing amount of $380,000. In keeping with her lifelong practice of generosity, May gave each of her brothers and sisters a "Swenson Fellowship" of $3,000 and smaller amounts to her many nieces and nephews.[27] Fittingly, she was in Logan with her family when she received notice of the MacArthur. The occasion was the celebration of double honors conferred on her by her alma mater—an honorary PhD and the Centennial Recognition Award.

The graduation ceremony and the conferral of May's honorary PhD survive on videotape.[28] A dour May, flanked by three male co-recipients who tower over her, marches in procession along a tree-lined path to the strains of "Pomp and Circumstance," the "Triumphal March" from *Aida*, and finally Handel's "Music for the Royal Fireworks." Bedecked in traditional academic regalia, May wears a robe that partially covers her plain black pants but reveals her sensible shoes. May, who had never aspired to a PhD, earned or honorary, regarded contrived touches of grandeur as unimportant. In an interview conducted by her old friend Edith Welch Morgan for the *Herald Journal*, May said:

FIGURE 28. May Swenson, March 1982. *Photo by Candy MacMahon.*

I have not built my career by the usual academic route and have not sought a master's degree or doctorate degree nor accepted offers of a tenured position, and so it was with special surprise and pleasure that I learned of my university's intention to confer an honorary degree upon me.[29]

In the video, May accepts the honor awkwardly. "I just want to say that I feel as if I know a great deal more than before. Thank you, all."[30] This wryly humorous remark was a quietly discordant affirmation that an honorary degree could not have made her more knowledgeable than she already was.

May's ambiguous discomfort that day became the subject of "My Name Was Called," which she began composing in Logan shortly after the ceremony and completed four months later in Sea Cliff. In the poem, May conflates her baptismal and her award ceremonies and emphasizes the uneasiness she felt in both situations, as a child and sixty years later as a mature woman:

My Name Was Called

. . . .

Old teetering monkeylike babylike head
under black gold-tasselled stiff platter-
like hat, sixty years later, the naked ears
stick out. My name is called. Pulled up,
out of the deafening bubbles, boosted up
to sit in the white chair. Murmured over
my head the rapid redundant prayer. Wet
head bowed beneath the hands laid heavy there.
Warm, suggestively wet, my white ruffled
panties streamed in the slick seat.
The silk and velvet lifted. My spotted
hand went up. Awkward. Huge in merciless
light my face on TV in front of my
actual face. My little ignorant ugly patient
helpless head on screen the freshest horror.
The greatest honor. Forced to confront,
but not forced to smile. Child eyes behind
old pouched lashless eyes, never again able
to soften the truth of my future face.
Face immersed, but still afloat over the years.
Head pressed under and blessed. Pulled up
and invested. I didn't know what would be
done, in the white dress or in the black,
when my name was called.

Later that same year, May published her ninth collection of poems,
In Other Words, and in 1988 she was named a Literary Lion of the New
York Public Library, whose stone lions flanking the entrance steps had
given her strength and consolation during those difficult early years
in New York.

May and Zan continued living at home during the summer and
traveling at other times. In Sea Cliff they socialized with a small cir-
cle of younger friends, including Alice Geffen and her partner Carole

Berglie, both of whom were involved in the literary world as editors and authors. May and Alice first met in 1975 at Author Appreciation Day, an event sponsored by the Sea Cliff Library.[31] Alice, who had a special interest in poetry, owned a bookstore and played chess. May, Zan, Alice, and Carole became an easy foursome, and with May as their mentor they frequently made birdwatching expeditions together. Alice and Carole visited May and Zan in Arizona, Florida, and Delaware, both at Unsubdued and at the house Zan later built in Ocean View. And when Zan was away from Sea Cliff, Carole and Alice looked in on May and drove her on errands and outings or into the city.

A fellow writer, birdwatcher, and chess player named Sallie Reynolds became another Sea Cliff friend. Sallie knew May in her last years and had spent the weekend before May's death with her. In 2020 she recounted her memories.

I have been slowly remembering May. Indeed, to the point that I have dreamed about her. It is both emotionally wonderful and terrible. May came to my shoulder, maybe an inch above. I'm now about 5'4", but then I was nearly 5'7"—so short, yes, and very small. With a small round head she denigrated but I loved. She was a little walnut of a person. Or acorn, the ones with the slightly fuzzy caps. I loved May, her little nut self and that wonderful brain, wildly adventurous yet so precise. I always came away from May *feeling* something new, seeing the thing in its ecosystem down to the very cells. And then the sense of kinship.

I met her at a reading, somewhere on Long Island, that Alice Geffen invited me to. It must have been about 1983–84, maybe 1985. It may even have been at the Sea Cliff library. . . . We'd discovered we were neighbors on the waterfront. May and Zan invited me to go birding with them. . . . I started playing chess with May. She liked it, probably because she won!

I was in a swivet over something, once, and I asked May, "What I should do?" It was a personal thing and very painful (whatever it was, it's gone!). And May thought for a long moment, and then said: "I find that doing nothing is often the best thing." Zan said May had a genius for relationships. That she could hold on to them, hold them together. And that quiet capacity of not stirring someone else's flames may have been an important part of that.

In 1987–89, I visited them in Delaware several times, once to experience thousands of migrating Snow Geese. It was a cacophony. I saw my one and only Tricolored Heron there. Their house, Zan's house, in Ocean View, was tall and small. The bottom floor was a garage and workshop. I think Zan had a motorcycle. They lived on the second floor, which had a view of the ocean from one or two windows. There was a balcony where May and I played chess if it was warm enough. The living quarters had a large living / dining / kitchen area and one bedroom, and a bath. May and Zan went down every winter for several years.

During the last two visits there, May and I talked about death, I am not sure what started that. And that's when she told me that if Elvis could die, then so could we all. And that she felt she herself was near death. As I said on the phone, it is to my eternal sorrow that I said the usual "comforting" things rather than listening. . . . But I was horrified at the thought of May's death.

May sometimes spoke of herself as old and ugly. She didn't like anything about getting old, it seemed to diminish her. Yet she made no attempt to disguise what was happening. She kept her hair very short and straight and wore not even a touch of lipstick.

She was not a bitter person yet was truly bitter about her waning capacities for walking and exploring. Some of our birding hikes were uncomfortable for that reason. I see now that she was clearly struggling to come to grips with her aging, and not being terribly successful. I was twenty-five years younger and maybe that made these things come out. She would say, "You and Zan go on ahead, I'll catch up." And I'd say, "I don't want to."[32]

Sallie visited May in Ocean View on the weekend of December 2–3, 1989. The following morning May died at the age of seventy-six of a heart attack brought on by chronic asthma and high blood pressure. Sallie traveled to Logan to attend the memorial service on December 9, 1989, but not being a Mormon like Zan, she was excluded from the ceremony.

I have a few moving letters to me from Zan after May's death, one right after we got back from the Mormon services in Logan (since I am not Mormon, I was not allowed in the temple to hear her eulogy, and I sat on a bench outside the closed temple door, in a rage!). The letters from Zan are heart-breaking, in Zan's wild way. The grief she felt is so controlled.

Sallie recalled another especially significant memory of May.

I was thinking about how much May liked Sappho. I couldn't find my Sappho, translated by Mary Barnard. But got it from the library and sure enough, I remembered May and Sappho. We were walking along the beach in front of her house—and it was a mess from a storm. I was picking through the plastic and dead stars and empty horseshoe crab shells and she laughed and said, "If you're squeamish, don't prod the beach rubble!"

May never hesitated to prod any aspect of life, nor was she squeamish about anything, including her own death. "Guilty" was one of May's last poems:

Guilty

I hadn't finished being young,
hadn't learned how to be,
when I noticed I'd been semi-old
for some time.
And now that, beyond that,
I've arrived—or, *gone*
is the right word—far
beyond "beyond the shadow
of a doubt" to that low state
labeled "old," I'm incredulous
at the extent of my self-blindness
since the beginning.

Guilty, I declare myself.
And, too late at this final state
to begin to learn how
to begin to be.
Self-condemned, confined
to the cell of old age, I'm
sentenced to . . . life!
A term pityfully short.
Time of execution, any early
morning. It's a secret.
It'll be a surprise.

ACKNOWLEDGMENTS

I EXTEND HEARTFELT THANKS TO:

Emily Williamson, my literary agent, for her steadfast optimism and diligence; Anne Savarese, my editor at Princeton University Press, for her insight, patience, and kindness; the entire editing, production, and design teams at PUP, especially James Collier, Emma Wagh, Theresa Liu, Katie Osborne, Haley Chung, and copyeditor Daniel Simon; Carole Berglie, literary executor of the Swenson estate and my Sea Cliff neighbor, for her invitation to undertake this project and for providing access to May's diaries and related material; Paul Crumbley and David Hoak, the dynamic and indispensable duo, for saving me from errors (any that remain are my own), unfailingly urging me on, and graciously writing the foreword; Peter Amram, my longtime friend and colleague, for nimbly, cheerfully, and relentlessly punching up my prose.

Lisa Turetsky, May's niece, for answering my questions instantly and for sending me packages of photographs and difficult-to-find printed material; the staff of the Special Collections Department at Washington University's Olin Library, particularly Joel Minor, curator of modern literature and manuscripts, and Kate Goldkamp, reference supervisor, for pampering me in St. Louis and sending me scans when I was back in New York; Clint Pumphrey, manuscript curator, University Libraries, Utah State University, for helping me navigate the Swenson Papers in Logan; Sallie Reynolds, Ed Field, Grace Schulman, and Andrew Rudin, May's dear friends whose adoration of May has been contagious, for their warmth and accessibility; Barbara Kates-Garnick and Stephen Carter for their kind help and encouragement.

My many friends, particularly Carol Poll, Mary and Floyd Linton, Raymond Derrien, Jessie Arner, Matthew Stevenson, Betsy Miller, Mary Ann Clark, Alexandra Troy, and Ned Ligon, for having done what dear friends do: they listened, gave sound advice, and always supported me.

Finally, I am thankful that my husband, Jim Campbell; our children, Angela Campbell and Benedict Campbell; and my sister, Christina Brucia, who have been my personal powerhouse of protean helpmates, can now reclaim my full attention.

Alice Helen Methfessel. Robert Lowell letters copyright © by Harriet Lowell and Sheridan Lowell. Compilation copyright © 2008 by Thomas J. Travisano. Reprinted by permission of Farrar, Straus and Giroux. All rights reserved.

Letters from James Laughlin to Alfred Kreymborg, February 8, 1949; and James Laughlin to May Swenson, September 25 [1950], copyright © 2024 by Leila Laughlin Javitch, Amelia Laughlin, and Walker Laughlin. Reprinted by permission of New Directions Publishing Corp.

ABBREVIATIONS

People:
AKa = Arnold Kates
AKr = Alfred Kreymborg
BSH = Beth Swenson Hall
DAS = Dan A. Swenson
DHS = Dan H. Swenson
EF = Edward Field
GFS = George F. Swenson
GHG = Gladys Hobbs Goodall
GR = Grant Redford
IR = Ione Redford
JL = James Laughlin
MHS = Margaret Hellberg Swenson
MS = May Swenson
MSW = Margaret Swenson Woodbury
PES = Paul E. Swenson
PS = Pearl Schwartz
RK = Rozanne Knudson
RSE = Ruth Swenson Eyre
SB = Suzzanne Bigelow
SN = Sylvia Norman
TT = Tomas Tranströmer

Archives & Literary Estate:
WUSC = Washington University, Olin Library, Special Collections
USUSC = Utah State University, Merrill-Cazier Library, Special Collections
LEMS = Literary Estate of May Swenson

Other:
LHA = Look Homeward, Angel
OTATR = Of Time and the River

NOTES

Chapter 1. My Life in a Narrative

1 The details of the lives of Swen and Thilda Swenson are taken from "A Short Biography of Swen Swenson and His Wife Thilda Pehrson" (1953), by Dan Arthur Swenson, LEMS.
2 DAS, "A Short Biography," 7.
3 DAS, "A Short Biography," 8.
4 DAS, "Autobiography of D. A. Swenson," 16, WUSC, Box 167, Folder 5393.
5 DAS, "Autobiography," 28.
6 DAS, "Autobiography," 35.
7 DAS, "Autobiography," 35–36.
8 DAS, "Autobiography," 61.
9 DAS, "Autobiography," 69.
10 DAS, "Autobiography," 80.
11 DAS, "Autobiography," 79–80.
12 DAS, "Autobiography," 82.
13 DAS, "Autobiography," 100–102.
14 RK and SB, *May Swenson*, 9.
15 RK and SB, *May Swenson*, 13.
16 RK and SB, *May Swenson*, 12.
17 DAS, "Autobiography," 108.

Chapter 2. An Innocent Era

1 DAS, "Autobiography," 113.
2 DAS, "Autobiography," 113.
3 DAS, "Autobiography," 114.
4 DHS, Taped interview conducted by Mary Weaver, June 11, 1994, WUSC, Box 222.
5 MSW, Taped interview conducted by Mary Weaver, May 31, 1994, WUSC, Box 222.
6 RSE, Taped interview conducted by Mary Weaver, June 11, 1994, WUSC, Box 222.
7 DHS said that he was five years old when he moved into the house at 669 E 5th Street N; Dan was born on February 5, 1916, thus placing the Swenson family's move in 1921. RSE, however, in *The Immigrants*, sets the date for the move in the spring of 1922. May's equating of "mechanical engineering" with "woodworking" can be found in MS, "An Interview with Karla Hammond," 134.
8 DAS, "Autobiography," 120; RSE, *The Immigrants*, 141–48.
9 GFS, Taped interview conducted by Mary Weaver, June 8, 1994, WUSC, Box 222.
10 DHS, RSE, MSW, Interviews.
11 RSE, Interview; RK and SB, *May Swenson*, 28.
12 GFS, Interview.
13 MSW, Interview.
14 BSH, Taped interview conducted by Mary Weaver, June 9, 1994, WUSC, Box 222; GFS, Interview; PES, Taped interview conducted by Mary Weaver, June 9, 1994, WUSC, Box 222.
15 MS, "An Interview with Karla Hammond," 134.
16 GFS, Interview.
17 MS, "An Interview with Cornelia Draves and Mary Jane Fortunato," 113–14.
18 RK, *The Wonderful Pen*, 22.

19 RK, *The Wonderful Pen*, 16, 19; RSE, Interview.

20 MS, "An Interview with Karla Hammond," 134.

21 RK and SB, *May Swenson*, 30–31.

22 RK, *The Wonderful Pen*, 16, 18.

23 RK and SB, *May Swenson*, 27.

24 RK, *The Wonderful Pen*, 22.

25 Jason Cornelius, adult fiction and special collection librarian, Logan Library, email to the author, April 29, 2020.

26 Details and quotations taken from MSW to RK, n.d., LEMS.

27 George R. Hill, patriarchal blessing for May Swenson, October 19, 1925, USUSC, May Swenson Papers Addendum, Series I, Box 1, Folder 1.

28 BSH, Interview.

29 DHS, Interview.

30 GFS, Interview.

31 MHS to MS, n.d., LEMS.

32 RSE, Interview.

33 RK and SB, *May Swenson*, 27.

34 As quoted in RK and SB, *May Swenson*, 26–27.

Chapter 3. Creature Both Male and Female

1 MSW, Interview.

2 The Logan Library has digitized a complete set of *The Amphion*, the Logan High School yearbook, beginning with the year 1924, http://library.loganutah.org/archives /Yearbooks.

3 An undated page from *The Grizzly* bearing May's story "Christmas Day," in the literary estate of May Swenson, also features the winning poem in the school's Christmas Poem Contest. The references to Christmas indicate that this issue of *The Grizzly* was published in 1928, shortly before Christmas, during the first semester of May's junior year.

4 RK, *The Wonderful Pen*, 28.

5 See USAC yearbook, *The Buzzer* (1932), 236, https://issuu.com/usudigitalcommons/docs /scaua-25p05s07-1932.

6 As quoted by Parson in "'Leftward March,'" 167.

7 McCormick, "The Great Depression."

8 "Campus Gayety Hit by Slump," *New York Times*, October 3, 1932.

9 Parson, "'Leftward March,'" 165–66.

10 Parson, "'Leftward March,'" 170.

11 DHS, Interview.

12 Yearbook page, LEMS.

13 MSW, Interview.

14 RSE, Interview.

15 RK and SB, *May Swenson*, 34.

16 MSW, Interview.

17 GFS, Interview.

18 MS, "Fruits."

19 "Popular Couple Wed in Church," *Salt Lake Tribune*, May 7, 1940.

20 MS to AV, November 12, 1947, WUSC, Box 100, Folder 3905.

21 RK and SB, *May Swenson*, 34.

22 Parson, "'Leftward March,'" 174–80.

23 DHS, Interview.

24 Parson, "'Leftward March,'" 174.

25 For biographical information about Ray West, see the Ray B. West Papers, USUSC; "Death: Ray B. West," *Deseret News* (Salt Lake City), April 8, 1990.

26 RK, *The Wonderful Pen*, 38.

27 MSW, Interview.

28 RK, *The Wonderful Pen*, 31.

29 RK and SB, *May Swenson*, 27.

30 Celebrated musicians in later years would set some forty of May's poems to music.

31 RK, *The Wonderful Pen*, 74, 80.

32 Logan History–Historic Photo Collection, Logan Library, Picture ID 312, 845.

33 *Provo Daily Herald*, September 5, 1928.

34 PES, Interview.

35 Some examples of Eugene Gant's pursuit of glory in Wolfe's *Look Homeward, Angel* and *Of Time and the River* include: "The proud horns blared, he tasted glory" (*LHA*, 220); "In Eugene's mind, wealth and love and glory melted into a symphonic noise" (*LHA*, 554); "he would make all of the glory, power, and beauty of the earth his own" (*OTATR* 929); "knowing only that we were young, and drunk, and twenty, and that the power of mighty poetry was within us, and the glory of the great earth lay before us!" (*OTATR*, 1045).

36 See, for example, Christopher C. Burt, "North America's Most Intense Heat Wave," *Weather Underground*, August 28, 2018, www.wunderground.com/cat6/North-Americas-Most-Intense-Heat-Wave-July-and-August-1936; "Heat Wave of 1936," https://project.geo.msu.edu/geogmich/sig_weath_events.html; "All-Time Extremes Central Park, NY," *Weather*, www.weather.gov/media/okx/Climate/CentralPark/extremes.pdf.

37 "The Jacob's Pillow Story."

38 Jack Anderson, "Barton Mumaw, 88, Dancer; Member of Ted Shawn Troupe," *New York Times*, June 21, 2001.

Chapter 4. The Taste of Love

1 "Women of USU: Then and Now, Classics, Grace Fisher and Frances Titchener." *Utah State Today*, June 24, 2020, www.usu.edu/today/story/women-of-usu-then-and-now-classics -grace-fisher-and-frances-titchener.

2 Regina Jais is best known for two travel books: *Legendary Germany* (1897) and *Legendary France* (1931).

3 Jessie Tarbox Beals, the celebrated New York photographer, was Regina Jais's neighbor. The New-York Historical Society owns a photograph of Jais's rooftop garden, taken by Tarbox in 1936 or 1937.

4 For information about Charles Zig Shye, see Miller, "The Robert Burnett Smith House."

5 Knudson, "The Love Poems of May Swenson," in *Body My House*, 23.

6 MS, "Music Maker."

7 *Ansel Adams, Exhibition of Photographs. William Einstein, Paintings and Drawings; Arthur G. Dove New Oils and Water Colors.*

8 Frank S. Nugent, "At the Filmarte," *New York Times*, April 21, 1937.

9 John Nerber, "Stories to Tell," *New York Times*, January 27, 1952.

10 The details of Anzia Yezierska's life between her affair with John Dewey in 1917 and her hiring of May Swenson in 1937 are taken from Dearborn, *Love in the Promised Land*, 140–61.

11 Mangione, *The Dream and the Deal*, 45.

12 Banks, *First-Person America*, xviii; Mangione, *The Dream and the Deal*, 47–48.

13 MS to GHG, September 8, 1937, LEMS.

14 For information about Hugh Stix, Friederike Beer-Monti, and the Artists' Gallery, see "Artists' Gallery Records, 1936–1966," Archives of American Art, Smithsonian American Art Museum; "One for the Show," *Time* 66, no. 13 (September 26, 1955); "Hugh Sylvan Stix, 85, Art Gallery Founder," *New York Times*, July 30, 1992.

15 Nothing more is known of this poem by Swenson.

16 "John Opper"; "John Opper, 85, Abstract Painter," *New York Times*, Oct. 7, 1994.

17 "Ralph Rosenborg."

18 For information on Ferry's early career, see "Thetas in the News: Alpha Lambda's Artist."

19 Sterling appears to have vanished from the art scene; I found no trace of him in museum or gallery records.

20 Papers of Jennings Yehudah Tofel (1891–1959), "Biographical Note," Center for Jewish History. https://archives.cjh.org/repositories/7/resources/3280; "Yude (Jennings) Tofel."

21 From Robert Frost's poem "Two Tramps in Mud Time," *Saturday Review of Literature*, October 6, 1934, reprinted in *A Further Range* (1936).

22 "Anti-Hitler March Blocks Times Sq.," *New York Times*, March 20, 1938, 35.

Chapter 5. I Have Yet to Find My Love

1 Mangione, *The Dream and the Deal*, 193–94.

2 Steinbeck, *Travels with Charley*, 134; Mumford, "Writers' Project," 306 (quoted in Mangione, *The Dream and the Deal*, 216).

3 Mangione, *The Dream and the Deal*, 172.

4 Mangione, *The Dream and the Deal*, 272.

5 Banks, *First-Person America*, xvii.

6 Frank Byrd as quoted in Banks, *First-Person America*, xvi–xvii.

7 Mangione, *The Dream and the Deal*, 255.

8 Mangione, *The Dream and the Deal*, 271–72.

9 May's thirty-three interviews in the Library of Congress can be read online at www.loc .gov/collections/federal-writers-project/?fa=location:new+york%7Ccontributor:swenson, +may&sp=1.

10 May Swenson and Mrs. John Elterich, "Bronx 1885," Library of Congress, www.loc.gov /item/wpalh001607.

11 *Investigation and Study of the Work Projects Administration*, 212.

12 Dorn, preface to *The Gate beyond the Sun*, by Vrbovska, iii.

13 Swenson and Vrbovska, *Czechoslovakian Lore*.

14 MS to AKa, n.d., WUSC, Box 84, Folder 3144.

15 RK, notes, LEMS.

16 For information about Harry Kemp, see Wetzsteon, *Republic of Dreams*; Brevda, *Harry Kemp*; Mangione, *The Dream and the Deal*; "Harry Kemp, 76, Poet Producer," *New York Times*, August 9, 1960; MS and Harry Kemp, "Tramp Poet," Library of Congress, www .loc.gov/item/wpalh001639.

17 MS and Kemp, "Tramp Poet."

18 MS and Kemp, "Tramp Poet."

19 Later published as "Nightly Vision" and "Dream of Diligence."

20 For information about the Raven Poetry Circle, see "Guide to the Raven Poetry Circle of Greenwich Village Collection"; Maxwell, "Village Poets," 15; Kiter, "Quoth the Raven Poetry Circle."

21 "Guide to the Raven Poetry Circle."

22 "Poets in Village Get Day in the Sun," *New York Times*, May 22, 1933.

23 Maxwell, "Village Poets," 15.
24 Bradley, *The Yale Younger Poets Anthology*, xxix.
25 "The Salty Thing I Taste," WUSC, Box 224, Folder 5133.2.
26 "Stewart's Cafeteria."
27 *The WPA Guide to New York City*, 140.
28 Gordon, *Live at the Village Vanguard*, 27.

Chapter 6. Dreams and Ashes

1 MS to DAS, September 24, 1940, WUSC, Box 98.
2 GFS, Interview.
3 Ralph Thompson, "Books of the Times," *New York Times*, August 24, 1939.
4 Fred T. Marsh, "A New Novel by Vardis Fisher," *New York Times*, August 27, 1939.
5 MS to DAS, September 24, 1940, WUSC, Box 98.
6 MS to DAS, September 24, 1940, WUSC, Box 98.
7 MS to DAS, September 24, 1940, WUSC, Box 98.
8 MS, "Without having to phrase it," WUSC, Box 149, Folder 5088.
9 MS, "How can I get it all down," WUSC, Box 144, Folder 4937.
10 RK and SB, *May Swenson*, 45.
11 "Guide to the Raven Poetry Circle of Greenwich Village Collection," MS 2921.
12 MS, "About the Baizermans," WUSC, Box 42, Folder 4879.
13 RK and SB, *May Swenson*, 45.
14 For information about the life of Alfred Kreymborg, see AKr, *Troubadour*; Norris, "American Troubadour"; "Alfred Kreymborg," Poetry Foundation.
15 AKr, *Troubadour*, 125–26.
16 AKr, *Troubadour*, 128.
17 For information about *Glebe* and *Others*, see Allen, "*Glebe* and *Others*."
18 MS to GFS, April 4, 1941, WUSC, Box 98, Folder 3813.
19 MS to GFS, April 24, 1941, WUSC, Box 98, Folder 3813.
20 As quoted by RK and SB, *May Swenson*, 48–49.
21 MS to AV, September 6, 1942, LEMS.
22 "Surrealist," also titled "In a Mirror," "Tiger's Passion" and "Tiger's Ghost."
23 See AKr's introduction to *Seventeen and One*.
24 AKa to MS, February 23, 1944, WUSC, Box 28, Folder 1116.
25 MS to GFS, December 1944 or January 1945, WUSC, Box 98, Folder 3813.
26 AKa to MS, July 25, 1945, WUSC, Box 28, Folder 1116.
27 MS to GFS, September 1945, WUSC, Box 98, Folder 3813.
28 Letter from Margit and her husband, Dezso, to AV, October 4, 1945, LEMS.
29 MSW, Interview.
30 RK and SB, *May Swenson*, 49.
31 This and the next ten quotations are from MSW, Interview.
32 See RK and SB, *May Swenson*, 49.
33 Knudson, *The Wonderful Pen*, 59.
34 RK, *The Wonderful Pen*, 61; RK and SB, *May Swenson*, 55–56.
35 AV to MS, October 28, November 3–5, 1947, WUSC, Box 63, Folder 2293.
36 MS to AV, November 12, 1947, WUSC, Box 100, Folder 3905.
37 LEMS.
38 AV to MS, February 1, 1948, WUSC, Box 63, Folder 2293.
39 AV to MS, February 2, 1948, WUSC, Box 63, Folder 2293.
40 AV to MS, February 3, 1948, WUSC, Box 63, Folder 2293.

Chapter 7. I Can Live Free Inside

1 Cantwell, *Manhattan*, 100.

2 Cantwell, *Manhattan*, 98.

3 SN to MS, September 1948, UWSC, Box 42, Folder 1603.

4 "The Bad Luck Diary," 1985, LEMS.

5 "Neither Wanting More" and "Dreams and Ashes," in *The Complete Love Poems of May Swenson*; "In Love Made Visible," *Ms.* 1, no. 4 (1991), and in *The Complete Love Poems*.

6 AKa to MS, December 1948, WUSC, Box 28, Folder 1116.

7 JL to AKr, February 8, 1949, WUSC, Box 107, Folder 4030.

8 Mel Gussow, "James Laughlin, Publisher with Bold Taste, Dies at 83," *New York Times*, November 14, 1997. The details of James Laughlin's life are taken from this obituary and from "James Laughlin," Poetry Foundation.

9 AKr to MS, March 15, 1949, WUSC, Box 30, Folder 1194.

10 PES, "A Figure in the Tapestry," 33.

11 PES, "A Figure in the Tapestry," 29.

12 DAS to MS, March 9, 1950, WUSC, Box 59, Folder 2162.

13 RK and SB, *May Swenson*, 74.

14 May Sarton, a year older than May Swenson, was born in Belgium. She fled with her family after Germany invaded Belgium in 1915 and grew up in Cambridge, Massachusetts. Sarton was a prolific writer who published more than forty volumes of prose and poetry.

15 Lion Feuchtwanger was a German novelist and a harsh critic of Adolf Hitler. *Success*, written in 1930, is the story of the persecution of a curator at an art museum. It is the first volume in his Wartesaal Trilogy. Feuchtwanger was rescued from Nazi Germany with the help of Eleanor Roosevelt and the American diplomat Harry Bingham.

16 As quoted by Norris, "American Troubadour," 69.

17 David Bird, "Elizabeth Ames, Creator of Yaddo, Upstate Cultural Haven, Dies at 92," *New York Times*, March 30, 1977.

18 Yaddo Records, Manuscripts and Archives Division, New York Public Library.

19 JL to MS, September 25 [1950], WUSC, Box 30, Folder 1231.

20 MS, "Appearances," in *Made with Words*, 31–45.

21 MS, "Appearances," *New Directions in Prose and Poetry* 13 (1951): 69–82.

22 MS, "Appearances," in *Made with Words*, 31.

23 As quoted in Bishop and Lowell, *Words in Air*, 110.

24 MS to PS, October 19, 1950, USUSC, Box 1, Folder 17.

25 AKr to MS, April 13, 1951, WUSC, Box 30, Folder 1195.

26 AKr to MS, April 19, 1951, WUSC, Box 30, Folder 1195.

Chapter 8. I Am One of Those to Whom Miracles Happen

1 MS to DAS, May 29, 1951, WUSC, Box 98, Folder 3810.

2 MS, "Chronology," in *Collected Poems*, 718.

3 MS to DAS, May 29, 1951, WUSC, Box 98, Folder 3810.

4 MS to AKr, July 6, 1951, WUSC, Box 85, Folder 3912.

5 MS to AKr, n.d., WUSC, Box 85, Folder 3912.

6 MS to EB, June 24, 1958, WUSC, Box 103, Folder 4003.

7 MS to EB, October 11, 1951, WUSC, Box 103, Folder 3996.

8 MS to EB, on or about October 18, 1951, WUSC, Box 103, Folder 3996.

9 MS to SN, April 14, 1952, WUSC, Box 90, Folder 3452.

10 MS to SN, April 14, 1952, WUSC, Box 90, Folder 3452.

11 MS to SN, April 21, 1952, WUSC, Box 90, Folder 3452.

12 MS to SN, April 21, 1952, WUSC, Box 90, Folder 3452.

13 MS to SN, April 14, 1952, WUSC, Box 90, Folder 3452.

14 Moe, "The Songs of Howard Swanson," 67.

15 MS to EB, March 10, 1953, WUSC, Box 103, Folder 3996.

16 EB to MS, February 12, 1953, WUSC, Box 103, Folder 3996.

17 MS to EB, April 7, 1953, WUSC, Box 103, Folder 3996.

18 MS to EB, March 10, 1953, WUSC, Box 103, Folder 3996.

19 MS to EB, March 10, 1953, WUSC, Box 103, Folder 3996.

20 MS to EB, March 10, 1953, WUSC, Box 103, Folder 3996.

21 EB to MS, March 20, 1953, WUSC, Box 103, Folder, 3996.

22 EB to MS, July 27, 1953, WUSC, Box 103, Folder 3997.

23 EB to MS, August 10, 1953, WUSC, Box 103, Folder 3997.

24 MS to EB, September 14, 1953, WUSC, Box 103, Folder 3997.

25 MS to EB, October 16, 1953, WUSC, Box 103, Folder 3997.

26 MS to EB, October 16, 1953, WUSC, Box 103, Folder 3997.

27 MS to EB, December 11, 1953, WUSC, Box 103, Folder 3997.

28 EB to MS, December 26, 1953, WUSC, Box 103, Folder 3997.

29 EB to MS, November 20, 1953, WUSC, Box 103, Folder 3997.

30 MS to EB, December 11, 1953, WUSC, Box 103, Folder 3997.

31 MS to EB, January 25, 1954, WUSC, Box 103, Folder 3998.

32 MS to Family, June 15, 1954, WUSC, Box 98, Folder 3808.

33 RSE, Interview, June 11, 1994.

34 MSW, Interview, May 31, 1994.

35 BSH, Interview, June 9, 1994.

36 EB to MS, October 15, 1954, WUSC, Box 103, Folder 3998.

37 MS to EB, December 5, 1954, WUSC, Box 103, Folder 3998.

38 MS to EB, February 6, 1955, WUSC, Box 103, Folder 3999.

39 MS to EB, June 22, 1955, WUSC, Box 102, Folder 3999.

40 For an account of the increased tension between May and Pearl, see EF, *The Man Who Would Marry Susan Sontag*, 90–91.

41 EF, *The Man Who Would Marry Susan Sontag*, 90.

42 EF, *The Man Who Would Marry Susan Sontag*, 90–91.

43 MS to EB, August 24, 1955, WUSC, Box 103, Folder 3999.

44 EB to MS, September 6, 1955, WUSC, Box 103, Folder 3999.

45 EB to MS, February 18, 1956, WUSC, Box 103, Folder 4000.

46 MS to EB, February 29, 1956, WUSC, Box 103, Folder 4000.

47 "The Centaur," written in 1954, was first published in *Western Review* in 1956.

48 MS to Family, May 6, 1956, WUSC, Box 98, Folder 3807.

49 MS to EB, February 13, 1956, WUSC, Box 103, Folder 4000.

50 MS to EB, January 6, 1957, WUSC, Box 103, Folder 4002.

51 MS to EB, January 6, 1957, WUSC, Box 103, Folder 4002.

52 RK, *The Wonderful Pen*, 88–89.

53 MS to EB, January 7, 1958, WUSC, Box 103, Folder 4002.

54 MS to EB, March 7, 1958, WUSC, Box 103, Folder 4002.

55 MS to EB, August 14, 1958, WUSC, Box 103, Folder 4003.

56 MS to EB, March 7, 1958, WUSC, Box 103, Folder 4002.

57 MS to EB, August 14, 1958, WUSC, Box 103, Folder 4003.

58 GR to MS, October 15, 1954, WUSC, Box 47, Folder 1777.

59 GR to MS, September 11, 1958, WUSC, Box 47, Folder 1777.

60 DHS, Interview, June 9, 1994.

61 MS to EB, October 15, 1958, WUSC, Box 103, Folder 4003.

62 MS to EB, March 18, 1959, WUSC, Box 103, Folder 4003.

63 Ed Field, friend of May Swenson, telephone conversation with author, March 27, 2022.

64 Margalit Fox, "Tobias Schneebaum, Chronicler and Dining Partner of Cannibals, Dies," *New York Times*, September 25, 2005.

65 Field's book was published in 1963 by Grove Press.

66 Interview with author, November 4, 2019.

67 EB to MS, March 26, 1959, WUSC, Box 103, Folder 4003.

68 MS to EB, April 21, 1959, WUSC, Box 103, Folder 4003.

69 MS to EB, May 26, 1959, WUSC, Box 103, Folder 4003.

70 MS to EB, January 10, 1960, WUSC, Box 103, Folder 4003.

71 MS to EB, June 15, 1960, Vassar College Special Collections, EB, Folder 21.5.

72 MS to RW, January 12, 1961, WUSC, Box 101, Folder 3940.

73 Postcard Collection, WUSC, Box 134.

74 MS to EB, December 5, 1960, WUSC, Box 103, Folder 4004.

75 EB to MS, December 26, 1960, WUSC, Box 103, Folder 4004.

76 MS to EB, August 29, 1961, WUSC, Box 103, Folder 4005.

77 EB to MS [November or December 1961], WUSC, Box 103, Folder 4005.

78 MS to Parents, May 14, 1963, WUSC, Box 98, Folder 3808.

79 MS to EB, June 6, 1963, WUSC, Box 104, Folder, 4008.

80 Hecht, review of *To Mix with Time*, 33.

81 EB to MS, June 17, 1963, WUSC, Box 104, Folder 4008.

82 MS to EB, July 12, 1963, WUSC, Box 104, Folder 4008.

83 MS to EB, September 25, 1963, WUSC, Box 104, Folder 4009.

84 MS to EB, June 17, 1964, WUSC, Box 104, Folder 4010.

85 MS to EB, October 2, 1964, WUSC, Box 104, Folder 4010.

86 MS to EB, December 2, 1964, WUSC, Box 104, Folder 4010.

87 MS to EB, June 1, 1965, WUSC, Box 104, Folder 4011.

88 EF, email to author, April 28, 2022.

89 GR to MS, November 5, 1965, WUSC, Box 47, Folder 1777.

90 "Grant H. Redford, Playwright, Found Dead in Automobile," *Seattle Times*, November 28, 1965, Box 47, Folder 1448.

91 MS to EB, December 29, 1965, WUSC, Box 104, Folder 4011.

92 IR to MS, March 12, 1966, WUSC, Box 47, Folder 1778.

93 MS, "I am the first," WUSC, Box 144, Folder 4939.

Chapter 9. It Is Squaresville Here

1 MS to EB, May 1, 1966, WUSC, Box 104, Folder 4012.

2 MS to EB, May 1, 1966, WUSC, Box 104, Folder 4012.

3 MS to MHS, September 18, 1966, WUSC, Box 98, Folder 3808.

4 MS to PS, October 4, 1966, WUSC, Box 95, Folder 3660.

5 Marshall and Travisano are good sources for this difficult period of Elizabeth Bishop's life.

6 EB to MS, May 21, 1965, WUSC, Box 104, Folder 4011.

7 EB to MS, November 10, 1965, WUSC, Box 104, Folder 4011.

8 MS to EB, February 23, 1966, WUSC, Box 104, Folder 4012.

9 EB to MS, November 10, 1966, WUSC, Box 104, Folder 4012.

10 MS to EB, November [16], 1966, WUSC, Box 104, Folder 4012.

11 EB to MS, November 16, 1968, WUSC, Box 104, Folder 4014.

12 MS, "An Interview with Cornelia Draves and Mary Jane Fortunato," 118.

13 MS to EB, November 16, 1966, WUSC, Box 104, Folder 4012.

14 EB to MS, November 29, 1966, WUSC, Box 104, Folder 4012.

15 The details of RK's early life and her relationship with May are taken from a draft of a manuscript by Carole Berglie about May's years with Rozanne Knudson, which she kindly made available to me.

16 MS to EB, January 5, 1967, WUSC, Box 104, Folder 4013.

17 PS to MS, March 14, 1967, WUSC, Box 53, Folder 1940.

18 MS to EB, March 21, 1967, WUSC, Box 104, Folder 4013.

19 PS to MS, May 14, 1967, WUSC, Box 53, Folder 1940.

20 PS to MS, May 24, 1967, May 25, 1967, Box 53, Folder 1940.

21 EB to MS, June 18, 1967, WUSC, Box 104, Folder 4013.

22 MS to EB, June 29, 1967, WUSC, Box 104, Folder 4013.

23 Marshall, *Elizabeth Bishop*, 196; Travisano, *Love Unknown*, 306.

24 Marshall, *Elizabeth Bishop*, 218.

25 EB to MS, August 25, 1967, WUSC, Box 104, Folder 4013.

26 Marshall, *Elizabeth Bishop*, 218.

27 MS to EB September 25, 1967, WUSC, Box 104, Folder 4013.

Chapter 10. If Distinction Comes, Can Extinction Be Far Behind?

1 MS to MHS, November 8, 1967, WUSC, Box 98, Folder 3808.

2 MS to MHS, December 11, 1967, WUSC, Box 98, Folder 3808.

3 MS to EB, March 25, 1968, WUSC, Box 104, Folder 4014.

4 MS to EB, October 27, 1969, WUSC, Box 104, Folder 4014.

5 EB to MS, November 2, 1969, WUSC, Box 104, Folder 4014.

6 MS to MHS, January 17, 1970, WUSC, Box 98, Folder 3808.

7 MS to MHS, May 22, 1970, WUSC, Box 98, Folder 3808.

8 MS, "Chronology," *Collected Poems*, 721.

9 MS to MHS, [Summer] 1970, WUSC, Box 98, Folder 3808.

10 MS to EF, August 24, 1970, WUSC, Box 77, Folder 2872.

11 MS to EB, October 21, 1970, WUSC, Box 104, Folder 4014.

12 MS to TT, February 17, 1971, WUSC, Box 99, Folder 3851.

13 MS to EB, December 2, 1971, WUSC, Box 104, Folder 4104.

14 EB to MS, February 8, 1972, WUSC, Box 104, Folder 4015.

15 MS to EB, March 9, 1973, WUSC, Box 104, Folder 4015.

16 Dennis Hevesi, "R. R. Knudson, Writer Whose Subject Was Sports, Dies at 75," *New York Times*, May 10, 2008.

17 MS to EB, November 3, 1971, WUSC, Box 104, Folder 4014.

18 MS to MHS, December 20, 1971, WUSC, Box 98, Folder 3808.

19 MS to EB, March 19, 1973, WUSC, Box 104, Folder 4015.

20 Taken from May's remarks as speaker at her mother's funeral service on June 7, 1972, LEMS.

21 MS to EB, February 24, 1975, WUSC, Box 104, Folder 4015.

22 MS to EB, December 2, 1978, WUSC, Box 104, Folder 4015.

23 MS to EB, February 12, 1979, WUSC, Box 104, Folder 4016.

24 EB to MS, March 22, 1979, WUSC, Box 104, Folder 4016.

25 EB to MS, April 12, 1979, WUSC, Box 104, Folder 4016.

26 Yale University News Release, January 14, 1981, WUSC, Box 199, Folder 5595.

27 RK and SB, *May Swenson*, 121.
28 VHS Tape, WUSC, Box 222, Item 4.
29 As quoted in RK and SB, *May Swenson*, 119.
30 VHS Tape, WUSC, Box 222, Item 4.
31 For information about May and Zan's friendship with Carole and Alice, see Berglie, introduction to the "Bibliography of the Works of May Swenson," in *Body My House*, 205–8.
32 Sallie Reynolds, email to author, February 18, 2020.

BIBLIOGRAPHY

"Alfred Kreymborg." The Poetry Foundation. www.poetryfoundation.org/poets/alfred
   -kreymborg.
Allen, Charles. "*Glebe* and *Others*." *College English* 5, no. 8 (1944): 418–23. www.jstor.org
   /stable/371449.
*Ansel Adams, Exhibition of Photographs. William Einstein, Paintings and Drawings:
   October 27–November 25, 1936.* New York: An American Place, 1936.
Arthur G. Dove New Oils and Water-Colors, March 23–April 16, 1937. New York: An Amer-
   ican Place, 1937.
"Artists' Gallery Records, 1936–1966: Description." Archives of American Art, Smithsonian
   American Art Museum. www.aaa.si.edu/collections/artists-gallery-records-9555.
"Artists: John Opper." Smithsonian American Art Museum. https://americanart.si.edu
   /artist/john-opper-3627.
Banks, Ann. *First-Person America.* New York: Alfred A. Knopf, 1980.
Berglie, Carole. Introduction to the "Bibliography of the Works of May Swenson," in *Body
   My House: May Swenson's Work and Life,* edited by Paul Crumbley and Patricia M.
   Gantt, 205–8. Logan: Utah State University Press, 2006.
Bigelow, Christopher Kimball, and Jonathan Langford. *The Latter-day Saint Family En-
   cyclopedia.* San Diego: Thunder Bay Press, 2019.
Bishop, Elizabeth. *Elizabeth Bishop: Poems, Prose, and Letters.* Edited by Robert Giroux
   and Lloyd Schwartz. New York: Library of America, 2008.
Bishop, Elizabeth, and Robert Lowell. *Words in Air: The Complete Correspondence between
   Elizabeth Bishop and Robert Lowell.* Edited by Thomas Travisano with Saskia Hamilton.
   New York: Farrar, Straus and Giroux, 2008.
Bowman, Matthew. *The Mormon People.* New York: Random House, 2012.
Bradley, George, ed. *The Yale Younger Poets Anthology.* New Haven: Yale University Press,
   1998.
Brevda, William. *Harry Kemp, the Last Bohemian.* Lewisburg, PA: Bucknell University
   Press, 1986.
Brucia, Margaret A. "'Are These Not My Streets?': May Swenson, New York City, and the
   Federal Writers Project." *Gotham: A Blog for Scholars of New York City History,* Decem-
   ber 7, 2021. www.gothamcenter.org/blog/nbspare-these-not-my-streets-may-swenson
   -new-york-city-and-the-federal-writers-project.
———. "'I Have Shoes to My Feet This Time': May Swenson, New York City, and the FWP." *Go-
   tham: A Blog for Scholars of New York City History,* December 9, 2021. www.gothamcenter
   .org/blog/i-have-shoes-to-my-feet-this-time-may-swenson-new-york-city-and-the-fwp.
Bushman, Richard Lyman. *Mormonism: A Very Short Introduction.* New York: Oxford
   University Press, 2008.
Cantwell, Mary. *Manhattan, When I Was Young.* New York: Penguin, 1995.
Crumbley, Paul and Patricia M. Gantt, eds. *Body My House: May Swenson's Work and Life.*
   Logan: Utah State University Press, 2006.
Dearborn, Mary V. *Love in the Promised Land: The Story of Anzia Yezierska and John Dewey.*
   New York: Free Press, 1988.
Eyre, Ruth Swenson, ed. *The Immigrants: Dan's and Greta's Families in the New Land.*
   Directed by Gwen H. Haws. Published by the Living Children of Dan and Greta Hell-
   berg Swenson, 2010.

Field, Edward. *The Man Who Would Marry Susan Sontag*. Madison: University of Wisconsin Press, 2005.

Frost, Robert. *Robert Frost: Poetry and Prose*. Edited by Edward Connery Lathem and Lawrence Thompson. New York: Holt, Rinehart and Winston, 1972.

Gordon, Max. *Live at the Village Vanguard*. New York: St. Martin's Press, 1960.

"Guide to the Raven Poetry Circle of Greenwich Village Collection: Biographical Note." New York Historical Society Museum and Library. http://dlib.nyu.edu/findingaids/html/nyhs /Raven/Raven.html.

Hans Böhler: 1884–1961. London: Marlborough Fine Art, 1968.

Hecht, Anthony. Review of *To Mix with Time*, by May Swenson. *New York Review of Books* 1, no. 3 (1963): 33.

Hoak, David. "Dear Elizabeth, Dear May: Reappraising the Bishop/Swenson Correspondence." In *Elizabeth Bishop and the Literary Archive*, edited by Bethany Hicok, 99–114. Amherst: Lever Press, 2019.

Howard, Richard. "Elizabeth Bishop—May Swenson." *Paris Review* 36, no. 131 (1994): 171–86.

Investigation and Study of the Work Projects Administration (formerly Works Progress Administration): Hearings before the Subcommittee on Appropriations, Third Session. Washington, DC: United States Printing Office, 1940.

"The Jacob's Pillow Story." Jacob's Pillow. www.jacobspillow.org/about/pillow-history /jacobs-pillow-story.

"James Laughlin." The Poetry Foundation. www.poetryfoundation.org/poets /james-laughlin.

Johansson, Carl-Erik. "History of the Swedish Mission of the Church of Latter-Day Saints, 1905–1973." MA thesis, Brigham Young University, 1973. BYU ScholarsArchive (4830).

Kiter, Tammy. "Quoth the Raven Poetry Circle." *New York History*. April 23, 2014. http:// blog.nyhistory.org/quoth-the-raven-poetry-circle.

Knudson, R. R. "The Love Poems of May Swenson." In *Body My House: May Swenson's Work and Life*, edited by Paul Crumbley and Patricia M. Gantt, 11–26. Logan, Utah: Utah State University Press, 2006.

———. *The Wonderful Pen of May Swenson*. New York: Macmillan, 1993.

Knudson, Rozanne, and Suzzanne Bigelow. *May Swenson: A Poet's Life in Photos*. Foreword by Richard Wilbur. Logan: Utah State University Press, 1996.

Kreymborg, Alfred, ed. *Seventeen and One*. New York: Bruce Fitzgerald, 1943.

———. *Troubadour*. New York: Sagamore Press, 1957.

Lyman, E. Leo. "The Political Background of the Woodruff Manifesto." *Dialogue: A Journal of Mormon Thought* 24, no. 3 (Fall 1991): 21–39.

Mangione, Jerre. *The Dream and the Deal*. Syracuse: Syracuse University Press, 1996.

Marshall, Megan. *Elizabeth Bishop: A Miracle for Breakfast*. Boston: Houghton Mifflin Harcourt, 2017.

Maxwell, William. "Talk of the Town: Village Poets." *New Yorker*, June 5, 1937, 13.

McCormick, John S. "The Great Depression." *Utah History Encyclopedia*. www.uen.org/utah _history_encyclopedia/d/DEPPRESSION_GREAT.shtml.

Miller, Tom. "The Robert Burnett Smith House." *Daytonian in Manhattan*, October 29, 2019. http://daytoninmanhattan.blogspot.com/2019/10/the-robert-burnett-smith -house-104-west.html.

Moe, Orin. "The Songs of Howard Swanson." *Black Music Research Journal* 2 (1981–82): 57–71.

Mumford, Lewis. "Writers' Project." *New Republic* 92 (October 20, 1937): 306–7.

Norris, Benjamin Dwight. "American Troubadour: The Career and Life of Alfred Kreymborg as a Modernist and Beyond." Undergraduate honors thesis, College of William & Mary, 2011. Paper 444. https://scholarworks.wm.edu/honorstheses/444.

Parson, Robert. "'Leftward March': 1930s Student Liberalism at the Utah State Agricultural College." *Utah Historical Quarterly* 75, no. 2 (Spring 2007): 164–82.

"Ralph Rosenborg." Caldwell Gallery. www.caldwellgallery.com/artists/ralph-rosenborg /biography.

Sappho. *Sappho: A New Translation.* Translated by Mary Barnard. Berkeley: University of California Press, 1958.

Schulman, Grace. "Life's Miracles: The Poetry of May Swenson." *American Poetry Review* 23, no. 5 (September–October 1994): 9–13.

Smith, Martha Nell. "That Never Told CAN Be: May Swenson's Manuscript Witnesses." In *Body My House: May Swenson's Work and Life,* edited by Paul Crumbley and Patricia M. Gantt, 107–19. Logan: Utah State University Press, 2006.

Steinbeck, John. *Travels with Charley.* New York: Viking Penguin, 1962.

"Stewart's Cafeteria." NYC LGBT Historic Sites Project. www.nyclgbtsites.org/site/stewarts -cafeteria.

Swenson, May. "Another Animal: Poems." In *Poets of Today,* introduction by John Hall Wheelock, 103–79. New York: Charles Scribner's Sons, 1954.

——. *A Cage of Spines.* New York: Rinehart, 1958.

——. *Collected Poems.* Edited by Langdon Hammer. New York: Library of America, 2013.

——. *The Complete Love Poems of May Swenson.* Boston: Houghton Mifflin, 2003.

——. *The Complete Poems to Solve.* New York: Macmillan, 1993.

——. *Dear Elizabeth: Five Poems and Three Letters to Elizabeth Bishop.* Afterword by Kristin Hotelling Zona. Logan: Utah State University Press, 2000.

——. *Earthlight on the Moon: Space Poems by May Swenson.* Edited by Carole Berglie. Sea Cliff, NY: Dasher, 2021.

——. "Fruits." *Scribble* 8, no. 1 (1932): 18.

——. *The Guess and Spell Coloring Book.* Drawings by Lise Gladstone. New York: Charles Scribner's Sons, 1976.

——. *Half Sun Half Sleep: New Poems.* New York: Charles Scribner's Sons, 1967.

——. *Iconographs: Poems.* New York: Charles Scribner's Sons, 1970.

——. *In Other Words: New Poems.* New York: Alfred A. Knopf, 1987.

——. "An Interview with Cornelia Draves and Mary Jane Fortunato." In *Made with Words,* edited by Gardner McFall, 104–20. Ann Arbor: University of Michigan Press, 1998.

——. "An Interview with Karla Hammond." In *Made with Words,* edited by Gardner McFall, 121–37. Ann Arbor: University of Michigan Press, 1998.

——. *The Love Poems of May Swenson.* New York: Houghton Mifflin, 1991.

——. *Made with Words.* Edited by Gardner McFall. Poets on Poetry Series. Ann Arbor: University of Michigan Press, 1998.

——. *May out West: Poems of May Swenson.* Edited by R. R. Knudson and Peter Davison. Logan: Utah State University Press, 1996.

——. *More Poems to Solve.* New York: Charles Scribner's Sons, 1971.

——. "Music Maker." *Rocky Mountain Review* 8 (1937): 5.

——. *Nature: Poems Old and New.* Edited by R. R. Knudson and Peter Davison. New York: Houghton Mifflin, 1994.

——. *New & Selected Things Taking Place.* Boston: Little, Brown, 1978.

——. *Poems to Solve.* New York: Charles Scribner's Sons, 1966.

———. *To Mix with Time: New and Selected Poems*. 2nd ed. New York: Charles Scribner's Sons, 1964.

Swenson, May, and Harry Kemp. "Tramp Poet" (1938). Federal Writers' Project. www.loc.gov /item/wpalh001639.

Swenson, May, and Anca Vrbovska. *Czechoslovakian Lore*. New York, 1938, Manuscript / Mixed Material, Library of Congress. www.loc.gov/item/wpalh001610.

Swenson, Paul. "A Figure in the Tapestry." In *Body My House*, edited by Paul Crumbley and Patricia M. Gantt, 27–39. Logan: Utah State University Press, 2006.

"Thetas in the News: Alpha Lambda's Artist." *Kappa Alpha Theta Journal* 53, no. 3 (March 1939): 221–22 (reprint of article in *Seattle Times*, December 7, 1938). https://archive.org /details/19390300/page/n37/mode/2up?q=%22Frances+Ferry%22.

Tranströmer, Tomas. *Windows & Stones*. Translated by May Swenson and Leif Sjöberg. Pittsburgh: University of Pittsburgh Press, 1972.

Travisano, Thomas. *Love Unknown: The Life and Worlds of Elizabeth Bishop*. New York: Viking, 2019.

Vrbovska, Anca. *The Gate beyond the Sun: New and Selected Poems*. Preface by Alfred Dorn. Brooklyn: Theo Gaus' Sons, 1970.

Wakefield, Dan. *New York in the '50s*. New York: St. Martin's Press, 1992.

Wetzsteon, Ross. *Republic of Dreams: Greenwich Village, the American Bohemia, 1910–1960*. New York: Simon & Schuster, 2002.

Wolfe, Thomas. *Look Homeward, Angel*. New York: Scribner, 1929.

———. *Of Time and the River*. New York: Scribner, 1935.

The WPA Guide to New York City. 1939. New York: New Press, 1992.

"Yude (Jennings) Tofel." Translated by Joshua Fogel. *Yiddish Leksicon: Biographical Dictionary of Modern Yiddish Literature*, October 5, 2016. http://yleksikon.blogspot.com /2016/10/yude-jennings-tofel.html.

Zona, Kirstin Hotelling. *Marianne Moore, Elizabeth Bishop, and May Swenson: The Feminist Poetics of Self-Restraint*. Ann Arbor: University of Michigan Press, 2002.

INDEX

Note: Page numbers in *italic* type indicate illustrations. "MS" refers to May Swenson.